THE ARDEN SHAK

GENERAL EDITORS: HAR<

AND HAROLD JENKINS

THE FIRST PART OF
KING HENRY VI

THE FRANCE OF *HENRY VI*

THE ARDEN EDITION OF THE
WORKS OF WILLIAM SHAKESPEARE

THE FIRST PART OF
KING HENRY VI

Edited by
ANDREW S. CAIRNCROSS

ARDEN SHAKESPEARE PAPERBACKS

METHUEN & CO LTD
11 NEW FETTER LANE LONDON EC4

The general editors of the Arden Shakespeare have been W. J. Craig (1899–1906), succeeded by R. H. Case (1909–44) and Una Ellis-Fermor (1946–58). Present general editors: Harold F. Brooks and Harold Jenkins.
King Henry VI, Part I was first published in the Arden Shakespeare in June 1909 edited by H. C. Hart.
Second edition 1930
This edition, completely revised and reset, first published 1962

First published as a University Paperback 1969

Printed and bound in Great Britain by
Richard Clay (The Chaucer Press), Ltd, Bungay, Suffolk
Type set by The Broadwater Press

SBN 416 27840 X

CONTENTS

Frontispiece: The France of *Henry VI*

PREFACE

As with _2 Henry VI_, the original Arden edition, by H. C. Hart, has been entirely rewritten. It was based on a theory of collaboration that seems to me no longer in keeping with the progress of Shakespearean criticism; and the space formerly devoted to parallels with Greene, Nashe, Marlowe, and others, and to conjecturing their respective shares, may now, I suggest, be more profitably spent in examining the text as a text, and the play as a play by William Shakespeare.

It is refreshing to leave the labyrinth of such conjectural criticism and to see the play more as Shakespeare and his audience must have seen it—to watch the manipulation of a mass of difficult chronicle material, accepted (Joan and all) much as he received it from Hall and Holinshed, into a grand design and part of a still grander tetralogy; the construction of a new type of drama. This is the drama of England—not a tragedy, and therefore without a hero, even Talbot —which is concerned with the external and political rather than the subjective and personal, and which varies in style and treatment with the variation of the matter, from the prosaic, artificial, or rhetorical to the idyllic, pastoral, or tragic. Viewed in this light, most of the alleged inconsistencies and shortcomings of _1 Henry VI_ vanish or take on a new significance.

The finest expression of this point of view is the perceptive short study of the structure of the play by Hereward T. Price,[1] to which, with Professor Peter Alexander's critical work, I am chiefly indebted.

In the course of editing, I have become increasingly convinced on every side of the integrity of the play. If I have omitted much of the detailed case made by the disintegrationists, and the detailed answers required, it is mainly for want of space, and not, I hope, that I have not given the case due weight. There are still, obviously, many questions to be solved; in particular, we need to know more of the compositors, and the scribe or scribes, and the peculiarities of act- and scene-division in the Shakespeare First Folio. I have, however, found the study of the play, within these limits, most re-

1. _Construction in Shakespeare_ (University of Michigan, 1951).

vii

warding both as regards understanding of the text and deeper appreciation of the dramatic intention.

I have to thank the general editors for their 'care and pain', from which, as the notes and introduction will testify, I have greatly benefited; and Dr Alice Walker and Mr J. C. Maxwell for criticism and suggestions.

ANDREW S. CAIRNCROSS

UDDINGSTON
GLASGOW
  December 1960

ABBREVIATIONS

The abbreviations for Shakespeare's plays, and customary terms, are from Onions, *Shakespeare Glossary*. References to the plays (other than *1 Henry VI*) are to the *Cambridge Shakespeare*, 1891–3.

Abbott	E. A. Abbott, *A Shakespearian Grammar*, 1869, edn of 1878.
Adams	Joseph Quincy Adams, *Shakespearean Playhouses*, 1917.
Armstrong	Edward A. Armstrong, *Shakespeare's Imagination*, 1946.
Baldwin	T. W. Baldwin, *Shakespere's Small Latine and Lesse Greeke* (Urbana), 1944.
Boswell-Stone	W. G. Boswell-Stone, *Shakespere's Holinshed*, 1896.
Brooke	*1 Henry VI*, ed. C. F. Tucker Brooke, Yale, 1918.
Carter	Thomas Carter, *Shakespeare and Holy Scripture*, 1905.
Cooper	Thomas Cooper, *Thesaurus Linguae Romanae & Britannicae*, 1565 (repr. 1578).
Evans	Sir Ifor Evans, *The Language of Shakespeare's Plays*, 1952, repr. 1959.
F (F1)	The First Folio (1623).
Fabyan	Robert Fabyan, *The New Chronicles of England and France*, 1516 (repr. 1811).
F.Q.	Edmund Spenser, *The Faerie Queene*.
Franz	W. Franz, *Shakespeare-Grammatik*, Heidelberg, 1909, repr. of 1924.
French	George R. French, *Shakespeareana Genealogica*, 1869.
Gaw	Allison Gaw, *The Origin and Development of '1 Henry VI'* (University of Carolina Studies, 1), 1926.
Greg, *EDD.*	Sir Walter W. Greg, *Elizabethan Dramatic Documents*, 1931.
——, *Sh. FF.*	Sir Walter W. Greg, *The Shakespeare First Folio*, 1955.
Hall	Edward Hall, *The union of the two noble and illustre famelies of Lancastre & Yorke, 1548*, repr. 1809.
Harbage	Alfred H. Harbage, *As they liked it: An Essay on Shakespeare and Morality*, New York, 1947.
Hart	*Henry VI (Part I)*, ed. H. C. Hart, (old) Arden edn, 1909.
Hodges	C. Walter Hodges, *The Globe Restored*, 1953.
Hol.	Raphael Holinshed, *Chronicles of England, Scotland, and Ireland*, 1577, 1587.
Homilies	*Certain Sermons or Homilies, . . .* repr. 1844.
Irving	*The Works of William Shakespeare*, ed. by Sir Henry Irving & Frank A. Marshall, 1922 (edn of 1922).

Knight	G. Wilson Knight, *The Olive and the Sword*, 1944.
Madden	D. H. Madden, *The Diary of Master William Silence*, 1897, new edn 1907.
Malone	Boswell's Variorum edn of *Malone's Shakespeare*, 1821.
Man. Voc.	*Manipulus Vocabulorum*, 1570, repr. *EETS*, 1867.
Metam.	Ovid, *Metamorphoses*.
Mirror	*The Mirror for Magistrates*, ed. Lily B. Campbell, Cambridge 1938.
MSH	J. Dover Wilson, *The Manuscript of Shakespeare's 'Hamlet'*, 1934
Noble	Richmond Noble, *Shakespeare's Use of the Bible*, 1935.
North's Plutarch	Thomas North, *Lives of the Noble Grecians and Romanes compared together by . . . Plutarke*, 1579. Nonesuch Press, 1929–30.
N.Q.	*Notes and Queries.*
NSS.	*Transactions of the New Shakespere Society.*
OED.	*Oxford English Dictionary*, 1888–1928, Suppl. 1933.
Onions	C. T. Onions, *A Shakespeare Glossary*, 1911, repr. 1951.
PMLA.	*Publications of the Modern Language Association of America* (Baltimore).
PQ.	*Philological Quarterly* (Iowa).
Price	Hereward T. Price, *Construction in Shakespeare*, University of Michigan, 1951.
Ribner	Irving Ribner, *The English History Play in the Age of Shakespeare*, Princeton, 1957.
Rossiter	*Woodstock, a Moral History*, ed. A. P. Rossiter, 1946.
Rothery	Guy Cadogan Rothery, *The Heraldry of Shakespeare*, 1930.
SB.	*Studies in Bibliography* (University of Virginia).
Schmidt	A. Schmidt, *Shakespeare Lexicon*, Berlin and London, 1874–5 (2nd edn 1886).
Scott-Giles	C. W. Scott-Giles, *Shakespeare's Heraldry*, 1950.
Sewell	Arthur Sewell, *Character and Society in Shakespeare*, 1951.
Sh. Bawdy	Eric Partridge, *Shakespeare's Bawdy*, 1947, repr. 1955, 1956.
Sh. Eng.	*Shakespeare's England: an Account of the Life and Manners of his Age*, 1916.
Sh. Qu.	*Shakespeare Quarterly* (Washington).
Spurgeon	Caroline F. E. Spurgeon, *Shakespeare's Imagery and what it tells us*, 1935, repr. 1958.
Theobald[4]	Theobald's fourth edn of Shakespeare, 1757: see *PQ.*, 1949, 425–8.
Tilley	M. P. Tilley, *A Dictionary of the Proverbs in England in the 16th and 17th Centuries*, 1950.
Tillyard, *EWP.*	E. M. W. Tillyard, *The Elizabethan World Picture*, 1943.
——, *Sh. Hist. Plays*	E. M. W. Tillyard, *Shakespeare's History Plays*, 1948.
Vaughan	Henry H. Vaughan, *New Readings and Renderings of Shakespeare's Tragedies*, 1886.

Venezky	Alice S. Venezky, *Pageantry on the Shakespearean Stage*, New York, 1951.
Wilson	*Henry VI*, ed. J. Dover Wilson, New Shakespeare, 1952.
W.S.	Sir Edmund K. Chambers, *William Shakespeare*, 1930.

Elizabethan authors are cited from the following editions:

Dekker	Fredson Bowers, Cambridge, 1953–8.
Greene	Plays: J. C. Collins, Oxford, 1905.
	Prose: A. B. Grosart, Huth Library, 1881–3.
Kyd	F. S. Boas, Oxford, 1901.
Lyly	R. W. Bond, Oxford, 1902.
Marlowe	C. F. Tucker Brooke, Oxford, 1910.
Nashe	R. B. McKerrow, Oxford, 1910, repr. 1958.
Spenser	J. C. Smith and E. de Selincourt, Oxford, 1912.

INTRODUCTION

THE TEXT

As a text, *1 Henry VI* has hitherto had little critical attention.
Like *2* and *3 Henry VI*, it has attracted textual study of its peculiarities mainly as a counter in controversy over authenticity, collaboration, and revision. Such controversy, apart from some suggestive
remarks by Professor J. Dover Wilson[1] and the late Philip Williams,[2] has contributed little towards determining the nature of the
copy for the text, and the history of its transmission. I therefore
propose to turn aside for the moment, and look at the text for itself.

There is only one text of *1 Henry VI*, that of the First Folio (F1),
published in 1623, seven years after Shakespeare's death. The Folio
was '*Printed at the Charges of W. Jaggard, Ed. Blount, I. Smithweeke,
and W. Aspley, 1623.*' Jaggard was the printer, but, since he had been
blind for a long time, the work was carried out by his son Isaac,
who, with Blount, made the entry of the book in the Stationers'
Register, of 'Mr William Shakspeers Comedyes Histories, and
Tragedyes soe manie of the said Copies as are not formerly entred
to other men. viz[t] . . . The thirde parte of Henry ye Sixt. . .' The
previous publication of corrupt texts of *2* and *3 Henry VI* in quarto
form (as *The First Part of the Contention of the famous Houses, of Yorke
and Lancaster* and *The true Tragedie of Richard Duke of Yorke*) made it
unnecessary to enter them again for copyright purposes; but the
counting of these as two parts of *Henry VI* would sufficiently explain
the apparent inconsistency in the entry of *1 Henry VI* as 'The thirde
parte'.[3]

THE COPY

The main feature hitherto noticed in the text, and underlying
the various theories of its origin, is the number of irregularities and
inconsistencies. In particular, certain proper names, such as Bur-

1. New Shakespeare (Cambridge, 1952), *I–III Henry VI*.
2. *Studies in Bibliography* (University of Virginia), VIII (1956), pp. 8–9.
3. The phrase has been used, however, e.g. by Tucker Brooke, as an argument
for the priority of *2* and *3 Henry VI*. Cf. below, pp. xxxv, xlvii ff.

gundy, Pucelle, Joan, Reignier, and Gloucester, vary in form or spelling; the incidence of brackets, the use of 'Here' to introduce stage-directions, and the act- and scene-division, are somewhat erratic; the verse is now and then irregular;[1] and the historical facts are occasionally inconsistent or contradictory. Greg is representative of the main trend of textual criticism since Malone when he says that 'either composite authorship or revision would explain certain contradictions and inconsistencies in the text'.[2] Most critics, indeed, the latest being Dover Wilson, have inferred both factors together. Williams called the copy 'almost certainly heterogeneous'.[3]

Irregularities, contradictions, and inconsistencies, however, do not necessarily imply composite authorship or revision. All that has been shown so far is that these factors *might* have produced this sort of text. But other and various agents, themselves often inconsistent, might equally well have produced the same result; I shall suggest that they did, and that they account more satisfactorily and stringently for the phenomena. I suggest rather that the state of the text is consistent with a single author—Shakespeare—and a succession of factors, extending from his use of different sources, and a stage-adapter's annotation of the manuscript and adaptation of the cast, to the intervention of a scribe, and of compositors A and B[4] of the First Folio. It will not always be possible to isolate the phenomena due to each of these factors; but the evidence seems sufficient and unequivocal in a way that the evidence for revision or composite authorship is not.

(a) *The author*

Occasional errors and inconsistencies are to be expected, and are indeed characteristic, in authorial copy; and may survive a long process of transmission to show through the superimposed layers. Such inconsistencies, which may be attributable to the basic authorial manuscript, occur in *1 Henry VI*. The glaring example is, of course, Exeter's surprised greeting of the Bishop of Winchester as Cardinal (v. i. 28) though Winchester had already appeared (I. iii; III. i; III. iv; IV. i) in his Cardinal's robes when Exeter was present. Winchester was both bishop and cardinal; and it may be the author forgot what he had written earlier. The inconsistency is an argument for the authorial nature of the copy, since the prompter could be expected to iron out the discrepancy for the stage.

---

1. Dover Wilson finds 30 hypermetrical and 25 defective lines.
2. Sir Walter W. Greg, *The Editorial Problem in Shakespeare*, p. 139.
3. *SB.*, VIII. 9.   4. Or possibly another, yet unidentified.

Other inconsistencies, due to the chronicle sources and the author's dependence on them, occur within single plays in the tetralogy, and between pairs of them. Such, for example, is the death of Clifford in *3 Henry VI*, where he is described as 'by the hands of common soldiers slain' (I. i. 9), and as killed by the Duke of York (I. iii. 5, 45).[1] Such, again, are the accounts of Mortimer's death, which *2 Henry VI* places in Wales and *1 Henry VI* in the Tower; Hall, directly, or through the medium of Holinshed, is responsible for both.[2]

The stage-directions are mainly authorial in character, e.g. *Here Alarums, they are beaten back by the English, with great losse* (I. i. 21); *Enter to the Protector at the Tower Gates, Winchester and his men in Tawney coates* (I. iii. 28); *Here Glosters men beat out the Cardinals men, and enter in the hurly-burly the Maior of London, and his Officers* (I. iii. 56). Some are taken straight from the Chronicles, as where '*The French leape ore the walles in their shirts*' (II. i. 38; Hall, 143). Many, again, are missing when action is implicit in the text, and, to an author or even an actor, unnecessary. Thus there is no '*Exit*' for the funeral procession of Henry V or two of the messengers in I. i, or for the Governor, Falstaff, or Talbot in IV. i (8, 47, 77); there is no entry for Vernon and Basset at III. iv. 1, though they remain (*manent*) on the stage after the others have left; '*And others*' does duty for the entry of Gargrave and Glansdale in I. iv, and for Vernon and the Lawyer in II. iv.

Again, inconsistencies in speech-prefixes are characteristic of the author, though they may also be produced by other agents. It is not surprising, therefore, to find e.g. the speech-prefix *Charles* (I. ii. 47) becoming *Dolphin*; Yorke becoming *Rich*. at II. v. 35; and *Somerset* in the stage-direction at I. i. 1, but not in the text of the scene.

Some of the variant spellings of proper names, so far as they are not due to other agents of transmission, may also go back to the chronicles. Thus Hall has *Burgoyn* (e.g. 104, 105, 106) and *Burgonions* (e.g. 118); so has Fabyan; Holinshed has *Burgognie* and *Burgognions*. *Burgonie* is found in three pages of *1 Henry VI*, and also in *Henry V*. The commoner F form *Burgundie* may have come from Shakespeare himself, or a scribe, or a modernizing editor. Similarly Hall's *Pucelle* (e.g. 148) and *the puzell* (e.g. 109) and Holinshed's *le pusell* (e.g. iii. 604), may explain the variants in *1 Henry VI*. These, at any rate, do not seem to be compositorial.

1. Cf. *2H6*, v. ii.

2. Hall's *Chronicle* (reprint 1809), pp. 21, 23, and 128, and notes to II. v; and R. A. Law, 'Edmund Mortimer in Shakespeare and Hall', *Sh. Qu.*, v (1954), 425–6.

(b) The compositors

At the other end of the transmission are the compositors, to whom likewise some of the variations may be ascribed. The text seems to have been distributed between the two compositors, A and B,[1] as follows:

A	k 2^v—k 5^r col. a	pp. 96–101 a	Act I
B	k 5^r col. b	101 b	II. i. 1–44
A	k 5^v—l 3^r	102–9	II. i. 45—III. iv. end
B	l 3^v—l 4^v	110–12	IV. i. 1—IV. v. 12
A	l 5^r	113	IV. v. 13—IV. vii. 22
B	l 5^v—m 2^r	114–19	IV. vii. 23—end

The preponderance of brackets on l 3^v—fourteen, out of forty for the whole play—must be largely ascribed to compositor B; while their complete absence from Act I is not out of keeping with A's known habits. The spelling variants *Ioane/Ione* are compositorial (A/B), as are some at least of the variants of *Gloucester*, and, of course, the recognized characteristic spellings of both compositors. In the presence of other agents of transmission, and pending further compositorial study, it is impossible to assess accurately the influence of the compositors on the text. It is not likely, however, to account for more than a part of the textual irregularity.

(c) The book-keeper

In view of the number of inconsistencies which cannot be attributed to any later agent of transmission but must go back to the author, we may perhaps agree with Dover Wilson that 'the copy for F can never have been used as a prompt-book'.[2] The assumption is that the book-keeper or prompter would have cleaned up inconsistencies and normalized stage-directions and speech-prefixes, or had a fair copy made of the autograph in which this would have been done. Signs are not wanting, however, that a stage-adapter, probably the book-keeper, did leave his mark—the sort of annotations that he would normally add to the manuscript in pre-

---

1. While I here adopt these current assumptions, I am very doubtful of B's presence. In particular, the inconsistent pattern of spellings, speech-prefixes, and italics often seems uncharacteristic. B's normal *Glouster* (with *Glou.* speech-prefix) nowhere appears (*Gloucester* occurs once); A-forms for prefixes (e.g. *Mess.*, *Suff.*, *Talb.*, *Bass.*) crop up among the B-forms (*Mes.*, *Suf.*, *Tal.*, *Bas.*); and the italic *Aire*, *Naples*, *Aniou*, etc. after 'of', and *Douer*, are unlike B. These and other peculiarities are more reminiscent of compositor E's work in e.g. *King Lear*, *Romeo and Juliet*, and *Titus Andronicus* (for which see Charlton Hinman, in *SB.*, ix (1957), 3–20).

2, Wilson, *1H6*, p. 103.

paration for transcribing the 'plot' and the players' parts. This is suggested, for example, by the misplacement of some stage-directions for music, as at II. i. 7, where the English forces enter to a night-attack, '*Their Drummes beating a Dead March*'! This direction, as Dover Wilson points out,[1] is obviously intended for the funeral of Salisbury, at II. ii. 6 or 7, just after the entry of the same three characters, Talbot, Bedford, and Burgundy. The same sort of thing happened at IV. i. 181, where the *Flourish* should clearly follow the exit of the King at 173. Again, the duplication, *Alarum. / An Alarum.*, at III. ii. 35, illustrates the well-known phenomenon of an authorial stage-direction being carried into the margin where it will catch the eye of the prompter, but not deleted in its original position.

Adaptations in the cast, often indicative rather than complete, suggest the same hand at work. The cast was one of the largest and most varied in the canon; and even small economies, possibly for ease of doubling, if not for absolute reduction of numbers, were probably worth while. It seems, for example, as if an attempt had been made to delete Alençon or Reignier, and to give his lines to the other. At III. ii. 17, Reignier does not appear in the stage-direction but has two speeches (23, 33), *after* which he enters at l. 40; while Alençon, entering at l. 17, is mute, has no re-entry at l. 40, but then speaks (67). This attempt was obviously imperfect or confused, and may have resulted from provisional alterations noted, but not checked or completed, on the manuscript, as an indication in transcribing the players' parts.

Similarly, adaptation seems to have been attempted in the part of Sir William Lucy in the only scenes—IV. iii, iv, and vii—in which he appeared. At IV. iii. 16, the stage-direction *Enter another Messenger* is followed by the speech-prefix 2. *Mes.* (*Mes.* at l. 30, 34, and 47). At l. 43, however, York says to the Messenger, 'Lucie farewell', betraying a substitution. A few lines later, in what is usually marked as a separate scene (IV. iv), but is properly a continuation of IV. iii, the Captain and Somerset address Lucy by name (IV. iv. 10, 12), and his five speeches are prefixed by *Lu.* or *Luc.* It seems likely, then, that an adapter altered the first entry (IV. iii. 1) and the three following prefixes—enough to indicate the change to be made throughout the part—but omitted to carry the alteration of prefixes into IV. iv, or to alter the name of Lucy in the text of both scenes.

Again, at IV. vii. 50, the stage-direction is *Enter Lucie*. The first speech after the entry reads:

1. *Op. cit.*, p. 138.

> *Lu.* Herald, conduct me to the Dolphins Tent,   51
>   To know who hath obtain'd the glory of the day.
> *Char.* On what submissiue message art thou sent?

The presence of the (unannounced) herald, the metrical excess in l. 52, together with the awkward rhyme Tent/sent, suggest disturbance of some kind. The 'Herald' is obviously the superfluous metrical element. Again this suggests a substitution for Lucy; and if we apply the same procedure, it is natural to suppose that 'Herald' was written in above '*Lu.*' as an indication that the alteration should be made throughout the part; but the scribe included both, treating 'Herald' as part of the dialogue. Remove it, and everything reads easily:

> *Lu.* Conduct me to the Dolphins Tent, to know
>   Who hath obtain'd the glory of the day.
> *Char.* On what submissiue message art thou sent?

On this supposition, Lucy was to be entirely replaced by a Messenger and a Herald.

An alternative, which seems to me less likely, is that Shakespeare began with a messenger, unnamed, gave him a name as he proceeded to write the dialogue and wanted a vocative; and later did the same with the Herald. In that case, however, he must have continued to use the prefix *Mes.* at least once (in iv. iii) after he used the name *Lucie* in the text; and to have altered the entry in iv. vii from *Herald* to *Lucie* after he had begun that dialogue, in a way that he did not do with the entry in iv. iii. For these reasons, and in view of the Reignier/Alençon adaptations, which are unlikely to have been the author's, it is more natural to presuppose adaptation by a prompter rather than by the author in the process of composition.

The copy for *1 Henry VI* thus seems to have been based on Shakespeare's autograph as annotated by a stage-adapter, who, however, was indicative rather than exhaustive, and who allowed many authorial inconsistencies and omissions to stand; and not on a fair copy or prompt-book, in which most of them might have been expected to be ironed out.

(d) The scribe

I suggest that this annotated manuscript did not itself go to the printers, but was transcribed as literally as the ability and deliberate 'improvements' of the scribe allowed; that his literal transcription permitted authorial inconsistencies and the stage-adaptation to remain above the surface; while his own distinctive contribution of errors and alterations betrays his presence and main characteristics.

His hand is suggested by a large number of some types of error not nearly so common in other F texts—types of error for which neither the author, the adapter, nor the compositors can be blamed. When we take together such textual corruptions as are supported or made highly probable by the sense, the context, and Shakespearean usage and metre, a pattern emerges.

One may begin with 'improvements'. The commonest type is the transposition of words and phrases, generally in inversion and chiasmus, to a more normal prose order, e.g.:

	F	Emendation
II. iv. 41	The fewest Roses are cropt from the Tree,	. . . from the tree are cropt
III. i. 112	Yeeld my Lord Protector, yeeld *Winchester,*	My Lord Protector yield, . . .
III. ii. 71	Away Captaines, let's get vs from the Walls,	Captains, away, . . .
IV. i. 70	How say you (my Lord) are you not content?	My Lord, how say you? . . .

In other cases,[1] it is clear that some alteration has been made, but it is not possible to say exactly what. The habit, however, is widespread enough, and can hardly be other than scribal.

A more deliberate attempt at 'improvement' seems to have been made where F reads (II. iv. 91):

> For Treason executed in our late Kings dayes.

The metre points to an original disyllable for 'executed', which can only have been 'headed'. This was probably 'improved' or sophisticated by the scribe as being too harsh or crude.

This tendency may be equally exemplified from minor insertions —again too numerous to be compositorial—that supply an ellipsis, to the detriment of the metre, e.g. (the superfluous words are bracketed):

I. ii. 38	And hunger will enforce them [to] be more eager:
I. ii. 86	That beautie am I blest with [which] you may see.
I. iii. 30	Piel'd Priest, doo'st thou command me [to] be shut out?
I. iv. 109	Conuey me [=we] Salisbury into his Tent, And then [wee'le] try what these dastard Frenchmen dare.
II. v. 34	Richard Plantagenet, my friend, is [he] come?
III. i. 29	If [I were] couetous, ambitious, or peruerse,[2]

---

1. See e.g. I. i. 71, 112; I. ii. 97; I. iii. 1, 8; II. v. 76; etc.
2. Cf. also I. ii. 148; IV. i. 71 ; IV. vii. 85, 89, 94; etc.

So with titles, as (King) Henry, I. i. 6; (Sir) Iohn Falstaffe, III. ii. 104; the (Lord) Talbot, III. iv. 13; (Lord) Cromwell of Wingefield, (Lord) Furniuall of Sheffeild, IV. vii. 66. Whether from deliberate improvement, or unconscious familiarity with the fuller forms, an apparently incomplete title seems to have been sometimes filled out. In most such examples, there is also an element of influence from the context, such as will be found operating strongly elsewhere in the text; and one cannot be dogmatic as to the exact cause of corruption in any particular case.

Other signs of the same tendency may be found in 'reuerently', probably for 'reuerent', used as an adverb, at I. ii. 145; and 'knocks' for 'knocketh' at I. iii. 5. Many others must meantime remain conjectural; some could, of course, be compositorial or editorial.

The other outstanding characteristic of the text that suggests a scribe is one of association, a sign of an active but not too attentive memory. Susceptibility to the context—mostly immediate, but perhaps occasionally more remote—shows itself in (a) various degrees and forms of dittography, and in (b) errors due to the influence of the apparent sense of the context, so that a word or phrase is read as something *similar* to its general shape. These may even be combined with the 'improving' tendency already noticed; and the results are such that the *ductus litterarum* is seldom of great value in emendation.

Dittography occurs more frequently than one is entitled to expect of the compositors. Examples where the emendation suggests itself from the immediate context, are:

	F	*Emendation*
I. iii. 47	Blew *Coats* to Tawny [Coats]: Priest, beware your Beard,	*omit*
I. iv. 15–16	A Peece of Ordnance 'gainst it *I haue* plac'd And euen these three dayes [haue I] watcht, If I could see them.	*omit*
I. vi. 11	Why ring not [out the] Bells aloud, Through*out the* Towne?	*omit*
III. i. 163	If Richard will be true, not that [*all*] *al*one, But *all* the whole Inheritance I giue,	*omit*

The same tendency may be seen in one of its simplest forms—assimilation—where the ending of one word is affected by that of another in the immediate context:

| I. i. 176 | The King from Eltam I int*end* to *send*, | steal |
| II. v. 108 | Might but redeeme the pass*age* of your *Age*. | passing |

Three further passages may be taken as contaminated in a similar way, though it is not possible to say with any certainty how they should be emended, and it is also possible to defend the first and the last as authentic:

III. i. 167–8	Thy *humble* seruant vowes obedience,
	And *humble* seruice, till the point of death.
v. iii. 136	*Consent*, and for thy Honor giue *Consent*,
v. iv. 170	Nor be rebellious *to the Crowne of England*,
	Thou nor thy Nobles, *to the Crowne of England*.

The first example is A's, the other two B's; the scribe, therefore, rather than a compositor, is likely to be responsible.

In much the same way, a succession of repeated words or phrases may have influenced the scribe's interpretation of similar graphic forms. The following are representative:

IV. iii. 44	And curse the cause I cannot *ayde* the man,
IV. iv. 23	The leuied succours that should lend him *ayde*,
29	Yorke should haue sent him *ayde*.
41	Within six houres, they will be at his *ayde*. [= syde]

v. iii. 100	*Madam* . . .
106	Sweet *Madam* . . .
123	No gentle *Madam* . . .
126	How say you *Madam* . . .
129	And *Madam* . . .
175	Farwell sweet *Madam* [= maid] : but hearke you
	Margaret,
	No Princely commendations to my King?
	Mar. Such commendations as becomes a *Maide*,
180	But *Madame* . . .

It would not, of course, be impossible for a compositor to make these errors. Their frequency, however, in the work of both F compositors, points rather to the scribe.

Errors where the meaning, rather than the form, of the context seems to have misled the scribe, especially if an unusual word or sense was involved, and where he may also have indulged in a form of improvement at the same time, are equally common, e.g.:

| I. ii. 100 | . . . at Touraine, in S. Katherines *Church-yard*, |

Here the chronicles make it clear that the church, not the church-yard, is involved. The scribe, however, may have thought this an unlikely place for a 'deal of old iron'; and may further have been deceived by reading the final loop of the Elizabethan *h* followed by a final *e* as an abbreviation, 'y^d', of 'yard'. So with II. iv. 56–7:

> *Lawyer.* Vnlesse my Studie and my Bookes be false,
>   The argument you hold was wrong in *you*:   *law*

where the error may be set down to the graphical similarity of y or Y to L,[1] the influence of 'you' in the same line, and the un-familiarity of the phrase 'wrong in law'.

And again:

> IV. iv. 31   Swearing that you with-hold his leuied *hoast*,   *horse*
>   33   . . . he might haue sent, & had the Horse:

> V. iv. 114   . . . if we conclude a Peace
>   It shall be with such strict and *seuere*   *seueral*
>   Couenants,

where the influence of 'strict' in the context, the legal term 'seueral', and the general look of the word, would account for the error.

Most of the F readings could no doubt with some ingenuity be defended; in the absence of a second text we cannot be quite as certain of some emendations as we could wish, though we can be certain from the context that, as Dover Wilson points out,[2] many others less innocent have escaped observation. To take an extreme case, it is possible to find some sort of sense in 'ruine combate with their Pallaces' (V. ii. 7), and no editor, to my knowledge, has emended, though Dover Wilson finds it 'a strange expression'.[3] The nature of the corruption, however, emerges when, in conjunction with the earlier 'combat with' (I. i. 54), we examine the source in Ps. cxxii. 6–7, 'Peace be within thy walls, and prosperity within thy palaces.' Shakespeare presumably adapted the second clause, in some such form as:

> Peace be amongst them if they turn to vs,
> Else ruine come within their Pallaces.

Suppose an original 'be', altered for variety to 'come' and (though not necessarily) 'within' written with a superior bar for the 'in', and the scribe's recollection of the earlier phrase accounts for the rest. In other words, he glanced at the copy, not too closely, and his familiarity with the earlier phrase, of similar form, decided his interpretation.

(e) Omission

It is clear from the verse that omissions are very numerous. Since this again applies to the work of both compositors, and particularly

---

1. Cf. III. ii. 117 Yet/Let.   2. *MSH.*, I. 47.   3. *1H6*, 193.

of A, much of the omission must be attributed to the scribe. That some of the omissions were due to difficulty in the copy at some stage, rather than to carelessness, is suggested by gaps in the text, as at I. iv. 90:

> Thou shalt not die whiles——[1]

and omissions of proper names, as at I. i. 56:

> Then *Iulius Caesar* or bright——

where a long name, with many minims, may have baffled the reader. Even *Nero*, at I. iv. 94, was possibly omitted for illegibility, to judge by the number of cruxes in the immediate context. The misreading of *Patay* as *Poictiers* at IV. i. 19 may also have been due to difficulty in the script.

At least one misplaced line seems to have been omitted and wrongly re-inserted, more likely by the scribe than by any other agent of transmission:

I. iv. 86–8. Salisbury and Gargrave have been mortally wounded. Talbot speaks first to Salisbury, then to Gargrave, then to Salisbury again (in the F text):

> Heauen be thou gracious to none aliue,
> If *Salisbury* wants mercy at thy hands.
> Beare hence his Body, I will helpe to bury it.   86
> Sir *Thomas Gargraue*, hast thou any life?   87
> Speake vnto *Talbot*, nay, looke vp to him.   88
> Salisbury cheare thy Spirit with this comfort,

which is absurd. At l. 109 we have again

> Conuey we (*F* me) *Salisbury* into his Tent,

Clearly l. 86 ought to refer to Gargrave, and follow l. 88; Salisbury's body will be looked after in due course. Talbot has turned from Salisbury for a moment to speak to Gargrave (87–8). When Gargrave makes no reply, Talbot, realizing that he is dead, orders attendants to 'Beare hence his Body', and then resumes his words with the still living Salisbury. In the transcription l. 86 must have been omitted, and wrongly inserted after l. 85 on the mistaken supposition that the body concerned was Salisbury's.[2]

Scribal omission and consequential conjecture, editorial or compositorial, may account for some further errors.[3] When Winchester

1. Cf. also III. ii. 74 'That we are here.'

2. This emendation was suggested by Dr Brooks. For a similar case, see V. iii. 47–9 and n.

3. Cf. the well-known examples (with a previous editior instead of a scribe responsible for the omission) of *R3*, I. i. 65; IV. iv. 536; and *1H4*, V. iii. 11.

announces that Charles the Dauphin and his lords desire a general peace (v. iv. 94 ff.)[1] and are at hand to confer about 'some matter', there is an obvious conflict between the known subject proposed and the indeterminate phrase. The conference is clearly to be about the peace; and the expression required is 'the same'. What seems to have happened is that the scribe omitted 'the', leaving 'same', which was misread 'some', to which 'matter' was added conjecturally to complete the metre and the sense.

The scribe, then, seems to have been guilty of (a) a large number of omissions; (b) contextual errors, that is, allowing the context to influence his interpretation of the *look* of a word—a normal factor in ordinary reading—and the rather similar 'errors of recollection', as Dover Wilson calls them, often in the form of 'catching' or dittography from the immediate neighbourhood, but possibly sometimes in the form of recollection of a similar phrase at some distance; and (c) 'improvement' or normalization—filling in ellipses, eliminating inversions and other rhetorical or poetic forms, and all without much regard to the metre. These errors, alterations, and omissions occur in the stints of both the F compositors alike, and are therefore unlikely, taken together, to be due to either, especially the conservative and literal compositor A.

ACT- AND SCENE-DIVISIONS

The erratic divisions in *1 Henry VI* have generally been attributed to revision or multiple-authorship. Even by advocates of Shakespearean authorship, they are still used to explain or support the treatment of the Margaret–Suffolk episode as a Shakespearean addition to link a 'Talbot' play with *2* (and *3*) *Henry VI*. Here, however, we enter a region of hypotheses. All that can be finally concluded is that, while such an explanation is possible, it is not inevitable. It covers only a small part of a much larger problem common to other plays in the First Folio, and indeed, only a small part of the problem in *1 Henry VI* itself. Other explanations are equally, if not more, probable; and it may well be that the habits of the *1 Henry VI* scribe play no small part in the final solution. The facts are these:

Our Acts I, II, and IV mark the Act and the first Scene only. Act III is fully divided. Act V is irregular. The last two Acts are marked thus:

Folio	Editors
Actus Quartus. Scena Prima.	*Act IV*
	Seven scenes marked
Scena secunda.	*Act V. Scene i.*

1. Cf. v. i. 4 ff.

Folio	*Editors*
Scaena Tertia.	*Scene ii.*
	Scene iii.
	Scene iv.
Actus Quintus.	*Scene v.*

Pollard's explanation, endorsed by Professor Alexander, was that '*scene ii* is scene ii not of Act IV but of Act V [scene i having been omitted, carrying with it the Act V heading], and the heading before the concluding scene *Actus Quintus* is an error for *Scena Quinta*. There is a similar error in *King John* where *Actus Secundus* stands for *Scena Secunda*.'[1]

The parallel from *King John* is far from clear. The marking there runs thus:

Folio	*Cambridge*
Actus Primus, Scaena Prima.	I. i
Scaena Secunda.	II. i
Actus Secundus	III. i
Actus Tertius, Scaena prima.	
Scoena Secunda.	III. ii

On this marking, it would appear that the Act/Scene error is actually the other way round, i.e. *Scene* for *Act*. The further errors may be noticed: *Actus Quartus* for *Actus Quintus* (i.e. *Actus Quartus* appears twice); *Actus Tertius* does not mark any legitimate division at all, but only an entry; there is no division for III. iii, and *Scena Tertia* is accordingly III. iv. Thus the general impression is not that of a simple error of confusing acts and scenes, but of some widespread disease similar to that which affects *1 Henry VI*.

No explanation or hypothesis, therefore, can be considered satisfactory for either play (or for a number of others) unless it is something more than local and covers the whole body of phenomena. Pollard's suggestion that *Actus Quintus* is an error, in *1 Henry VI*, for *Scena Quinta*, though plausible enough, is unsatisfactory since it does not explain why Scene iv was not numbered and what it was. Similarly his assumption that *Scene ii* is correct, and his assumption that a first scene of Act V has been lost, is merely to build one hypothesis on another. There is no obvious omission or cut here; it is here, if anywhere, with the death of Talbot and the opening of negotiations, that Act V must begin. Why are all the scenes of Acts I and II, except the first, also unmarked; and similarly those of Act IV, whose Talbot scenes are of the essence of the play?

It seems more probable that we have to do here, as in *John*, with

1. *Op. cit.*, p. 185.

some agent doing his best with something he did not well understand; helped perhaps by some indications of act markings, but no indication of scenes. In *1 Henry VI*, with its numerous episodes often linked by *Alarms and Excursions*, he had little to guide him except a change of place—from e.g. Paris to London—or of nationality—the alternation of English and French, and even that often obscured. Such a person might well mark scenes or omit to mark them; and mark them in the wrong places when he did. He could treat the Talbot episodes of Act IV as one continuous scene, and wake up to the need for a second scene when the action suddenly changed to England (v. i), and mark it *Scena secunda*. The return to the French faction would then become *Scaena Tertia* (v. ii), while the following *Alarum* and *Excursions* justified him in omitting any division at v. iii, and similarly in not separating the Margaret–Suffolk episode. Joan's trial, though strictly a separate scene (v. iv), takes place so close after her capture that it could be assumed with some justification to occur in the same place and as part of the same series of events; it was therefore left unmarked. The sudden change to England at v. v demanded, or was recognized as, a new scene, but, as the end of the play was in sight and no Act v had yet appeared, it had to be so marked.[1]

This is all, of course, purely hypothetical; but at least it offers a more general and probable view of what happened. And since neither the author nor the compositors can be blamed for such an erratic and inconsistent procedure, it seems possible that here again we have the handiwork of the scribe.[2] The problem, as has been said, concerns other F plays, and a satisfactory solution will have to account for all such phenomena. But until such a solution has been achieved, it would seem unwise to use phenomena we do not fully understand as the basis of theories of revision,[3] interpolation, or multiple-authorship.

It seems reasonable, then, to suggest that the copy for *1 Henry VI* was a transcript of the author's manuscript, carrying some annotations by the stage-adapter or prompter—a transcript probably made expressly for the printers of the Folio, and perhaps for that reason 'improved' to a degree and in a way not permissible in Shakespeare's lifetime. The variations and inconsistencies in the text do not seem to go beyond what a combination of the various agents of transmission might be expected to produce, nor to justify

1. I owe these suggestions to Dr H. F. Brooks.
2. Or editor marking the copy.
3. For the theory that the Margaret–Suffolk scenes are a later addition, to link this play with *2 Henry VI*, see below, p. xlviii.

the elaborate theories of revision or of multiple-authorship that
have sometimes been founded upon them.

EMENDATION AND EDITORIAL POLICY

The main value of this theory of the copy for *1 Henry VI* is that
it makes possible a more systematic and unified approach to emendation. Whereas readings have been considered and emended on
their individual merits, and with excessive caution since they were
thought to be printed direct from autograph, they can now be regarded more as a body, with certain trends of scribal error running
throughout. Emendation can thus be attempted with somewhat
greater freedom and consistency where it would not have been
suggested by the *ductus litterarum*. It is unfortunate that, as must
happen in a one-text play, so many more readings almost certainly
corrupt cannot be emended with reasonable certainty; and in particular that omissions that could be filled with various alternatives
must remain omissions. Even so, and even though some of the present emendations may be disputed, the general gain to the text,
and to Shakespeare's text, seems not inconsiderable.

In accordance with Arden practice, the collation is selective. It
records spelling and punctuation variants only where they seriously
affect interpretation, and only such conjectures as seem valuable,
highly probable, or necessary to be taken into account for a proper discussion of the crux concerned.

In the text, some older forms (fift, Dolphin, etc.) have been
silently modernized or standardized. The forms *Falstaff* [1] and Joan
of *Aire* may surprise from unfamiliarity, but they seem to be what
Shakespeare wrote. The *Champaigne* of Shakespeare and the chronicles, where the reference is to *Compiègne*, has been retained as a
compromise. In the stage-directions, the various forms of *La Pucelle*
have been standardized, but in the text the forms with 'la' and 'de'
have been retained, and the variant spellings at I. iv. 106, where
they are necessary to the pun.

In the stage-directions, words without equivalent in F are enclosed in square brackets. A scene-heading (IV. iv), which should
probably not be marked, is removed to the right without the usual
spacing; but the separate lineation is not changed. Square brackets
have also been used in one instance (v. v. 60) where a word necessary to the sense, but not sufficiently certain as an emendation, has
been supplied.

1. Adopted, however, by Wilson.

2. HISTORICAL

AUTHORSHIP

The main trend of eighteenth- and nineteenth-century criticism was to doubt Shakespeare's sole authorship of *1 Henry VI*. It became part of the Shakespeare 'mythos' that anything unworthy of his genius or repulsive to the sensibilities of the critic's time should be removed from the canon, and fathered on some alternative writer, or even a 'symposium' of writers, with Shakespeare possibly adding a few scenes or revising the whole[1]. In *1 Henry VI*, 'the revolting treatment of Joan', and the 'mean and prosaical'[2] style were sufficient grounds, along with two or three shreds of contemporary evidence and some 'echoes' and inconsistencies in the play, for an elaborate theory involving the part authorship of Greene, Marlowe, and Nashe, or some of them.

The first indication of this trend came from Edward Ravenscroft, writing about *Titus Andronicus* in 1687;[3] 'I have been told by some anciently conversant with the Stage, that it [viz. *Titus*] was not Originally his, but brought by a private Author to be Acted, and he only gave some Master-touches...: this I am apt to believe, because 'tis the most incorrect and indigested piece in all his works; It seems rather a heap of Rubbish than a Structure.'[4] Theobald, in 1734, challenged the authenticity of *Henry VI* in a very similar strain; 'though there are several master-strokes in these plays, ... yet I am almost doubtful, whether they are entirely of his writing... I should rather imagine them to have received some finishing beauties at his hand ... the diction ... is more obsolete, and the numbers more mean and prosaical, than in the generality of his compositions.'[5] In 1747, Warburton shed all hesitation: *1 Henry VI* 'was certainly not Shakespeare's'. Johnson's sensible remarks that 'in the productions of genius there will be inequality', and that 'the diction, the versification, and the figures are Shakespeare's' were powerless to stem the tide. Malone, after accepting Johnson's verdict for a time, reverted to the *status quo*, and was 'decisively of the opinion that this play was not written by Shakespeare,'[6] but 'the entire, or nearly the entire, production of some ancient dramatist.'[7]

Shakespeare's total authorship was thus denied, in some form, by most eighteenth- and nineteenth-century critics. A few exceptions were Charles Knight (1842), Hudson (1851), Grant White (1859), and Thomas Kenny (1864).[8] As late as 1918, Tucker Brooke

1. *W.S.*, 1. 290.   2. Malone, xviii. 3.   3. *W.S.*, ii. 255.
4. Cf. further, *Titus Andronicus*, ed. J. C. Maxwell, revised edition, 1961, Appendix (a).
5. Malone, xviii. 3.   6. *Ibid.*   7. *Op.cit.*, 557.
8. *The Life and Genius of Shakespeare.*

could still write that this view 'has vastly the largest number of up-
holders . . . and is indeed the only one that can be brought into
reasonable harmony with the evidence. In regard to the particular
scenes to be ascribed to Shakespeare there has been no radical
variation among good critics.'[1] Jane Lee[2] was rash enough to ap-
portion the play among its supposed authors, in which procedure
she was followed by Fleay,[3] H. C. Hart,[4] and recently Dover Wilson.[5] The scenes generally given to Shakespeare, mainly on the
grounds of style, are those dealing with the Temple Garden quarrel
(II. iv), the death of Mortimer (II. v), the death of Talbot (IV. ii–vii),
and the Margaret–Suffolk wooing (V. iii. 45–195).

Most of the German critics, however, supported Shakespearean
authorship. And with the end of the nineteenth century, the tide
began to turn. In 1903, Courthope[6] lent powerful support. He
made the point that 'these plays [including 1 Henry VI] are the
work of a single mind',[7] and that Shakespeare 'was the one dramatist alive . . . who had sufficient grasp of mind to imagine that historic drama as a consistent whole'.[8] Shakespeare was therefore 'the
sole author of King Henry VI'.[9] Finally, in 1929, Professor Peter
Alexander convinced the great majority with his Shakespeare's
'Henry VI' and 'Richard III'.[10] In 1951, Hereward T. Price, in a bril-
liant monograph, felt justified, without more ado, in analysing the
structure of 1 Henry VI to illustrate Shakespeare's characteristic
methods of dramatic construction.

MALONE'S 'DISSERTATION'

It was Malone who first presented a reasoned and exhaustive
case against Shakespeare's authorship. The numerous classical
allusions, he pointed out, 'do not naturally arise out of the subject,
but seem to be inserted merely to show the writer's learning'.[11] The
stately and uniform versification Malone would attribute to one or
more of Lodge, Greene, or the author of Selimus, Solyman and Perseda,
The Spanish Tragedy, and Titus Andronicus (not considered to be
Shakespeare's either).[12] Nashe's favourable mention[13] suggested
that it was written by a friend of his; while the omission by Holinshed, 'who was Shakespeare's guide', of Hall's description of Talbot
as the 'terror of the French', furnished an additional proof'. Malone

1. Yale ed., 141; cf. Trans. Conn. Acad. (1912), XVII. 141.
2. NSS. (1876), 219.
3. 'Who wrote Henry VI?', Macmillan's Magazine, 1875.
4. Hart, p. xii.   5. 1H6.
6. A History of English Poetry, Appendix to vol. IV (1903).   7. Op. cit., 462.
8. Op. cit., 463.   9. Ibid.   10. Cambridge, 1929.
11. Malone, XVIII. 558.   12. Op. cit., 563.   13. See below, p. xxxviii.

then cited the dramatist's apparent ignorance of Henry's age;[1] Cambridge's raising of an army against Henry V, where in *Henry V* he merely conspired to assassinate him;[2] and the inconsistency between the accounts of Mortimer's death in *1 Henry VI* and *2 Henry VI* (in one, Glendower's captive, in the other, a state prisoner in the Tower).[3] The lack of rhyme, in an early play, was also against Shakespeare. In short, 'except in some scenes of the fourth Act, there is not a single print of the footsteps of Shakespeare'.[4] Heming and Condell therefore printed the play in the First Folio either through inaccurate memory, or because it was necessary to *2* and *3 Henry VI*, or because Shakespeare wrote a few lines at iv. ii. ff.

GREENE

Apart from the general grounds of style, inconsistencies, and learning, Malone found a more specific ground for his position on authorship in the related question of the authorship of *2* and *3 Henry VI*. There his main case rested on Robert Greene's allusion, in his pamphlet, a *Groats-worth of witte* (1592), to Shakespeare as 'an vpstart Crow, beautified with our feathers, that with his *Tygers hart wrapt in a Players hyde*, supposes he is as well able to bombast out a blanke verse as the best of you:'[5] and its parody of *3 Henry VI*, I. iv. 137, 'Oh Tygres Heart, wrapt in a Womans Hide'. This Malone held to imply that Shakespeare had appropriated the plays of Greene himself and the others he was addressing ('our feathers'), including the line from *3 Henry VI*, and made them his own by revision. The line also appears in the quarto version, which Malone took to represent the original play (though mutilated in report), of which the Folio text was the Shakespearean version. Malone found further support for this view in certain quarto passages which differed fundamentally from the corresponding passages in F. These indicated to him the presence of revision.[6] His case for *3 Henry VI* was easily extended to the similar phenomena in *2 Henry VI*, and by implication, because here no quarto existed, to *1 Henry VI*.

NASHE

In the same year as Greene's pamphlet appeared, Thomas Nashe, in his *Pierce Penilesse his Svpplication to the Divell* (S.R., 8 August 1592), wrote of 'braue *Talbot* (the terror of the French) ...

1. Cf. iii. iv. 17 ff. and n.   2. *1H6*, ii. v. 75; *H5*, ii. ii.
3. Malone, xviii. 567; *1H6*, ii. v; *2H6*, ii. ii.   4. Malone, xviii. 568.
5. G. B. Harrison's reprint: Bodley Head Quartos, 45–6.
6. See my *2 Henry VI* (New Arden), xvi ff.

that hee should triumphe againe on the Stage ... fresh bleeding.'[1]
This is generally agreed to refer to Talbot in *1 Henry VI*, where he
is described as 'the terror of the French' (I. iv. 42), enjoying a
'triumph' (III. iii. 5), and fresh bleeding (IV. vii). The play would
seem to have been very popular in 1592: Nashe refers to 'ten thousand spectators at least, (at seuerall times)'.[2]

HENSLOWE

This seems to agree nicely with the third contemporary reference
—an entry, in Philip Henslowe's *Diary*,[3] of 'Harey the vj', as performed by Lord Strange's Men on 3 March 1592. This play is
marked 'ne' (new?), and drew the relatively large sum of iij[l] xvj[s]
for Henslowe (compared with the previous day's xiij[s] for 'Matcha-
vell').[4] It was repeated on fourteen occasions to 19 June, by which
time the takings had fallen to xxxij[s], and the theatres were about
to close on account of the plague. 'The date', says Chambers, 'helps
to identify the play [*1 Henry VI*] with "Harey the vj". It was ...
either new, or substantially remodelled.'[5] At that time (1930) the
assumption seemed natural. It was then still generally believed that
Shakespeare's first company, with which he is already found associated as a leading member in 1594, was the Strange–Chamberlain's Men. To find in a list of Strange's plays a title so similar to
Henry VI seemed to clinch the matter.

In addition, *The Contention* and *The True Tragedy*, then assumed
to be, or represent, original plays later revised (as *2* and *3 Henry VI*),
had belonged to Pembroke's Men, as stated on the title-page of
The True Tragedy; and with Pembroke's, as Malone had emphasized,[6] Shakespeare was not known to have had any connection.
Strange's, the argument ran, must therefore have acquired from
Pembroke's *The Contention* and *The True Tragedy*, and had them
revised by Shakespeare. If *1 Henry VI* was indeed a new Strange
play in 1592, they probably had it adapted (with e.g. the addition
of the Margaret–Suffolk scenes) to form a fore-piece to their newly
acquired and revised *2* and *3 Henry VI*. This adaptation could
amount, as Chambers says, to having it 'substantially remodelled'.
Or *1 Henry VI* might equally have been acquired, like the others,
from a different company, and the subsequent revision by Shakespeare would account for the 'newness'.

Paradoxically, if we accept (what is now widely accepted)
Shakespeare's early connection with Pembroke's, it is equally pos-

1. McKerrow, *Nashe*, I. 212.   2. *Ibid*.   3. *W.S.*, I. 292; II. 308.
4. *W.S.*, II. 309; Greg, *Henslowe's Diary*, I. 13.   5. *W.S.*, I. 292.
6. Malone, XVIII. 570.

sible to use 'harey the vj' against Shakespeare's authorship. For if Shakespeare in 1592 had no connection with Strange's, *and* this is indeed *1 Henry VI*, it could not be Shakespeare's. Strange's must later have acquired *2* and *3 Henry VI* (in their 'older' forms) from Pembroke's, had Shakespeare revise them, and at the same time adapt 'Harey the vj', their own older play, to form a first part to fit them, presumably by adding the Suffolk–Margaret episode and perhaps other scenes like the Temple Garden quarrel. Either way, then, the Henslowe entry may be made to support non-Shakespearean authorship.

While the main case against Shakespeare rests on these three contemporary allusions, various subsidiary lines of argument have commonly been used, since Malone, to corroborate the presence of other hands in *1 Henry VI*, and sometimes to identify them. Most are of the vocabulary-clue type. H. C. Hart, for example, devotes much of his analysis to the search for words 'not again in Shakespeare', implying that they belong to another, for example Greene, Peele, or Nashe. Several more specific parallels, especially with the writings of Nashe, are cited by Dover Wilson, to imply that Shakespeare is unlikely to have been acquainted with their sources, in view of his limited scholarship.

THE ANSWER TO MALONE

We no longer take seriously Malone's view that Shakespeare's sole guide was Holinshed, or that he was ignorant of the classics; or the Romantic-Victorian view that anything horrible or disgusting to certain sensibilities was a slur on the fair name of Shakespeare and must be attributed to another; or the requirement that he must never nod, metrically or poetically. We are aware that he practised the recognized Renascence ideal of decorum, suiting the style to the action; and that there was a stock dramatic vocabulary which he knew and used. The case for revision based on the double texts of *2* and *3 Henry VI*, and on Greene's phrase about the 'upstart crow', is seen rather to imply Shakespeare's own entire authorship of these two plays, a line from one of which Greene is holding up to ridicule as the sort of bombast written by this upstart player-dramatist in competition with the University Wits. *The Contention* and *The True Tragedy* are now generally accepted as reports of *2* and *3 Henry VI*, not in any sense their originals.[1]

We are now reasonably certain, moreover, that Shakespeare did write some of his earlier plays for Pembroke's, and that he had no

1. Peter Alexander, *Shakespeare's 'Henry VI' and 'Richard III'*; *2H6* (New Arden), Introduction.

demonstrable connection, before 1594 (by which time all three parts of *Henry VI* must have been written) with Strange's. The identification of *Harey the vj* with *1 Henry VI*, so naturally assumed by Chambers, is now extremely doubtful, and can hardly bear the weight of the case against Shakespeare's authorship of *1 Henry VI*.

Professor Peter Alexander presented a strong case[1] against this identification. His arguments may be briefly summarized as follows:

(*a*) Many subjects were duplicated in the repertories of the Elizabethan companies, e.g. Richard II, Richard III, Henry IV, Henry V, Troilus and Cressida, Julius Caesar, etc.; to which it may be added that we actually have the 'plot' of a play among the Alleyn manuscripts at Dulwich, attributable to the Strange–Chamberlain's Men about this date, on the reign of Henry VI.[2]

(*b*) There is no evidence that Shakespeare wrote anything for the Strange–Chamberlain's Men—his later company—before 1594. Their repertory before that is known in considerable detail (134 entries).[3]

(*c*) There is evidence that Shakespeare was a member of, or at least wrote for, Pembroke's Men before they went on their disastrous tour of 1593.

(*d*) Recollections of *1 Henry VI* are found in the 'memorial' versions of *2* and *3 Henry VI* (*The Contention* and *The True Tragedy*)[4] the first of which appeared in print early in 1594 (S.R., March 12), as Pembroke's. The assumption is that *1 Henry VI* was also in their repertory and had been there long enough for them to become familiar with the text.

Hart's and similar parallels of vocabulary, at the best, do no more than lend some degree of plausibility, not proof, to the theory of non-Shakespearean authorship. They are of little evidential value as proof of authorship for an age when there was a common fund of dramatic diction and everybody borrowed from everybody else. Hart himself, in fact, reduces the whole method to absurdity when he says that certain correspondences 'may be reminiscences the other way'[5] as between e.g. Peele and Shakespeare.

Rather more precise are one or two derivative passages found in both Nashe's work and in *1 Henry VI*. The argument is that since these passages or references are found in Nashe's own works, and since Shakespeare is unlikely to have read the sources as well as Nashe, their presence in *1 Henry VI* is a sign of Nashe's hand in the play. Two of the strongest and most characteristic may serve for all.

1. *Op. cit.*, 188 ff.   2. Greg, *EDD.*, 113 ff.   3. *W.S.*, II. 307 ff.
4. Alexander quotes two of these: for others, see App. III.   5. P. xx.

1. Both Nashe and *1 Henry VI* quote a passage from Cornelius Agrippa's *De Incertitudine et Vanitate Scientiarum*, in Sandford's translation:

> Neither hathe the true mouinge of *Mars* bene knowen vntill this daie[1]   (Ch. 30, p. 43, ed. 1569)

Nashe, in his *Haue with you to Saffron-Walden* (1596; McKerrow, iii. 20. 13–15):

> . . . you are as ignorant in the true mouings of my Muse as the Astronomers are in the true mouings of *Mars*, which to this day they could neuer attaine too.

Compare *1 Henry VI*, I. ii. 1–2:

> *Mars* his true mouing, euen as in the Heauens,
> So in the Earth, to this day is not knowne.

Agrippa's book was widely known and read in the sixteenth century, as its frequent reprints, both in Latin and English, testify. There is thus no reason—except the old prejudice against Shakespeare's learning—why Shakespeare, as well as Nashe, should not have known it. If it appears surprising that both should quote this particular sentence, it may be replied that Nashe has shown his familiarity with *1 Henry VI* and Talbot on the stage. There is therefore the probability that the *1 Henry VI* allusion had drawn his attention to, or revived his memory of, the reference. The passage may also have become a commonplace, because of its allusion to one of the then outstanding mysteries of nature. Shakespeare is, in any case, nearer to Agrippa, with his 'mouing' and 'known'. Both may well derive independently from Agrippa. The parallel does not prove Nashe's hand in the play.

2. Similarly, when considering *1 Henry VI*, I. ii. 55–6, where it is said of Joan,

> The spirit of deepe Prophecie she hath,
> Exceeding the nine *Sibyls* of old Rome:

Professor Dover Wilson draws attention to references to the Sibyls by Nashe[2] and by his source, Henry Howard's treatise, *A Defensatiue against the poyson of supposed Prophecies* (1583). The play refers, he says, 'not to the ten Sibyls mentioned by Varro, or to the Cumean Sibyl, or to her nine books, but to the so-called Sibylline Oracles. . . Howard speaks more than once of these Sibyls; they must "haue been inspired with this gift [of prophecy] aboue their equals" '. Nashe was indeed 'shaky on the exact number . . . but Howard had

---

1. Cf. *Sh. Eng.*, I. 448–9.   2. McKerrow, II. 123, 29–30; 280, 10–12.

forgotten to supply him with that detail.'[1] (xxvi–xxvii). Again there is no reason why Shakespeare should not also have read Howard. Actually, the lines in *1 Henry VI* draw much more directly on one of Shakespeare's recognized sources, Cooper's *Thesaurus*, where the Glossary gives, under *Sibylla*, 'A generall name of all women which had *the spirite of prophecie*: of them (as Varro and Lactantius doe write) were tenne . . . euery one of these (as Lactantius sayth) prophecied of the incarnation of Christ.' Shakespeare was also shaky on the number, but he had at least taken one phrase, not in Nashe or Howard, from Cooper.

The final answer to Malone, of course, lies in the play itself. As will be argued in the Literary Introduction, and supported by head-notes to the scenes,

(*a*) it has every mark of being written deliberately as an integral part of a tetralogy, (i) using the same chronicles and chronicle-material, (ii) according to the same method, (iii) at the exact points where each play supplements the others, but duplicating where necessary to its own story, in addition to preparing for the sequel in *2 Henry VI*;

(*b*) it has a carefully constructed five-act plan, the theme of each act and the whole theme being clear and well-defined;

(*c*) it is full of Shakespeare's characteristic style and imagery;

(*d*) the inconsistencies are either such as are to be expected of an author using these methods, or of a particular type of scribe; and the explanation of most inconsistencies in these ways suggests that with fuller knowledge the rest could likewise be accounted for.

PRIORITY

A separate consequence of the case for non-Shakespearean origin has been founded on Henslowe's 'Harey the vj', acted from 3 March 1592, taken in conjunction with Nashe's reference to the popularity of Talbot on the stage (August 1592), and Greene's attack on Shakespeare about the same time. If the play was new in March, and the theatres were effectively closed for new writing in June until early in 1594, and *2* and *3 Henry VI* were also in existence by that time, as they must have been (since (*a*) Pembroke's collapsed in their provincial tour of 1593, and (*b*) the first of the two was pirated by March 1594), it follows that it must have been written after parts *2* and *3*. There would not have been time in the short period March to June 1592 to write and rehearse these parts; and they must therefore have been in existence already.

The sort of conjectural history of the play required by this theory

1. *1H6*, xxvi–xxvii.

may be seen in Dover Wilson's edition. He imagines Nashe and Greene writing all or most of the play for Strange's, with whom Shakespeare is supposed at that time to have been connected. Greene and Nashe were for some reason paid off, and Shakespeare asked to complete the play. This he did, perhaps with some help, and hurriedly; adapting the play, naturally, to the other two parts they had previously acquired.[1]

As we have seen, however, Strange's day-to-day performances include in a long list no other play except 'harey the vj' that has any suggestion of connection with Shakespeare.[2] There is no sign for example of *2* and *3 Henry VI*, to which the first part is supposed to have been adapted. Wilson suggests that they belonged to a different company.

What makes all this so improbable, indeed impossible, is that, as Professor Alexander has pointed out, the memorial versions of *2* and *3 Henry VI* (*The Contention* and *The True Tragedy*) contain a number of recollections from *1 Henry VI*, including such alleged additions as the Margaret–Suffolk episode.[3] The three plays must therefore have been in the hands of one company for long enough before the closure of the theatres in June 1592 to give the actors time to memorize them so that they were able, after breaking up, to report them with some fullness, and confuse similar passages between each pair by association of ideas. And since the reports of the second and third parts are clearly derived from Pembroke's (the second by inference from the title-page of the third), that company must have been Pembroke's. *1 Henry VI* must therefore be a distinct play from 'Harey the vj', and Shakespeare not yet a member of Strange's.

It is possible to concede all this, however, and yet to hold that *1 Henry VI* was written last of the three, and in any case adapted in various ways, including the insertion of the Margaret–Suffolk material, to act as a fore-piece to *2* and *3 Henry VI*. This affects the structure and integrity of the plays, and their relation to the sources, rather than the authorship, and will be better dealt with in the Literary Introduction.

Meanwhile, there seems no sufficient reason to doubt Shakespeare's authorship of the whole play, or that he wrote it in the natural chronological order. As often happens, one comes back to Johnson's massive common sense. In a note to *2 Henry VI*, he says:

1. *1H6*, xlviii–xlix.
2. I do not take seriously the identification of *Titus & Vespacia* in Henslowe with *Titus Andronicus*.
3. See App. III.

'It is apparent that this play begins where the former ends, and continues the series of transactions, of which it presupposes the first part already known. This is sufficient proof that the second and third parts were not written without dependence on the first.'[1]

DATE

Assuming, then, that these plays were written in natural sequence, the date of *1 Henry VI* (as of *2* and *3 Henry VI* and *Richard III*), can be fixed within narrow limits. All are subsequent to *The Faerie Queene*, I–III, the Preface and the Stationers' Register entry of which are both dated December 1589. All show the influence of Spenser.[2] The downward limit is set by Nashe's allusion to Talbot before 8 August 1592. This may be further narrowed by several converging and complementary lines of argument:

1. The theatres, as noted above, were effectively closed for new writing on 28 June 1592, by which time, it is clear (from the collapse of Pembroke's, for which they can all be assumed to have been written, the following summer, and from recollections of the other plays in the reported versions of the last three), all four were in existence. A reasonable margin of time must be allowed for all four to become familiar to the reporting actors, and for *1 Henry VI* to be followed by its three successors.

2. Marlowe's *Edward II* was entered on 6 July 1593, a month after his death. It was written for Pembroke's, and was heavily influenced by the Shakespearean series, which it was an attempt to imitate—it was something new for Marlowe, and not at all in his *Tamburlaine–Faust–Jew of Malta* line. It is full of Shakespearean echoes. This is made quite clear from the fact that some are integral to the subject or derived from the known chronicle source in Shakespeare, but contingent in Marlowe. It may be inferred that *Edward II* follows *Richard III*, and therefore *1 Henry VI*, and that other parallels show the same direction of influence. A. P. Rossiter[3] gives an example where Shakespeare derived from Hall the passages:

> *2H6*, II. iii. 28:
>> I see no reason, why a King of yeeres
>> Should be to be protected like a child.
> *1H6*, I. i. 35:
>> Whom like a Schoole-boy you may ouer-awe.

Marlowe imitates:

---

1. Johnson, v (1765), 3.
2. Cf. *1H6*, I. i. 11–13; I. i. 124 (and *Troil.*, v. v. 26); III. iv. 19; *R3*, I. iv. 26.
3. Rossiter, 54.

Ed. 2, 1336–7:
> As though your highnes were a schoole boy still,
> And must be awde and gouernd like a child.[1]

3. Again, if we admit that *The Troublesome Raigne* (1591) collects bits and pieces from many sources in the way Marlowe has done in *Edward II* from several of Shakespeare's plays, the gap may be further narrowed. For *Richard III*, the last of the series, seems clearly to be imitated in *The Troublesome Raigne*'s

> Set down, set down the load not worth your pain![2]

This is virtually Anne's order at the funeral of Henry VI:

> Set downe, set downe your honourable load,

which suggests that the most likely date for *1 Henry VI* is 1590.

3. LITERARY

CONFLICTING ESTIMATES

The Elizabethan verdict on the popularity of *1 Henry VI* is preserved by a spectator—the pamphleteer and playwright Thomas Nashe—who wrote, 'How it would haue ioyed braue *Talbot* (the terror of the French) to thinke that ... hee should triumphe againe on the Stage, and haue his bones newe embalmed with the teares of ten thousand spectators at least, (at seuerall times) who ... imagine they behold him fresh bleeding.'[3]

The post-Elizabethan verdict (until recently) has been rather different. To Maurice Morgann, in 1777, it was 'that Drum and trumpet Thing'.[4] To Professor Dover Wilson, in 1953, 'A thronged house and heavy gate-money seem hardly justified by the intrinsic merits... But, as the standing popularity of *Titus Andronicus* shows, Elizabethan audiences were not very critical when dramatists appealed to their emotions.'[5] In the interval, Coleridge had issued his 'rude comment' to anyone who dared to claim the play for Shakespeare, 'you may have ears—for so has another animal—but an ear you cannot have'.[6] Malone found it 'among the feeblest performances of Shakespeare';[7] while Marshall was repelled by the 'horrid atmosphere of bloodshed' and the treatment of Joan, that 'simple and heroic maid'.[8]

Although Courthope had tried to reassert a contrary view in

---

1. Cf. *2H6*, I. iii. 78 and *Ed.2*, 704; *3H6*, I. i. 239 and *Ed.2*, 970; *R3*, III. vii. 224 and *Ed.2*, 2077.
2. *2T.R.*, vi. 1.   3. *Pierce Penilesse*: McKerrow, I. 212.
4. *An Essay on the Dramatic Character of Sir John Falstaff*.   5. *1H6*, xv.
6. Quoted *op. cit.*, xxix.   7. Malone, XVIII. 37 n.   8. Irving, II. 184.

1903,[1] it was not until later that critics became generally alive to the dramatic value of the *Henry VI–Richard III* series. 'Two years ago,' wrote R. W. Chambers in 1937, 'by going to the shores of the Pacific, I had the exceptional good luck to see the three parts of *Henry VI* and *Richard III* acted as one series. . . To see this was to realize that Shakespeare began his career with a tetralogy based on recent history, grim, archaic, crude, yet nevertheless such as, for power, patriotism, and sense of doom, had probably had no parallel since Aeschylus wrote the trilogy of which the *Persians* is the surviving fragment.'[2] This verdict has been amply confirmed by the more recent productions at the Birmingham Repertory Theatre and the Old Vic. The producer, Sir Barry Jackson, had had a similar 'experience of a lifetime' when he saw F. R. Benson's 1906 performance of the whole chronological sequence of the history plays at Stratford.[3] From his own productions, of *2 Henry VI* in 1951 and *3 Henry VI* in 1952, and of all three parts in 1953, he concluded 'what is as clear as daylight from the practical view of stage production is that the author was a dramatist of the first rank, though perhaps immature. If the author was not Shakespeare, I can only regret that the writer in question did not give us more examples of his genius. In short, *Henry VI* is eminently actable.'[4]

A parallel reorientation was effected by Tillyard's study of the history plays[5] in relation to their chronicle sources. Where they had previously been regarded, in the Morgann tradition, as merely 'a succession or stringing together of scenes or episodes',[6] Tillyard showed in detail how they present or imply a comprehensive world picture, and a systematic development of one theme explicitly stated in Edward Hall's Chronicle, embracing the deposition of Richard II and its consequences as far as the succession of Henry VII. This line has now been further developed, chiefly in America.[7] Most recently, Hereward T. Price has shown the importance for Shakespeare's histories of the central design, rather than plot or character, and how carefully every 'episode' is subordinated to the central theme.

An outstanding example of the change of interpretation may be seen in the attitude to Joan. She is now no longer the 'simple and

1. *History of English Poetry*, App. to vol. IV.

2. 'The Jacobean Shakespeare and *Measure for Measure*'. Annual Shakespeare Lecture of the British Academy, 1937.

3. *Shakespeare Survey*, VI. 49.   4. *Ibid.*, 50.

5. *Sh. Hist. Plays*, 1944.

6. J. B. Henneman, *PMLA.*, xv (1900), 290–320, 'The Episodes in Shakespeare's *1 Henry VI*'.

7. By e.g. Harbage, Ribner, Kirschbaum, Lily B. Campbell.

heroic maid', nor St Joan. Shakespeare, it is recognized, took Joan as he found her in Hall and Holinshed, and did no more than reflect the current English attitude. *1 Henry VI*, as Harbage notes, 'is a play about the courage, prowess, and assumed righteousness of the English as represented by such loyal and able leaders as Salisbury, Bedford, Warwick, and, above all, Lord Talbot; and about the opportunism, treachery, and fox-like successes of the French as represented by the fraud and moral depravity of La Pucelle.'[1] Nor is there, as sometimes claimed, any inconsistency in the presentation of Joan. Leo Kirschbaum[2] has clearly shown that the 'holy' and 'divine' Joan, as she appears to the French, is, even to them, treated with consistent irony, so that almost every reference carries an equivocal meaning, and she is from the start witch, 'dame', strumpet, and trull; so that the final avowal of her condition is no more than the fulfilment of the earlier implications. The 'holy' Joan of i. ii. 55–7, for example, is, as he notes, negated by the pagan reference. Expressions such as 'She takes upon her bravely at first dash' are 'deliberately slangy and cynical'. She is a 'bright star of *Venus*', pucelle, sweeting, devil's dam. Regarded in this light, the picture is natural and consistent.

Clearly a revolution has been in progress, in which every aspect has combined to re-establish the Elizabethan verdict on the play.

A 'TALBOT PLAY'?

Nashe's appreciation, however, has itself assisted to some extent in creating and maintaining one minor misinterpretation—that *1 Henry VI* is a 'Talbot play', not originally written but adapted for the series by the addition of the Margaret–Suffolk scenes.[3] No doubt Talbot is the outstanding single figure, and so appealed to Nashe. Opposed to Joan, he is completely fearless and disinterested, representing the entire if rather narrow patriot; he gives his life to prevent the loss of France (England's natural possession or 'margin of safety'); he and his son, equally heroic, die 'martyred to England's internal dissension'.[4] His part has been elaborately amplified from the meagre record of the chronicles; as Joan's has been exaggerated to heighten Talbot's achievement. The nature of their opposition is clearly defined at the outset, by Talbot's 'Heavens, can you suffer Hell so to prevail?'[5] and forms a central and substantial theme of the play. But no more. Talbot has only 13 out of 27 scenes, and dies at the end of Act iv. His doings are

1. Harbage, 153.
2. *PMLA.*, vol. 67 (1952), pp. 809–22: 'The Authorship of *1 Henry VI*'.
3. See further below, p. xlviii. 4. Harbage, 153. 5. i. v. 9.

merely one aspect of a theme that has many others, part of a larger unity and plan.

As Price points out, 'Shakespeare is imposing upon a body of historical data a controlling idea, an idea that constructs the play. He does the same thing with all his historical plays, English or Roman.'[1] It is interesting to note, by way of practical corroboration, that the abridgement used in the television serial 'An Age of Kings' (25 August 1960) should have been able to dispense with the heroic Talbot, and yet retain a highly unified and developing theme, a design.

SHAKESPEARE'S PLAN

Such misapprehensions of the English history plays can be corrected only when the general plan and purpose is appreciated, and each play seen in the context of the whole. Within the limits of the historical material—whose content he could shape and adapt, but not fundamentally alter—there can be little doubt that Shakespeare, the 'Johannes fac totum', set himself, and achieved, the ambitious task of staging, in his country's finest hour, its quasi-Biblical story, from the original sin of Henry IV to the grand redemption of the Tudors. The theme was already there in Hall's Chronicle, though Shakespeare amplified from Holinshed and Fabyan.[2] In Hall and Shakespeare it therefore partakes of the nature of an epic or, as Harbage[3] wisely says, a comedy—he might have said a divine comedy—since it ends happily, while its constituent parts may contain all the variety of epic, each tending to tragedy, comedy, pastoral, satire, or any mixture of them. It is the epic of England, rather than of individuals. And it has the defects of an epic, of a continued story, or a cycle. It is inclined to be episodic. Some parts have dramatically weak endings. The instalments often recapitulate. But, so considered, the unity is there, and Shakespeare has everywhere taken great pains to draw the links tighter.

The theme was announced right at the beginning by Hall: 'What mischiefe hath insurged in realmes by intestine devision, what depopulacion hath ensued in countries by ciuill discencion, what detestable murder hath been committed in citees by seperate faccions, and what calamitee hath ensued in famous regions by domestical discord & vnnaturall controuersy ... what miserie, what murder, and what execrable plagues this famous region hath suffered by the deuision and discencion of the renoumed houses of Lancastre and Yorke, ...' of which the conclusion is the Tudor peace brought

1. *Op. cit.*, 26.   2. See App. I.   3. *Op.*, *cit.*, 158–9.

about by the marriage of Henry VII to Elizabeth of York. The moral is that 'as by discord great thynges decaie and fall to ruine, so the same by concord be reuiued and erected' and England 'by vnion and agrement releued pacified and enriched.'

Professor Harold Jenkins has shown in detail how the comprehensive plan of *1* and *2 Henry IV* has shaped the material, and limited and modified the dramatic form of both plays.[1] The same applies to the *Henry VI–Richard III* series. Each play suffers to some degree as a unit because it has, where appropriate, to

(*a*) prepare for its successors, and look back to its predecessors;
(*b*) stop somewhere in a continuous, still incomplete, or only partially complete, action;
(*c*) carry on the general theme;
(*d*) duplicate general material for the sake of the exposition in the individual play.

Thus the introduction of Richard of Gloucester is dramatically and historically unnecessary in *2 Henry VI*, like that of young Richmond in *3 Henry VI*, and, for many critics, that of Margaret in *1 Henry VI* and *Richard III*. It is the need to develop this general plan that makes the conclusions of the first three so dramatically inconclusive: they look forward to the next play; and the openings, however dramatically effective, often superfluous to the immediate plot. It is this that justifies, indeed demands, the constant back and forward reference, and the introduction of binding elements—curses, dreams, prophecies, allusions—otherwise dramatically unnecessary.

1 Henry VI develops the general theme of Hall—the retribution on Henry VI for the original sin of his grandfather. The first stage of that retribution consists in the turning of the tables on England by the French; it opens with England in effective control of France and ends with France (almost) completely lost and a French queen about to ascend the throne of England to dominate a boy king and the country. The play looks back to the greatness of Henry V and forward to the rule of Suffolk and Margaret, York's claim, and civil war. The action is far from complete; the internal dissensions and rivalries have still to be worked out. And out of its context, there is no need in the play for e.g. the Mortimer–Plantagenet scene and its genealogy, reported more fully in *2 Henry VI*, or the restoration of York 'to his blood', or the Temple Garden scene. The play has, of course, its own unity, but for full appreciation, it should be seen as a unit in a series concerning the events and the

---

1. *The Structural Problem in Shakespeare's 'Henry the Fourth'*, 1956.

dominant themes of Hall's grand conception of the struggle of York and Lancaster.

ORDER

It is thus typical and natural that *1 Henry VI* should open with the funeral of Henry V.[1] With his victorious career, after the uneasy fortunes of Henry IV, the 'English circle' ended. Nemesis, which had spared him, was about to fall with redoubled force on England. For he was succeeded by the boy king Henry VI—a major misfortune in itself, according to the ideas of those days, and doubly unfortunate in the midst of a war on foreign soil, and with such a band of self-interested nobles. No sooner is the strong hand of Henry V removed, and Henry VI's lack of authority apparent, than the latent dissensions break out in all sorts of places. Order dissolves into chaos. In spite of the heroism of the Talbots, and the patriotism of Bedford, Salisbury, and Warwick, and the traditional superiority of the English, all Henry V's work is undone. It is entirely in keeping that the play should end on a note of chaos, showing how far the natural order or degree has been inverted, when Suffolk can say,

> *Margaret* shall now be Queene, and rule the King:
> But I will rule both her, the King, and Realme.

It is ironically significant that it should be Henry VI himself, unaware how far he has been responsible for the collapse of order and the outbreak of dissension, who comments:

> Civil dissension is a viperous worm,
> That gnaws the bowels of the commonwealth.
>
> (III. i. 72–3)

a comment preceded only by Warwick's prophecy (II. iv. 124 ff.):

> this brawl to-day
> Grown to this faction in the Temple Garden,
> Shall send between the red rose and the white
> A thousand souls to death and deadly night.

For it is Henry who restores Richard Plantagenet to 'his blood' as Duke of York and thus advances his politic claim to the succession, allows Winchester to be made a Cardinal where Henry V had refused, plucks a red rose as if it were a thing of no account, and finally is persuaded into breaking his oath and pledge to the daughter of the Earl of Armagnac and putting himself under the baleful influence of Margaret and Suffolk.

---

1. For a fine structural analysis of this scene, see Price, 26–7.

As the English relapse into chaos, the French achieve unity. Their confidence is restored with the arrival of Joan, the recapture of most of France, and the reconciliation with Burgundy. In spite of the treaty imposed on them, they become effectively independent, and see one of themselves elevated to the English throne.

The English chaos is further thrown into relief by the family order and loyalty elaborated in the Talbots. They are, as Kirschbaum notes,[1] the microcosm of which England is the macrocosm. If all individual Englishmen had been loyal and true like them, there would have been no danger of foreign loss and internal disunion.

Typical of the collapse of political (and moral) order are the frequent oath-breaches and the adoption of politic attitudes. York is advised to be, and is, politic regarding his ultimate ambition to reign. Winchester effects a hypocritical reconciliation with Gloucester. Suffolk makes promises (v. iii. 89, 138) and statements that are false and misleading; and quibbles exactly in the later style of Richard of Gloucester on the breaking of oaths; and Henry himself is persuaded into breaking his contract with the Earl of Armagnac. The political order is thus, by the end of the play, on the road to complete collapse.

It is beside the point, in this political field, to ask for a central figure, as in tragedy, or for detailed character-analysis. The theme, as often pointed out, is England, and the characters are drawn firmly, but as political, not private, figures. Private, realistic touches do indeed break through the political formalism and rhetoric, but they are few. Most of them are Joan's, as her 'Done like a Frenchman!—turn and turn again.';[2] 'Are ye so hot?';[3] others are Winchester's equivocal 'as I intend it not',[4] and the mayor's 'I myself fight not once in forty year'.[5]

The aspects that matter are the public or external facts and characteristics. In these four historical plays, it is in the main true that, as Arthur Sewell points out, 'the moral nature of man is apprehended in terms of its political manifestations' . . . 'the primary activity of character is apprehended as shaping or mis-shaping political order . . . the characters have no truly private emotions. What inner feeling they may be thought to have is public emotion.' Sewell reinforces the points from what is 'almost an exception', the character of Henry VI. Henry has all the private virtues, the king-becoming graces: and by force of his holy character, in spite of his lack of authority 'nearly succeeded in accomplishing . . . an under-

1. *PMLA.* (1952), 822.   2. iii. iii. 85.   3. iii. ii. 58.
4. iii. i. 141.   5. i. iii. 91.

standing between the warring factions of Lancaster and York. Had it not been for that Amazon, Margaret of Lancaster, and that fiend in human shape, the younger Richard of York, he would have. As ... Edward IV says to Margaret as he looks back (*3H6*, II. ii. 160–2)

> Hadst thou been meek, our title still had slept
> And we, in pity of the gentle king,
> Had slipp'd our claim until another age.

An outstanding admission, and the highest tribute to the quiet power of Henry's character.'[1]

For the times, however, Henry has too much 'lenity'; he would retire to a pastoral simple life. His very private virtues have unfitted him to govern the warring factions in the state. There is 'no worse a vice than lenitie in Kings' (*The Misfortunes of Arthur*, III. i. 63).[2]

UNITY

The breakdown of order is itself a unifying theme in *1 Henry VI*. The loss of France, and the inversion of the English-French relation, is another. Shakespeare, however, has further taken many loose threads from Hall, and, without chronicle authority, woven them together. Where necessary, he has invented scenes to symbolize stages in the action (Mortimer–Plantagenet), to objectify the principles underlying a conflict (Temple Garden), or merely to amplify and illustrate a character (Talbot and the Countess of Auvergne).[3] The main threads woven into the plot are:

(*a*) The end of the 'English circle' with the death of Henry V.

(*b*) The rise and fall of Talbot, and his rivalry with Joan.

(*c*) The 'intestine divisions' of the nobility; first that of Gloucester and Winchester, supplemented later by that of York and Somerset, paralleled by that of their adherents Vernon and Basset.

(*d*) The disputed succession, discussed, by inference, in the Garden scene, in which the dying Mortimer's claim is passed on to Richard Plantagenet.

(*e*) Henry's marriage, the breach of the Armagnac contract, and Suffolk's wooing of Margaret for Henry, to the displeasure of Gloucester and Plantagenet, now Duke of York. These are closely linked, far beyond what is seen in Hall, by showing the fate of Talbot sealed by the rivalry of York and Somerset; by Suffolk's clash with Gloucester and York over Henry's marriage, the broken contract, and the cession of Anjou and Maine; and by the linking by York of his claim to the crown with Mortimer, 'restoration to his blood'

1. Sewell, 47, 51, 31.   2. Ribner, 233.   3. II. v; II. iv; II. iii.

(connecting with *Henry V*), rivalry with Somerset, objection to Henry's marriage to Margaret, and judgment on Joan.

To achieve this superior degree of unity in the action, Shakespeare had obviously to take considerable liberties with chronicle events. Joan, for example, was burned in 1431, Henry married in 1444, and Talbot died in 1453. To bring them together in his more complicated action, Shakespeare had therefore almost to annihilate historic time, and disregard chronological order. This he did,[1] because 'the necessary dramaturgic emphasis on the patriot-hero demands that he be created Earl and publicly denounce Fastolfe (i.e. Falstaffe) on the occurrence that dramatically marks the climax of his endeavours, the crowning of his King in the capital of the invaded country; and his death is advanced by nearly a quarter of a century. Emotionally, if not in stated terms, this prepares for the burning at the stake of his opponent and motivates the final coming of peace.'

The opening scene, as often in Shakespeare, not only sets the atmosphere of foreboding, and has the dramatic assets of a pageant followed by a clash of interests and a rapid succession of (reported) events, but touches on a number of the main themes so as to emphasize their importance and unity. On the funeral of Henry V and the panegyric of all present comes the first brief outburst of enmity between Gloucester and Winchester, and on that the succession of messengers announcing in effect the loss of the France Henry V had spent his life to win. This is reminiscent of the disasters of Job, and ends with the announcement of the supreme disaster, the capture of the heroic Talbot. The scene ends on a further note of foreboding in the soliloquy of Winchester. The second scene completes the picture with a contrast in the success and high spirits of the French and the arrival of Joan. These events are a concentration from the years 1422 to 1451. They have the effect of creating—in the study—some slight inconsistency; but the powerful dramatic effect more than justifies the liberty taken with chronology.

This is Shakespeare's regular practice, though perhaps not always to this degree. He constantly inverts historical order, compresses, expands, repeats, anticipates, transfers events and characters, omits, invents imaginary scenes and characters, and all for dramatic purposes.

An outstanding instance of Shakespeare's power of compression, adaptation, and combination may be studied in the defection of Burgundy from the English (III. iii. 41 ff.; IV. i). In Hall, this material is spread over some twenty years and half a dozen separate

1. Gaw, 25-6; cf. III. i. 71; v. i. 21; v. v. 81.

passages.[1] In *1 Henry VI*, it is compressed into one (unhistorical) appeal to Burgundy by Joan (burned some years previously), who effects a sudden conversion. This achieves at the same time the elimination of a long accumulation of Burgundy's grievances against the English—not particularly interesting or dramatic in themselves —and the expansion of the very thin part of Joan, as well as a further illustration of her power. The final touch of Burgundy's 'treachery'—the letter to Henry—is itself tied up by Shakespeare with the un-Gartering of Falstaff, the coronation of Henry in Paris, and another little touch of Talbot, who is sent to deal with Burgundy.

The part of Falstaff, like those of Joan and Talbot, was obviously expanded with some difficulty. His single historical act of cowardice at Patay is multiplied to cover an unspecified defeat of Talbot's as reported by a messenger (I. i. 131 ff.); a similar opprobrious reference to cowardice (I. iv. 35); another at Rouen, unhistorically, where he says, 'We are like to have the overthrow *again*' (III. ii. 105–6); and finally the Garter scene, which refers again to his cowardice at Patay.

In similar style York's quarrel with Somerset is multiplied, and further emphasized by its duplication in Vernon and Basset (III. iv. 28 ff.; IV. i. 78 ff.; IV. iii–vii). But what is even more impressive is the magnification of York, with the addition of the imaginary Temple Garden and Trial scenes—he has actually little or no part here historically—as the coming protagonist in the succeeding plays of civil war; and linking him with all the main threads of the plot. The quarrel appears repeated in five scenes (II. iv, III. i, III. iv, IV. i, IV. iii). Its first appearance, however, combines it with the germ of York's claim to the crown. On a mere hint in Hall of help delayed, the quarrel is, quite unhistorically, though in character, expanded into a cause for the defeat and death of Talbot. York, in place of the historical Bedford, then plays the chief rôle in the capture, trial, and condemnation of Joan. Finally, in fictitious matter in v. iv, he learns to his dismay of the treaty and foresees 'the utter loss of all the realm of France'—his France[2]—and cannot refrain from insulting the French peace mission. This is planning on a complicated scale.

The organized redistribution of chronicle material may be studied, again, in the scenes dealing with the sieges of Orleans and Rouen. With the relevant chronicle account, material from two other incidents is incorporated. From the capture of Le Mans (Hall, 143), the English assault on Orleans (II. i) takes the French

1. Hall, 147, 154, 160, 167–8, 173–4, 176, 194. (See App. 1.)
2. Cf. *2H6*, I. i. 215 ff.

carousing (though the French did celebrate at the relief of Orleans —Hall, 149—also), the battle-cry 'St. George! A Talbot!', and 'The French leap over the walls in their shirts'. Joan's capture of Rouen (III. ii) takes the burning torch or cresset of Le Mans (142), as well as the 'sacks and baskets' (197) of the capture of Cornill Castle. The attitude of the Bastard of Orleans to his illegitimacy and inheritance, part of the chronicle matter here (144–5), is omitted from *1 Henry VI*, but appears adapted in the Faulconbridge of *King John*.

TIME

As a natural consequence of throwing the events of thirty years into the melting-pot, and depicting a king who grows from infancy to young manhood in that period, Shakespeare had to avoid precise indications of time. Events must happen, as it were, in a great sea of time, with no fixed points of reference but the death of Henry V behind and the Wars of the Roses before. The events in the play seem to follow one another in rapid succession, yet Shakespeare had to create an illusion of extension. The very inconsistency of Henry's age ('When I was young', III. iv. 17) helps here; he is never *shown* as a child, but only at one fixed point and age. Otherwise extension is provided almost unnoticed. Back reference to the great days of Henry V is everywhere. There is the long backward vista of the succession from the time of Edward III, tracing York's claim to the crown through the Earl of Cambridge and the dying Mortimer who in turn looks back on his tragic history. The vision is carried forward in forebodings and prophecies to the impending Wars of the Roses and in York's politic silent anticipation of the time when his claim will be heard and achieved. Talbot returns from captivity and gives an account of his imprisonment, implying some duration. Joan describes her past in Touraine. The French watch the English soldiers lying near Orleans, who 'faintly besiege us one hour *in a month*' II. ii. 8). A forward reference anticipates 'the next parliament' (II. iv. 14), later shown in session (III. i). Talbot has been *long* resident in France (III. iv. 14). Other direct means are also used to imply extension in space and time, such as changes of locality, as from Bordeaux to London to Angiers to London; the loss of many listed English possessions in France; Henry's travel from London to Paris and back: and battles in widely separated parts of France.

THE MARGARET–SUFFOLK EPISODE

One further example of Shakespeare's comprehensive and integrating adaptation may be given, partly for itself, but partly also for its bearing on a point of controversy. Even some who admit Shakespearean authorship here, claim that the episode is not integral to the play, but was added afterwards to link it to *2* and *3 Henry VI*. To Allison Gaw, for example, the episode is 'artistically bad', and the play should properly omit this part to end with Winchester's peace in v. iv.

Gaw misses the point entirely. Other considerations apart, the conclusion of the peace with the French may no doubt seem a more natural and stable ending for the play, and the omission of Margaret might still seem to leave a complete story. But is it complete, either historically or artistically?

The theme of the play is the loss of France, and the ruin of England. The loss of France is completed with the *giving away* of the two remaining provinces (Normandy is another, later, matter) Maine and Anjou; the ruin of England, by the loss of France and the outbreak of civil war. Both are ensured with the breaking of the Armagnac contract, and the marriage of Henry with Margaret. This in turn ensures the dominance of the disastrous French influence in Margaret, Joan's immediate successor, who enters, with beautiful irony, on her baleful part in English affairs at the very moment that the work of her predecessor Joan has been perfected in the effectual loss of France.[1] This again leads direct, along with the intestine divisions it provokes and intensifies, to the civil wars of the Roses. The play does not, in fact, end in a peace treaty, and was not intended to; it ends the first main stage in the downfall of England, and prepares the beginning of another. Part of the English disaster is that the saintly Henry, who, though a child and powerless among his quarrelling nobles, is honourable and respected, is seduced into breaking his oath. And that breach, like others in the historical series,[2] is inevitably visited with retribution—the retribution of the French maid who becomes his queen and the fury, the 'bloody scourge', the she-wolf, of the later plays. As Marshall says,[3] 'Henry's marriage seems to have been the turning-point of his fortunes. From that moment nothing seems to have prospered with him or his army. The discontent which the cession of Maine

1. The thematic continuity from Joan to Margaret was brought to my attention by Dr H. F. Brooks, who points out that a comparable technique is used in *R3*, where Richmond (like Margaret here) is a latecomer to the action, but (like her) has had his place thematically prepared for him. In the theme of vengeance he takes over from his antitype, the Margaret of that play: she is the voice of all the revenges that have only provoked further revenges; he, the minister of divine retribution that brings the progression of vengeance to a stop.

2. E.g. Edward IV and Lady Bona in *3H6*.

3. Irving, II. 170.

excited . . . was increased by the ill success which the English met with in France [and in England] after that event.' The vital importance of this unhappy marriage made it, for Shakespeare, both a natural centre from which to radiate (*2H6*, 1. i) the various strands of *2 Henry VI*, and the natural climax to the misfortunes of *1 Henry VI*.

In *1 Henry VI*, Margaret's marriage is an integral part of v. i and v. ii; it is implicit in the whole structure of those parts admitted to be original and Shakespearean. In v. i, Gloucester mentions and supports the King's first marriage contract with the daughter of the Earl of Armagnac. Without the original presence of Margaret in the play, the reference is pointless. The loss of Anjou and Maine, Margaret's marriage dowry, threatens a fatal blow to York's ambition; and the conflicting attitudes of the nobles to the marriage are a factor in aggravating the rivalries already crystallized in the Temple Garden scene.

A consideration of the chronicle material and its adaptation supports this conclusion. In v. i, Shakespeare combines

(*a*) an abortive truce conference called by the Pope and the Emperor at Arras in 1434 (Hall, 166, 174);

(*b*) a marriage offer of the Earl of Armagnac's daughter (Hall, 202, 204) to Henry in 1442, and their affiance by proxy, with a large dowry. Gloucester was not involved;

(*c*) a truce diet at Tours in 1443 (Hall, 203–4), at which Suffolk effected the betrothal of Henry and Margaret: to which Gloucester objected the Armagnac contract.

Shakespeare attaches the later diet, (*c*), to the Pope's earlier peace conference (*a*), and makes it the scene, *through the mouth of Gloucester*, of a positive Armagnac proposal (*b*). This scene has therefore deliberately created, from Hall's Margaret–Suffolk material, a positive but fictitious rôle for Gloucester. It is intended to show Henry committed to accepting, as a further bond of the peace, the Armagnac contract; so that, when the Margaret–Suffolk episode, developed independently, causes him to break his oath, it will involve Gloucester's honour, further alienate York by giving away Anjou and Maine as part of his prospective possessions, and precipitate the ruin of Henry and England through the moral lapse and the surrender to passion and the French influence.

Gloucester's unhistorical announcement of the peace letter from the Pope and of the Armagnac proposal are thus necessary in the play as a step to the conclusion of the peace. But in fact, as Hall notes in advance (203), the Armagnac marriage never takes place; the peace is concluded and cemented with Henry's marriage to

Margaret (v. v. 42–5), and the truce is actually arranged in relation to this contract. All this, and Shakespeare's familiarity with the Margaret chronicle material, is implied in the admittedly original and Shakespearean scene v. i; without it, Gloucester's part there is quite meaningless.

In relation to *2 Henry VI*, the Margaret–Suffolk episode further explains what is not clear from that play alone—Gloucester's break-down on reading the terms of the truce (i. i), at the point where the cession of Anjou and Maine is mentioned. The personal relation of Margaret to Suffolk, again, as in *1 Henry VI*, is a dramatic elaboration of a mere hint in Hall—that Suffolk was 'the Queen's darling'—interpreted in both plays with the same peculiar unhistorical slant. In short, it seems plain that the story and relation of Margaret and Suffolk has been incorporated from the beginning in the dramatic conception of both plays, and by the same sort of adaptation of history as Shakespeare normally followed.

The straightforward explanation of this, as of the other links between *1 Henry VI* and the rest of the series, seems in the long run the most satisfactory; in fact, the whole argument against the priority of *1 Henry VI* can be applied more forcefully in favour of it.

(*a*) Gloucester's earlier affair, not elsewhere mentioned in the plays, but expressly mentioned in Hall's material on Gloucester, is tacitly assumed (v. v. 97) and used by Henry to quiet his opposition (cf. v. i. 15 ff.) to the Margaret marriage; while his wife Eleanor's pride, amply illustrated in *2 Henry VI*, is mentioned (i. i. 39) where it is dramatically unnecessary. In the same way, Margaret's father, Reignier, who is not particularly important in himself, has an earlier independent existence, as if in preparation for the Margaret–Suffolk episode.

(*b*) The *2 Henry VI* references to 'our ancient bickerings' (i. i. 42) of Gloucester and Winchester, and 'the last time' (i. iii. 170), are natural recollections of something already familiar.

(*c*) The Temple Garden scene leads up to and supplies a fictitious basis for the Wars of the Roses in the three following plays. It is the first statement of a theme integral to all, but least necessary here, and one that would not be required at all if this were a 'Talbot' play.

(*d*) The intestine divisions of the nobles are already there in *1 Henry VI*; a point which a comparison of the opening scenes of the two plays will confirm and illuminate.

(*e*) Bedford's death, before his historical time, and the transfer of his historical part to York in v. iv, can be seen as a device to bring forward York and his claim—supplemented by the appearance of Mortimer—to the crown, in preparation for the part he is to play in *2 Henry VI*.

(*f*) Margaret naturally follows Joan as part of the French rôle in the ruin of England through the beginning of the Wars of the Roses, and the aggravation of the nobles' rivalry; and her advent is prepared for, through her father, and through Gloucester's opposition to the breach of the contract implied in the proposal of her marriage to Henry, well before she appears.

DESIGN

So far from being a mere succession of drum-and-trumpet episodes, everything in the play bears witness to careful planning and controlled design. Not only has the amorphous historical material been sifted, rearranged, expanded, and compressed; but it has been arranged to contribute to the development of the dominating theme. The design follows precise patterns of contrast; repetition of theme, often with increment; rise, climax, and fall. It is all harmonized with great formality, like the tremendous pageant it was, with the chorus Exeter, usually, pointing the moral. Two illustrations may be useful:

(*a*) The careers of Joan and Talbot are closely linked. The stars favour Joan (II. i), as they frown on the English (I. i). There is a sort of ritual progression, as Tillyard points out,[1] in Joan's successive attempts to ruin Talbot at Orleans, Rouen, and Bordeaux; which are further supplemented by the Countess of Auvergne, and, in a sense, by the work of Margaret of Anjou after his death. The rise of Joan, backed by the unity of the French, including the adhesion of Burgundy, follows an alternate pattern of victory and defeat, and rises to its climax in the death of Talbot, left to himself by the rivalries of the English nobles. Her capture and death soon after is again contrasted with Talbot's.

(*b*) In the same way, the play has three interrupted ceremonies;[2] at the beginning of the first, third, and fourth acts. For Shakespeare, ceremony had a universal significance. Everything in nature, the state, and the individual, has its proper place or degree, to which outward order and ceremony correspond for their manifestation and preservation. Almost alone in *1 Henry VI*, Talbot observes the appropriate ceremonies of state. He comes 'to do my duty to my sovereign', and ascribes the glory of his conquest, in proper order,

First to my God, and next unto your Grace.[3]   (III. iv)

By contrast, and at this point a direct contrast, it is part of the de-

sign, and a natural part, that all ceremonies, in such a divided, dis-
ordered state as that of the English after the death of Henry V and
the succession of the politically incompetent Henry VI, should be
flouted or interrupted. Ceremony and degree have lost their hold.
Not only is an extended ceremony not wanted dramatically in a
play like this; there is just no place for it in the nature of things.

The play has hardly begun when the funeral of Henry V himself
is interrupted, first by the incipient quarrel between Winchester
and Gloucester, and then by the series of messengers announcing
defeat and loss. The proceedings in the Parliament House (III. i)
are similarly interrupted right at the start, when Winchester
snatches and tears Gloucester's bill. This interruption is again followed by a second, when the servants of the two nobles break in
fighting. The flouting of ceremony has gone a stage further—it has
spread from masters to servants; and it takes place in the presence
of the King himself. On the third occasion, the coronation (IV. i),
after Talbot's recent observations of ceremony, is again twice interrupted—by the irruption of the coward Falstaff bearing the
letter of defection from Burgundy, and by the demand for a duel
by Vernon and Basset, supported by their masters—a repetition,
with increment, of the previous example.[1]

In short, the play bears the stamp of a single mind in the orga-
nization of material, in its adaptation to the exposition of a grand
central design extending beyond the play itself, and in the rein-
forcement of the whole by a body of subsidiary devices and ideas,
to create a highly popular play in an original form.

ORIGINALITY

For *1 Henry VI* almost certainly marks the rise of an original type
of play, as F. P. Wilson notes. Did Shakespeare and Marlowe, he
asks, inherit a tradition of chronicle history plays, which they then

---

1. Cf. G. Wilson Knight, *The Crown of Life*, 215–16, 'Feasts are regularly
important throughout Shakespeare. . . In *Timon* there are two: the first (I. ii)
conceived as a sacrament of love and friendship . . . crowned by Timon's speech
and negatively underlined by Apemantus' cynicism; the second (III. vi) planned
as a deadly serious practical joke. . . In *Macbeth* we have . . . (III. iv) the feast to
which Banquo has been carefully invited and which he attends as a ghost,
smashing up the conviviality and social health so vividly emphasized in the text,
and thus denying to Macbeth's tyrannous and blood-stained rule all such
sacraments of brotherhood. These two *broken* feasts in *Timon of Athens* and
Macbeth . . . are key-scenes; and their shattering stage-power derives precisely
from the simplicity of the effects used, planted squarely as they are on funda-
mentals.

'The meaning of the feast offered but denied to Alonso, Sebastian, and Antonio
will now be clear.'

proceeded to raise above the chronicle level? 'So we have always been taught to believe; but when we look for these early chronicle plays written before the Armada, where are they?'[1] The only possible rival claimant is Marlowe's *Edward II*, written for the same company, Pembroke's Men, and published in 1594. But of course *Edward II*, foreign to Marlowe's manner in *Tamburlaine* and *Dr Faustus*, is only too clearly an imitation of Shakespeare's histories, as some of its imitative phrases confirm.[2] Greene's *James the Fourth* and Peele's *David and Bethsabe* hardly qualify for inclusion in the type.

Shakespeare's type of history is distinguished by its unity—both as single play and as member of a series—and, in spite, or perhaps because of, its manipulation of historical characters and events, preserves a general truth to the Elizabethan interpretation of English history, especially as represented in Hall's Chronicle. It freely incorporates fictitious material to supplement and body forth, drawing on ballad sources, on the old English as well as the Senecan tradition; and diverges freely into the comical, or pastoral, or tragical, or any other strain as the subject suggests or requires.

PAGEANTRY

In a play so much concerned with the outward, political, scene and with war, there is clearly great scope for pageantry and spectacle, as well as for action. The English-French conflict provides plenty of action—the so-called 'drum-and-trumpet aspect'—in the hand-to-hand fighting, with specially dramatic and varied touches in the cannon shot that kills Salisbury, the burning torch thrust out on the 'top', the night attack on Orleans, the pebble-throwing servants, Gloucester at the Tower Gate, and Winchester tearing Gloucester's bill. Spectacle and pageantry[3] there was also in plenty, full of colour and contrast. The play opens on such a pageant in the funeral of Henry V; the sieges and attacks offer tableaux on the walls, with e.g. Warwick as the traditional presenter, supplying the commentary; the Temple Garden scene has the contrast of red and white as the basis of its symbolism; and there are other elements of colour like the blue and tawny coats of the factions, and red robe of the Cardinal.

STYLE

In keeping with the subject and material, the style is formal, con-

1. *Marlowe and the Early Shakespeare* (1953), 105.
2. E.g. the O'Neill reference, natural in *2H6*, irrelevant in *Edward II*.
3. See Venezky.

ventional, rhetorical. It is a practical style, rather than a poetic.
There are few purple patches, and little strong personal emotion.
All the figures and devices of classical rhetoric, the Senecan sticho-
mythia, the soliloquy, classical similes and allusions, appear in profusion, when appropriate. Much of the play is concerned with exposition, narrative, and debate; and the verse is naturally direct,
and often stilted, but suited to the action. In this respect it is, as
Sir Ifor Evans remarks, 'the least exciting'[1] of the plays.

This is, of course, not altogether unintentional. Shakespeare observes decorum. There is a specially rich exotic vein of allusion and
imagery in the early Joan of Arc scenes; and it is there we find the
outstanding 'Glory is like a circle in the water'. Suffolk and Margaret, too, convey, across their highly artificial dialogue, a sense of
luxury.[2] There is, again, a special dignity in the Mortimer episode,
and the familiar Biblical strain in the language of Henry. The Talbot scenes, highly formal as they are, express a deeper emotion than
the rest and produce memorable touches.

IMAGERY

The imagery both confirms the integrity of the play as Shakespeare's, and like all the other elements reinforces the general impression. The main groups thus naturally cluster round the ideas
of discord and chaos. Looking back, at the end of *Richard III*, on
the whole conflict of the Roses, Richmond notes how the heavens
'long have frown'd vpon their Enmity'.[3] They begin frowning in
the first line of *1 Henry VI*, as 'change' at once supervenes on the
death and funeral of Henry V, whose sun has set:[4]

> Hung be the heavens with black, yield day to night;
> Comets importing change of times and states,
> Brandish your crystal tresses in the sky,
> And with them scourge the bad revolting stars,
> That have consented unto *Henry's* death:

The 'planets of mishap' (l. 23) and the 'adverse planets' (54)[5] carry
on the figure, while Bedford already, without specific cause, ex-

1. Evans, 33.
2. Joan refers to—Caesar's insulting ship; Saint Martin's summer; the sword
of Deborah; the sibyls of old Rome; Mahomet; Constantine; St Philip's daughters; Venus; Rhodope of Memphis; the rich jewel-coffer of Darius; the English
nobles to—Hecate, Circe; the Countess of Auvergne to—Cyrus and Tomyris;
and Margaret to—this diamond . . . / In golden palaces . . . v. iii. 169–70.
3. Cf. *R3*, I. i. 4, 'The clouds that lowr'd upon our house'; *3H6*, v. iii. 4, 'a
black suspicious threat'ning cloud'.
4. *1H6*, I. i. 8–16; cf. *H5*, I. ii. 279; and see Knight, 33, and Spurgeon, 225 ff.
5. Cf. IV. v. 6.

presses the fear of 'civil broils' (53); there is thunder and lightning
at the death of Salisbury; Talbot's life is 'eclips'd';[1] Icarus (young
Talbot) falls from heaven.[2] These are 'the ill aspects of planets evil'
that 'In evil mixture to disorder wander', when changes 'rend and
deracinate / The unity and married calm of states / Quite from
their fixture', and when 'degree is shak'd', as in *1 Henry VI*.[3] By
contrast, the planets, beginning with Mars, favour Joan, 'bright
star of Venus', 'Astraea's daughter'.

The other main group of imagery is that of disease, possibly suggested by Hall's 'intestine deuision'. Of the death of Salisbury, and
the consequent decline in their fortunes, Hall says the English 'felt
it grow like a pestilent humor, which succesciuely a litle and litle
corrupteth all the membres, and destroyeth the body'.[4] So, says
Exeter,

> This late dissention grown betwixt the peers, . . .
> As fester'd members rot but by degree,
> Till bones and flesh and sinews fall away,
> So will this base and envious discord breed.[5]

'The Vulture of sedition / Feeds in the bosom' of the 'great commanders';[6] 'Civil dissention is a viperous worm, / That gnaws the
bowels of the commonwealth.'[7]

A more scattered, but at times pervading, body of imagery is
concerned with the general atmosphere of gloom and disaster, pre-
sided over by Talbot's apocalyptic 'three attendants'—'lean Famine, quartering Steele, and climbing Fire'.[8] The English are
'hunger-starved men',[9] and 'famish'd . . . like pale ghosts'.[10] They
are exhorted to turn, like stags at bay, on the 'bloody hounds with
heads of steel'.[11] And with 'quartering steel' go blood and death.
The play, opening with a funeral, is full of death, from age, or the
sword, or fire. Death stalks through parts of the play—'hard favoured death',[12] 'Triumphant Death, smear'd with captivity'.[13] The
death-darting eye of the basilisk, so familiar in many other plays,
has a natural place.[14]

The slaughter-house imagery of *2* and *3 Henry VI* does no more
than suggest itself[15]—that is reserved for the civil war. Blood, however, natural enough in a war-play, is additionally linked with the
'sanguine' red rose; and Talbot sweats the 'bloody sweat' of the

---

1. IV. v. 53.   2. IV. vii. 15–16.
3. *Troil.*, I. iii. 85 ff.; Tillyard, *EWP.*, 7–8; and cf. *Lr.*, I. ii. 138 ff.
4. Hall, 146.   5. III. i. 189 ff.   6. IV. iii. 47–8.   7. III. i. 72–4.
8. IV. ii. 11.   9. I. v. 16.   10. I. ii. 7.   11. IV. ii. 51.
12. IV. vii. 23.   13. IV. vii. 3.   14. V. iv. 120–2.
15. II. v. 109–10; and perhaps IV. vii. 76, 'fly-blown'.

Crucifixion.[1] Others of the subsidiary images, in keeping, are drawn from the chase[2] and the cock-fight.[3] Imagery of the garden and the orchard is the natural product of the roses scene (II. iv) and of reference to the genealogical tree of York and Lancaster.[4]

I Henry VI is thus not a 'Talbot' play; nor does the evidence suggest that any part of it is by another hand; nor that it is adapted. It is of the same stuff and conception as the other parts of the series, which portrays, in itself, as in each member, a unity not of plot or character, but of idea and design and imagery—a conception, as Price notes,[5] never seen before except in Aeschylus, with his 'controlling moral idea'. Greene spoke more truly than he knew when he called Shakespeare 'the onely Shake-scene in a countrey'.

1. IV. iv. 18.   2. IV. ii. 45 ff.   3. II. iv. 87, 'craven'.
4. Cf. Spurgeon, 216 ff.
5. Price, 26, citing Kitto, *Greek Tragedy* (1939), 36.

THE FIRST PART OF
KING HENRY VI

DRAMATIS PERSONÆ[1]

KING HENRY THE SIXTH
DUKE OF GLOUCESTER, *Uncle to the King, and Protector.*
DUKE OF BEDFORD, *Uncle to the King, and Regent of France.*
DUKE OF EXETER, *Great-uncle to the King.*
BISHOP OF WINCHESTER, *Great-uncle to the King, and afterwards Cardinal.*
DUKE OF SOMERSET.
RICHARD PLANTAGENET, *afterwards Duke of York.*
EARL OF WARWICK.
EARL OF SALISBURY.
EARL OF SUFFOLK.
LORD TALBOT, *afterwards Earl of Shrewsbury.*
JOHN TALBOT, *his Son.*
EDMUND MORTIMER, *Earl of March.*
SIR JOHN FALSTAFF.
SIR WILLIAM LUCY.
SIR WILLIAM GLANSDALE.
SIR THOMAS GARGRAVE.
Mayor of London.
WOODVILE, *Lieutenant of the Tower.*
VERNON, *of the White-Rose or York Faction.*
BASSET, *of the Red-Rose or Lancaster Faction.*
A Lawyer. Mortimer's Keepers.
A Papal Legate, and two Ambassadors.
CHARLES, *Dauphin, and afterwards King of France.*
REIGNIER, *Duke of Anjou, and titular King of Naples.*
DUKE OF BURGUNDY.
DUKE OF ALENÇON.
BASTARD OF ORLEANS.
Governor of Paris.
Master-Gunner of Orleans, and his Son.
General of the French Forces in Bordeaux.
A French Sergeant. A Porter.
An old Shepherd, Father to Joan la Pucelle.

MARGARET, *Daughter to Reignier, afterwards married to King Henry.*
COUNTESS OF AUVERGNE.
JOAN LA PUCELLE, *commonly called Joan of Aire.*

Lords, Warders of the Tower, Heralds, Officers, Soldiers, Messengers, and Attendants.

Fiends appearing to Joan la Pucelle.

Scene: *Partly in England and partly in France.*

1. First given imperfectly by Rowe; corrected by Cambridge Editors; and revised.

THE FIRST PART OF
KING HENRY THE SIXTH

ACT I

SCENE I.—[*Westminster Abbey.*]

Dead March. Enter the Funeral of KING HENRY *the Fifth, attended on by the* DUKE OF BEDFORD, *Regent of France; the* DUKE OF GLOUCESTER, *Protector; the* DUKE OF EXETER, [*the* EARL OF] WARWICK, *the* BISHOP OF WINCHESTER, *and the* DUKE OF SOMERSET.*

Bed. Hung be the heavens with black, yield day to night!

ACT I
Scene 1

Title. *King Henry*] edd.; *Henry | F.*   Act I Scene I] *edd.; Actus Primus. Scœna Prima. | F.   Westminster Abbey.*] *Theobald; not in F.*   S.D. *the Earl of Warwick*] edd.; *Warwicke | F.*

S.D. the Funeral] see Hall, 113–14 (App. 1). '*1 Henry VI* opens, with a note of high irony, on the funeral of Henry V' (H. C. Goddard, *The Meaning of Shakespeare*, 1951, p. 29). The choice of opening connects the play with the tetralogy *Richard II–Henry V*; provides a contrast for the coming 'change of times and states'; and offers a theme from which the latent 'intestine divisions' of the English nobles can at once break out. Now that the strong hand of Henry V, the conqueror of France, is removed, his conquests immediately begin to crumble. The pageantry and spectacle of the mourning scene, in black—a touch from Marlowe's *Tamburlaine*—is built up, through the quarrels, into the consequent rapid succession of reported disasters, unhistorically anticipated and telescoped, with a conscious reminiscence of Job. The theme is thus announced as the loss of France, whose evil influence will triumph at the end by the replacement of the sorceress Joan by the no less malignant Margaret of Anjou.

The collapse of order and ceremony is indicated by the double interruption of the funeral (cf. III. i and IV. i, and Intro., p. liii), by the 'jars' of the nobles, and the bad news of the messengers.

1. *Hung . . . black*] The stage was draped with black for a tragedy (Malone); see Hodges, 47–8, and cf. Marston, *Insatiate Countess*, IV. v. 4–5: 'The stage of heauen is hung with solemn black, / A time best fitting to act tragedies.' Shakespeare may have taken the hint from Hall, 114, who speaks of 'black barnes & . . . horses bearded with blacke'.

heavens] the projecting roof or pent-

3

Comets, importing change of times and states,
Brandish your crystal tresses in the sky,
And with them scourge the bad revolting stars,
That have consented unto Henry's death—   5
Henry the Fifth, too famous to live long!
England ne'er lost a king of so much worth.
Glou. England ne'er had a king until his time.
Virtue he had, deserving to command:
His brandish'd sword did blind men with his beams: 10
His arms spread wider than a dragon's wings:
His sparkling eyes, replete with wrathful fire,
More dazzled and drove back his enemies
Than mid-day sun fierce bent against their faces.
What should I say? His deeds exceed all speech: 15
He ne'er lift up his hand but conquered.
Exe. We mourn in black: why mourn we not in blood?

6. Henry] *Pope; King Henry / F.*

house over the rear of the Elizabethan stage, which naturally suggested clouds, night, etc., when suitably draped.

2. *Comets . . . change*] a common classical and Elizabethan superstition. Hall, 113, calls Henry 'the blasyng comete . . . of his daie'; Lyly, *Euphues*, i. 293, has 'blasing Commettes, which euer prognosticate some straunge mutation'. The imagery is significant of coming disaster for England.

importing] in the literal L. sense, bringing in.

states] (*a*) conditions, (*b*) countries or governments (L. *res*).

3. *Brandish*] cause to flash, or glitter, like a brandished sword.

crystal tresses] bright hair; cf. *1 Tamburlaine*, v. ii, 'Flora in her mornings pride, / Shaking her siluer tresses in the air' and Ovid, *Metam.*, xv. 849–50, 'Flammiferumque trahens spatioso limite crinem / Stella micat'. Cf. 56 n. below.

4. *scourge*] The crystal tresses are now transformed into the snaky hair of Medusa.

As Tamburlaine was the 'scourge of Asia' and the 'scourge of God', Tal-

bot, later, is the 'scourge of France'.

revolting] rebellious.

5. *consented*] acted in concert, conspired together to bring about; the original L. sense.

6 ff.] This *laudatio* is based on Hall, 112–14, a passage that Shakespeare draws on elsewhere, e.g. *2H6*, i. i. 80.

6. Henry] 'King' was probably added by the scribe under the influence of the title. It is extra-metrical and unnecessary; cf. 52 below, and see Intro., p. xx.

too famous . . .] a version of the good dying young?

9. *Virtue*] L. *virtus*, the quality of a *man*; excellence; ability.

12. *replete with*] full of.

14. *fierce*] adj. used adverbially; cf. *H5*, ii. iv. 9.

15. *What should I say?*] I cannot express it: cf. Hall, 113: a common Latinism.

16. *lift*] common omission of *-ed* in inflections ending in *t* or *d*; cf. Abbott, 341.

17. *mourn . . . in blood*] viz. by making war against the French.

Henry is dead and never shall revive.
Upon a wooden coffin we attend;
And Death's dishonourable victory   20
We with our stately presence glorify,
Like captives bound to a triumphant car.
What! shall we curse the planets of mishap
That plotted thus our glory's overthrow?
Or shall we think the subtle-witted French   25
Conjurers and sorcerers, that, afraid of him,
By magic verses have contriv'd his end?
Win. He was a king bless'd of the King of kings.
Unto the French the dreadful judgment-day
So dreadful will not be as was his sight.   30
The battles of the Lord of Hosts he fought;
The Church's prayers made him so prosperous.
Glou. The Church! Where is it? Had not churchmen
        pray'd,
His thread of life had not so soon decay'd.
None do you like but an effeminate prince,   35

33.] *As Pope;* The . . . it? / Had . . . pray'd, *F.*   not] *F;* but *conj. Vaughan.*

18. *revive*] original L. sense = live again.

19. *wooden*] The literal sense is extended to include 'unfeeling; expressionless'.

20 ff. *Death's . . . victory . . . planets . . . overthrow*] cf. Judges, v. 20, the victory of Barak and Deborah, where 'even the stars in their courses fought against Sisera'; cf. I. ii. 105, 'the sword of Deborah'.

22.] cf. Marlowe, *Ed. 2*, 174, 'With captiue kings at his triumphant Carre'; and *2 Tamb.*, IV. iii. S.D.

23. *planets of mishap*] planets that bring mishap; cf. *Alphonsus, King of Arragon*, 1392.

25. *subtle-witted*] of clever, acute intelligence (like the serpent?).

26. *Conjurers and sorcerers*] cf. Roger Bolingbroke and Marjory Jourdain, *2H6*, I. iv, who at the request of Eleanor, Duchess of Gloucester (cf. 39 below), 'deuised an image of waxe, representyng the kynge, whiche by their

sorcery, a litle and litle consumed, entendyng therby in conclusion to waist, and destroy the kynges person, and so to bryng hym death' (Hall, 202). The terms anticipate the rôle assigned to Joan.

27. *contriv'd*] plotted.

28. *King of kings*] Rev., xix. 16.

29. *dreadful judgment-day*] a dominant theme in Shakespeare, as in the Middle Ages.

30. *his sight*] objective use = the sight of him.

31.] Henry V is compared with David, 1 Sam., xxv. 28, 'because my lord fighteth the battels of the Lord' (Noble).

Lord of Hosts] Isa., xiii. 14.

33. *not*] cf. 43, below. Winchester is being accused of 'praying against' Henry as a 'foe' and hence of having 'contriv'd to murder' him.

34. *thread of life*] alluding to the three classical Fates, who respectively spin, measure, and cut the thread of life.

Whom like a school-boy you may overawe.

Win. Gloucester, whate'er we like, thou art Protector,
And lookest to command the Prince and realm.
Thy wife is proud; she holdeth thee in awe
More than God or religious churchmen may.   40

Glou. Name not religion, for thou lov'st the flesh,
And ne'er throughout the year to church thou go'st
Except it be to pray against thy foes.

Bed. Cease, cease these jars, and rest your minds in peace;
Let's to the altar; heralds, wait on us. [*Exit Funeral.*] 45
Instead of gold, we'll offer up our arms,
Since arms avail not; now that Henry's dead,
Posterity, await for wretched years,
When at their mothers' moist eyes babes shall suck,
Our isle be made a nourish of salt tears,   50

---

45. S.D.] *This edn; not in F.*   47. not; now . . . dead,] *This edn;* not, now . . .
dead, *F;* not, now . . . dead. *edd.*   48. for] *F;* fond *conj. this edn.*   49. moist]
F2; moistned *F1.*   50. nourish] *F;* marish *Pope.*

---

36. *school-boy . . . overawe*] cf. *2H6*,
II. iii. 28–9, and Marlowe, *Ed. 2*, 1336–
7, 'As though your highnes were a
schoole boy still, / And must be awde
and gouernd like a child.' Shakespeare's source is Hall, 208; cf. Rossiter, 54–5.
    38. *lookest*] expectest.
    to command . . . realm] an indication
of the coming reversal of order, rea-
lized and similarly expressed by Suffolk in the last lines of the play.
    Prince] L. *princeps* = ruler; the regu-
lar Elizabethan term.
    39. *Thy wife*] Gloucester's second
wife, Eleanor Cobham (Hall, 129).
The reference, dramatically unnecessary, is an indication of Shakespeare's
overall plan for the *H6–R3* tetralogy,
and of the priority of *1H6*. Her dramatic rôle comes in *2H6*.
    41. *lov'st the flesh*] compare Winches-
ter's character as developed in *2H6*;
and 1 John, ii. 15–16, 'Love not this
world . . . as the lust of the flesh'.
    44. *jars*] Hall, 130.
    45. *wait on us.*] Clearly this in-
structs the 'funeral' to move on to the
altar and exit. The subsequent refer-

ence (62) is not inconsistent, whether
the procession has left the stage or not;
the corpse is still in the abbey, and
Bedford's progress is in any case interrupted by the messengers. It is in-
conceivable dramatically that the
'funeral' should remain motionless
there throughout the rest of the scene;
and the final speech is clearly a soliloquy. Here, as in so many other places
(Intro., p. xv), the S.D. has been over-
looked, or considered unnecessary, by
the stage-adapter.
    48. *for*] The conj. 'fond(e)' is based
on the presence of the superfluous 'ned'
in 49. (Cf. 'fond wretch', *Meas.*, v. i.
108.) These letters may belong to
'fonde', the remaining 'fo' having been
rationalized to 'for', not elsewhere used
by Shakespeare with 'await'.
    50. *nourish*] Elizabethan form of
nurse. Three ideas seem to be presented: (*a*) the men will all be killed, only
the women left; (*b*) the women will
nurse their babes at their weeping
eyes; (*c*) England (i.e. the women)
will be one 'nourish', feeding her off-
spring (at her weeping eyes) on salt
tears (instead of milk). H.F.B.

And none but women left to wail the dead.
Henry the Fifth, thy ghost I invoke:
Prosper this realm, keep it from civil broils,
Combat with adverse planets in the heavens.
A far more glorious star thy soul will make   55
Than Julius Caesar or bright——

Enter a Messenger.

Mess. My honourable lords, health to you all!
      Sad tidings bring I to you out of France,
      Of loss, of slaughter, and discomfiture:
      Guienne, Champaigne, Rheims, Rouen, Orleans,   60
      Paris, Guysors, Poictiers, are all quite lost.
Bed. What say'st thou, man! Before dead Henry's corse
      Speak softly, or the loss of those great towns
      Will make him burst his lead and rise from death.
Glou. Is Paris lost? Is Rouen yielded up?   65

56. ——] *F;* Charlemagne *conj. anon.* (*in Camb.*)*;* Hercules *conj. Lloyd;* Constantine *conj. Perring.*   60. Champaigne] *F;* Champagne *edd.*   Rouen] *Capell; not in F.*   62. man!... corse] *Staunton;* man, ... Coarse? *F+edd.*

52. *ghost*] spirit; cf. *R3*, I. ii. 8.
invocate] invoke (L. *invocare*); call upon.

53. *civil broils*] cf. 'jars' above—one of the main themes of the historical plays; the first explicit reference to civil war.

54. *adverse planets*] unfavourable influences; cf. Hall, 74, 'the aspect of the planet reigned contrary to his purpose'; and 'the bad revolting stars' in 4 above.

56. *Caesar*] cf. Ovid, *Metam.*, xv. De Iulio Caesare in Cometam, 843–5, 'Venus . . . suique / Caesaris eripuit membris . . . / coelestibus animam intulit artis.'

bright—] The F dash probably indicates illegibility of the copy or MS.; cf. Intro., p. xxiii.

S.D.] The entry of this and the 'other' messengers (88, 102) with news of successive disasters is modelled on the beginning of Job, with which this passage is comparable for cumulative

dramatic effect. Shakespeare uses the device elsewhere, e.g. *R3*, IV. iv. 500 ff.

60–1.] see map; and previous note. The collocation of losses ranging historically from 1427 to 1450 is typical of Shakespeare's technique of telescoping historical events for dramatic effect. The result is, of course, a certain inconsistency when the same events are later introduced in their historical context, e.g. for the loss of Paris, cf. IV. i. 1; V. ii. 2–3.

60. *Champaigne*] Compiègne (not Champagne); 'the toune of Champeigne' (Hall, 156; Fabyan, 601), where Joan was captured.

Rouen] The emendation is justified by the metre and by the reference (65) in Gloucester's reply.

62. *Before ... corse*] imagined as still in the abbey, though in fact off-stage, or on its way there; cf. 45 n.

64. *his lead*] the inner coffin, or lining of the 'wooden coffin', 19; cf. Hall, 113; and *Mer. V.*, II. vii. 49–51.

If Henry were recall'd to life again,
These news would cause him once more yield the ghost.
Exe. How were they lost? What treachery was us'd?
Mess. No treachery, but want of men and money.
Amongst the soldiers this is muttered—   70
That here you maintain several factions:
And whilst a field should be dispatch'd and fought,
You are disputing of your generals;
One would have lingering wars, with little cost;
Another would fly swift, but wanteth wings;   75
A third thinks, without expense at all,
By guileful fair words peace may be obtain'd.
Awake, awake, English nobility!
Let not sloth dim your honours new-begot.
Cropp'd are the flower-de-luces in your arms;   80
Of England's coat one half is cut away.   [*Exit.*]
Exe. Were our tears wanting to this funeral,
These tidings would call forth her flowing tides.
Bed. Me they concern; Regent I am of France:
Give me my steeled coat: I'll fight for France.   85
Away with these disgraceful wailing robes!
Wounds will I lend the French instead of eyes,
To weep their intermissive miseries.

---

76. third thinks] *F1;* third man thinks *F2;* third, he thinks *conj. Orger.*   80–1.
arms; / . . . coat] *As Pope;* Armes / . . . Coat, *F.*   81. S.D. *Exit.*] *Dover Wilson;
not in F.*   83. her] *F;* their *Theobald.*

67. *yield the ghost*] Biblical, e.g. Gen.,
xlix. 33; Acts, v. 10; with a play on
'yield' in 65.

70. *this is muttered*] Hall, 130.

71. *maintain . . . factions*] The chief
cause of the loss of France, as emphasized throughout the play, and of the
Wars of the Roses, was the ability of
the nobles to keep bodies of retainers,
or private armies, in 'livery'. Henry
VII later curbed this by the Statute
against Maintenance and Livery.

several] separate—the legal sense,
e.g. *Tp.*, III. i. 42; very likely with
further overtones of 'private', as when
land in common is contrasted with
land in several: 'More profit is found

when pastures in several be' (Thomas
Tusser).

72. *field . . . dispatch'd*] battle . . . prepared, organized.

80. *flower-de-luces*] the fleur-de-lis, or
lily of France, which the English kings
from Edward III had quartered
with the English lions. Hence 'half'
in 81.

81. S.D.] The omission is typical of
the basic authorial copy for F. See
Intro., p. xv.

83. *tidings . . . tides*] note the pun.

85. *steeled*] of steel; cf. *2 Tamb.,* 2874,
'steeled crests'.

88. *intermissive*] coming at intervals
(*OED.*); having a temporary cessation

Enter to them another Messenger.

2 Mess. Lords, view these letters full of bad mischance.
   France is revolted from the English quite,   90
   Except some petty towns of no import:
   The Dauphin Charles is crowned king in Rheims:
   The Bastard of Orleans with him is join'd:
   Reignier, Duke of Anjou, doth take his part:
   The Duke of Alençon flieth to his side.   *Exit.* 95
Exe. The Dauphin crowned king! All fly to him!
   O, whither shall we fly from this reproach?
Glou. We will not fly but to our enemies' throats.
   Bedford, if thou be slack, I'll fight it out.
Bed. Gloucester, why doubt'st thou of my forwardness?   100
   An army have I muster'd in my thoughts,
   Wherewith already France is overrun.

Enter another Messenger.

3 Mess. My gracious lords, to add to your laments,
   Wherewith you now bedew King Henry's hearse,
   I must inform you of a dismal fight   105
   Betwixt the stout Lord Talbot and the French.
Win. What! Wherein Talbot overcame, is't so?
3 Mess. O no: wherein Lord Talbot was o'erthrown:

89. *2 Mess.] Rowe; Mess. / F.*   94. Reignier] *Rowe; Reynold / F.*   95. Duke of]
F; Duke conj. S. Walker.   96. crowned] *Rowe;* crown'd *F.*   103. *3 Mess.*
Rowe; Mes. / F.

(Schmidt); interrupted by the death
of Henry V?
   91. *petty*] small (Fr. *petit*) in size and
value.
   import] importance.
   92. *The Dauphin . . . crowned*] in 1429
(Hall, 150); he had already been
crowned at Poitiers as a child in 1422.
   93. *Orleans*] Jean, Count Dunois
(1402–68), illegitimate son of the Duke
of Orleans, and first cousin to Charles
VII (Hall, 144–5).
   94. *Reignier*] F *Reynold* may be a misreading due to the scribe's copy. Dover
Wilson has pointed out that his presence thus early in the play, dramatically unnecessary, is an argument for

the priority of *1 Henry VI* over *2* and *3*
Henry VI; see Intro., pp. xxxv ff.
   96–8. *fly*] playing on several senses
of the word, with the use of Ænigma
(Baldwin, II. 143), or sudden turn of
the meaning in 98.
   102. *overrun*] harried and destroyed
by a hostile force.
   105. *dismal*] savage, terrible; cf.
Macb., I. ii. 53, 'a dismal conflict'.
   fight] the battle of Patay (Hall, 150);
see I. v. 13 ff.; III. ii. 104 ff.; and IV. i.
9 ff.
   107.] Note the preparatory build-up
of Talbot's reputation.
   is't so?] didn't he? The phrase is
part of the question.

The circumstance I'll tell you more at large.
The tenth of August last this dreadful lord,   110
Retiring from the siege of Orleans,
Having scarce full six thousand in his troop,
By three and twenty thousand of the French
Was round encompassed and set upon.
No leisure had he to enrank his men;   115
He wanted pikes to set before his archers;
Instead whereof sharp stakes pluck'd out of hedges
They pitched in the ground confusedly
To keep the horsemen off from breaking in.
More than three hours the fight continued;   120
Where valiant Talbot, above human thought,
Enacted wonders with his sword and lance:
Hundreds he sent to hell, and none durst stand him;
Here, there, and everywhere, enrag'd he flew:
The French exclaim'd the devil was in arms;   125
All the whole army stood agaz'd on him.
His soldiers, spying his undaunted spirit,
'A Talbot! a Talbot!' cried out amain,
And rush'd into the bowels of the battle.

112. scarce full] *Rowe;* full scarce *F.*   124. flew] *Rowe*[2]*;* slew *F.*   126. the]
F; their *conj. Capell.*

109. *circumstance*] the relevant details
(the L. sense). It was part of the mediaeval training in rhetoric to add
'circumstance' to a general proposi-
tion.
110. *tenth of August*] actually 18 June
(Wilson).
dreadful] the literal sense—causing
dread, i.e. the terror of the French.
111. *Retiring . . . Orleans*] an apparent inconsistency, since the siege is described in the later scenes I. iv–II. i.
The order has been altered to add the
capture of Talbot as the crowning disaster to the English. He is, however,
freed in time to take his part in the
siege.
112. *scarce full*] The F version is
probably one of the scribe's frequent
transpositions. Holinshed has 'not past
6000'.

116–17. *pikes . . . stakes . . . hedges*]
'*stakes* bound with yron sharpe at both
endes of the length of v. or vi. fote to
be pitched before the Archers and
of euery side the fote men so that
the fotemen were *hedged* about',
Hall, 67; cf. also 122 (Henry V at
Agincourt).
124. *Here . . .*] cf. *F.Q.,* III. i. 66,
'Wherewith enrag'd she fiercely at
them flew, / . . . Here, there, and every
where about her swayd / Her wrathfull
steele'; cf. III. xi. 28; and *Troil.,* v. v. 26.
flew] see n. above.
126. *agaz'd*] astounded, amazed; cf.
at gaze.
128. *A Talbot!*] = à Talbot; cf. *2H6,*
IV. viii. 53 and n. The line reads better
if the words are read with the French
accentuation suggested by this interpretation.

Here had the conquest fully been seal'd up   130
If Sir John Falstaff had not play'd the coward.
He, being in the vaward, plac'd behind
With purpose to relieve and follow them,
Cowardly fled, not having struck one stroke.
Hence grew the general wrack and massacre: 135
Enclosed were they with their enemies;
A base Walloon, to win the Dauphin's grace,
Thrust Talbot with a spear into the back,
Whom all France, with their chief assembled strength,
Durst not presume to look once in the face.   140
Bed. Is Talbot slain? Then I will slay myself,
For living idly here, in pomp and ease,
Whilst such a worthy leader, wanting aid,
Unto his dastard foemen is betray'd.
3 Mess. O no, he lives, but is took prisoner,   145
And Lord Scales with him, and Lord Hungerford;
Most of the rest slaughter'd, or took likewise.
Bed. His ransom there is none but I shall pay:
I'll hale the Dauphin headlong from his throne;
His crown shall be the ransom of my friend;   150
Four of their lords I'll change for one of ours.

131. Falstaff] *F, Wilson;* Fastolfe *Theobald+edd.*   137. Walloon] *F* (Wallon).
141. slain? Then] *Theobald*[4]*;* slaine then? *F.*

130. *seal'd up*] completed, made perfect.

131. *Falstaff*] Hall, 149–50. F has *Falstaffe* throughout, but editors from Theobald onwards (except Wilson) have restored *Fastolfe* from the chronicles. See J. B. Henneman, *PMLA.,* xv (1900), 290–320; and *Library* (1946), 12–16.

The original name of Falstaff in *H4, H5,* and *Wiv.* was clearly Oldcastle; the choice of the coward Falstaff as a substitute is probably therefore not without significance.

132. *vaward*] vanguard.

plac'd behind] presumably = posted behind the vanguard, in support; cf. Greene, VI. 276, 'foremost in the vawarde' (Hart).

133. *With purpose*] on purpose,

designedly; cf. *Mer. V.,* I. i. 91.

135. *wrack*] destruction, ruin.

137. *Walloon*] an inhabitant of the border country between the Netherlands (then including Belgium) and France.

139. *chief*] the main body of.

139–40.] Hall, 229, 'killed him, . .. whome they neuer durste loke in the face, whyle he stode on his fete'; cf. Hol. iii. 640.

143–4.] Note the further build-up of Talbot; cf. 107 and 121.

145–6.] Hall, 150.

148.] ambiguous; but presumably means, 'I alone will pay . . .'

149. *hale . . . headlong*] an Elizabethan commonplace; cf. e.g. *2 Tamb.,* 4021, 'Haling him headlong to the lowest hell'.

Farewell, my masters; to my task will I;
Bonfires in France forthwith I am to make
To keep our great Saint George's feast withal.
Ten thousand soldiers with me I will take,   155
Whose bloody deeds shall make all Europe quake.

3 Mess. So had you need; 'fore Orleans besieg'd
The English army is grown weak and faint;
The Earl of Salisbury craveth supply
And hardly keeps his men from mutiny,   160
Since they, so few, watch such a multitude.   [*Exit.*]

Exe. Remember, lords, your oaths to Henry sworn,
Either to quell the Dauphin utterly,
Or bring him in obedience to your yoke.

Bed. I do remember it, and here take my leave   165
To go about my preparation.   *Exit.*

Glou. I'll to the Tower with all the haste I can
To view th' artillery and munition;
And then I will proclaim young Henry king.   *Exit.*

Exe. To Eltham will I, where the young King is,   170
Being ordain'd his special governor;

---

157. 'fore Orleans besieg'd] *Hanmer; for Orleance is besieg'd F.*   161. *Exit.*]
Dover Wilson; not in F.   166. *Exit.*] *edd.; Exit Bedford. | F.*   169. *Exit.*] *edd.;*
Exit Gloster. | F.   170, 176. Eltham] *Steevens;* Eltam *F.*

154. *Saint George's feast*] held regularly on 23 April in Shakespeare's
time. Nichols, II. 455–7, has a full account of the ceremonies and banquet-
ing (Hart).
  withal] with them, therewith.
  155. *Ten thousand soldiers*] Hall, 151.
  157. *'fore Orleans besieg'd*] cf. 60–1;
I. ii. 5–8; and I. iv. 1. F conveys the
contrary impression that the English
are beseiged in Orleans. For *'fore,* cf.
I. iii. 22.
  The source is Hall, 143–6, which
describes the siege of Orleans in 1428–
9 (Wilson). For the construction, cf.
III. iii. 72, and see Abbott, 418.
  159. *supply*] munitions of war etc.;
reinforcements.
  160. *hardly*] with difficulty.
  161. Exit.] cf. 81 and n.
  162–4. *oaths . . . sworn . . .*] to Henry
on his death-bed; Hall, 112. The refer-

ence is to *one* oath taken by many
people.
  163. *quell*] destroy, overcome.
  165. *it*] i.e. my oath; cf. n. to 162
above.
  168. *munition*] war materials; cf.
John, v. ii. 98 (Hart).
  169. *proclaim . . . king*] i.e. in England
(1431).
  170. *Eltham*] nine miles S.E. of London, on the road to Canterbury. The
palace there was a residence of the
English kings from the 13th to the 16th
century (Brooke).
  171. *special governor*] Exeter and Winchester had joint charge of the king;
but Shakespeare has followed Hall,
131 and 143 (as against 115), to limit
the office to Exeter, throw Winchester
into opposition, and emphasize the
division among the nobles, with Winchester as chief of one faction.

And for his safety there I'll best devise.   *Exit.*
Win. Each hath his place and function to attend:
  I am left out; for me nothing remains;
  But long I will not be Jack out of office.   175
  The King from Eltham I intend to steal,
  And sit at chiefest stern of public weal.   *Exit.*

[SCENE II.—*France. Before Orleans.*]

Sound a Flourish. Enter CHARLES, ALENÇON, *and* REIGNIER,
marching with Drum and Soldiers.

Cha. Mars his true moving, even as in the heavens
  So in the earth, to this day is not known.
  Late did he shine upon the English side;

176. steal] *Singer, conj. Mason;* send *F.*   177. S.D. *Exit.] F; Exeunt. | edd.*

SCENE II] *Capell; not in F.*   France. Before Orleans.] *Theobald + edd.; not in F.*

174–6.] Hall, 131, item 2 of Gloucester's accusations against Winchester.

175. *Jack out of office*] proverbial; Tilley, J23; a person who has been dismissed from his office, *OED.* Cf. 38 above; here is another threat to political order.

176. *steal*] 'steal' is required by the rhyme of the final couplet; while 'send' is a typical error of the scribe, under the influence of 'intend'; see Intro., p. xxi.

177. *chiefest stern*] L. *gubernator* = (*a*) governor, (*b*) steersman.

public weal] state; cf. common weal. S.D.] see n. to 45. Obviously all these concluding soliloquies would not be made before a funeral procession standing still on the stage.

Scene II

The scene contrasts with scene i, emphasizing the weakness of the English, and the pride and confidence of the French, favoured by the stars. The French boasting suffers a quick ironical reverse (22 ff.), but their pride is restored with the introduction and build-up of Joan and her supernatural powers.

The scene is based on Hall, 145, 148, and 156 ff. (Hol., iii. 599, 600, 604).

S.D. Flourish.] fanfare of trumpets to announce the approach of a great person.

1–2.] from Sandford's translation of Cornelius Agrippa, *De Incertitudine et Vanitate Scientiarum,* often reprinted, in Latin and English: 'Neither hathe the true mouinge of *Mars* bene knowen vntill this daie' (ch. xxx, p. 43, ed. 1569). Nashe also quotes the passage in *Haue with you to Saffron-Walden* (1596); see Intro., p. xxxiv.

1. *Mars . . . moving*] The planet Mars has an eccentric orbit, which puzzled astronomers till Kepler; see *Sh. Eng.,* I. 448.

his] a mistaken form of *'s,* formerly quite common, and generally used after nouns ending in s, where the inflexional genitive would have been awkward; see *OED.*; and cf *Ham.,* II. ii. 484—Q2 Marses; F Mars his—for the sophistication.

Now we are victors, upon us he smiles.
What towns of any moment but we have?   5
At pleasure here we lie near Orleans,
The whiles the famish'd English, like pale ghosts,
Faintly besiege us one hour in a month.
Alen. They want their porridge and their fat bull-beeves:
Either they must be dieted like mules   10
And have their provender tied to their mouths,
Or piteous they will look, like drowned mice.
Reig. Let's raise the siege: why live we idly here?
Talbot is taken, whom we wont to fear;
Remaineth none but mad-brain'd Salisbury,   15
And he may well in fretting spend his gall—
Nor men nor money hath he to make war.
Cha. Sound, sound alarum; we will rush on them.
Now for the honour of the forlorn French!
Him I forgive my death that killeth me   20
When he sees me go back one foot or fly.   *Exeunt.*

Here Alarum; they are beaten back by the English with great loss.
Enter CHARLES, ALENÇON, *and* REIGNIER.

---

7. The whiles] *Capell;* Otherwhiles *F.*   13. live] *F;* lie *Hudson, conj. S.*
Walker.

4. *Now*] ambiguous, and possibly =
now that.
5. *towns of . . . moment*] cf. i. i. 60 ff.
7. *The whiles*] The F 'otherwhiles'
does not occur elsewhere in Shakespeare; and the *e/er* confusion as well
as trouble with initial *T* seems characteristic of the scribe; cf. Intro., p. xxii,
and v. iii. 83. Cf. *Ham.*, iii. ii. 86, 'The
whilst this play is playing'.
8. *faintly*] feebly, weakly; cf. *1 Tamb.*,
520, 'with vnwilling souldiers faintly
arm'd'; and above, i. i. 158.
9–12.] Cf. Nashe, *Foure Letters Con-*
futed (S.R., 12 Jan. 1593), i. 331. 28–
33, 'mutton and porridge . . . this colde
weather our souldiors . . . haue need
of it, and, poore field mise, they haue
almost got the colicke and stone with
eating of prouant.'
Another parallel in Nashe is in

Summer's Last Will and Testament (S.R.,
1600; written *c.* 1592), iii. 270. 1152–3,
'Except the Cammell haue his prouen-
der / Hung at his mouth, he will not
trauell on.' On such parallels have
been based claims for Nashe's hand in
the play; see Intro., pp. xxxii ff.
9. *porridge . . . bull-beeves*] supposed
to produce strength and courage.
14. *Talbot . . . taken*] Hall, 150.
wont] a rarer form of *were wont*.
16. *fretting*] impatience, ill-temper.
spend his gall] wear out his bitterness
of spirit (Hart).
17. *Nor men nor money*] cf. i. i. 69.
19. *forlorn*] as in 'forlorn hope'; men
who perform their duty at the imminent risk of life, *OED.*, 3b; cf.*Cymb.*, v.
v. 405, 'The forlorn soldier that so
nobly fought' (E. E. Duncan-Jones in
N.Q., ccii (Feb. 1957), 64).

Cha. Who ever saw the like? What men have **I**!
　　Dogs! cowards! dastards! I would ne'er have fled
　　But that they left me 'midst my enemies.
Reig. Salisbury is a desperate homicide;　　　　　　　25
　　He fighteth as one weary of his life:
　　The other lords, like lions wanting food,
　　Do rush upon us as their hungry prey.
Alen. Froissart, a countryman of ours, records
　　England all Olivers and Rolands bred　　　　　　　30
　　During the time Edward the Third did reign.
　　More truly now may this be verified;
　　For none but Samsons and Goliases
　　It sendeth forth to skirmish. One to ten!
　　Lean raw-bon'd rascals! Who would e'er suppose　　35
　　They had such courage and audacity?
Cha. Let's leave this town; for they are hare-brain'd slaves,
　　And hunger will enforce them be more eager:
　　Of old I know them; rather with their teeth
　　The walls they'll tear down than forsake the siege.　　40
Reig. I think by some odd gimmers or device
　　Their arms are set, like clocks, still to strike on;
　　Else ne'er could they hold out so as they do:

---

29. Froissart] *F* (*Froysard*).　　30. bred] *Rowe;* breed *F.*　　37.] *as Pope;* Let's …
Towne, / For … Slaves, *F.*　　38. be] *Pope;* to be *F.*　　41. gimmers] *F* (Gim-
mors), *Alexander.*

---

22 ff.] Hall, 145. Note how quickly the French pride has had a fall (cf. 20–1).

25. *homicide*] manslayer.

26. *weary of his life*] cf. Gen., xxvii. 46; Eccles., ii. 17 (Noble).

27–8. *lions … prey*] Ps., xvii. 12, 'like as a lion that is greedy of his prey'.

28. *their hungry prey*] transferred epithet = the prey of them (who are) hungry.

29–30. *Froissart … Olivers … Rolands*] Wilson refers to Berners' *Froissart* (Tudor Translations, iv. 429) where every Englishman in the victory over the French in 1367 is accounted 'worth a Rowlande or an Olyvere'.

33. *Samsons and Goliases*] typical O.T.

strong men; cf. Judges, xv. 16; 1 Sam., xvii. 23–4.

34. *to skirmish*] to battle—a stronger term than now (Hart).

35. *raw-bon'd*] skeleton-like.

rascals] lean worthless deer; cf. Madden, 237.

37. *hare-brain'd*] cf. 'mad as a March hare', in use from 1500.

slaves] a term of contempt.

38. *be*] cf. I. iii. 30. The F *to* was probably a sophistication by either scribe or compositor.

eager] L. *acer* = sharp, keen.

41. *gimmers*] a corruption of *gimmels*; cf. *H5*, IV. ii. 49; joints, links, connecting parts (in machinery), especially for transmitting motion (as in clockwork) *OED.*, 2.

By my consent, we'll even let them alone.
Alen. Be it so.   45

Enter the Bastard of ORLEANS.

Bast. Where's the Prince Dauphin? I have news for him.
Cha. Bastard of Orleans, thrice welcome to us.
Bast. Methinks your looks are sad, your cheer appall'd.
     Hath the late overthrow wrought this offence?
     Be not dismay'd, for succour is at hand: 50
     A holy maid hither with me I bring,
     Which, by a vision sent to her from heaven,
     Ordained is to raise this tedious siege
     And drive the English forth the bounds of France.
     The spirit of deep prophecy she hath,   55
     Exceeding the nine sibyls of old Rome:
     What's past and what's to come she can descry.
     Speak, shall I call her in? Believe my words,
     For they are certain and unfallible.
Cha. Go call her in. [*Exit Bastard.*] But first, to try her skill, 60
     Reignier, stand thou as Dauphin in my place;
     Question her proudly; let thy looks be stern;
     By this means shall we sound what skill she hath.

Enter [*the Bastard of* ORLEANS *with*] JOAN [LA] PUCELLE.

Reig. Fair maid, is't thou wilt do these wondrous feats?

47. *Cha.*] *edd.; Dolph.* | *F* (*and throughout the rest of the scene*).   48. appall'd] *F*
(appal'd).   60. S.D.] *Capell; not in F.*   63. S.D.] *Dyce* (*subst.*); *Enter Ioane
Puzel.* | *F.*

45. S.D. Bastard of Orleans] Hall,
144–5. This is the source of Faulconbridge and his choice in *John*.
   48. *Methinks*] it seems to me.
   cheer] countenance; cf. *MND.*, III.
ii. 96, 'pale of cheer'.
   appall'd] made pale.
   49. *overthrow*] defeat, reverse.
   offence] harm, injury.
   51. *A holy maid*] Hall, 148; Hol.,
III. 600, 104.
   54. *forth*] out of; cf. Sc. *furth of*; and
2H6, III. ii. 89.
   55–6. *spirit . . . prophecy . . . sibyls*] cf.
Cooper, *Thesaurus*, s.v. sibylla, 'A

generall name of all women which had
the spirit of prophecie'. But they were ten.
Shakespeare may, as Brooke suggests,
have transferred the number of the
Cumaean Sibyl's nine books 'to the
sibyls themselves, of whom various
numbers (but not nine) are reckoned'.
   59. *unfallible*] the older, alternative
form, obsolete after the 17th century;
see Abbott, 442.
   63. S.D. Pucelle] Fr. = maid. See
Intro., p. xv, for the spelling variations.
   64. *wilt*] attracted into the second
person singular by 'thou'.

Puc. Reignier, is't thou that thinkest to beguile me?   65
       Where is the Dauphin? Come, come from behind;
       I know thee well, though never seen before.
       Be not amaz'd, there's nothing hid from me.
       In private will I talk with thee apart:
       Stand back, you lords, and give us leave awhile.   70
Reig. She takes upon her bravely at first dash.
Puc. Dauphin, I am by birth a shepherd's daughter,
       My wit untrain'd in any kind of art.
       Heaven and our Lady gracious hath it pleas'd
       To shine on my contemptible estate.   75
       Lo, whilst I waited on my tender lambs,
       And to sun's parching heat display'd my cheeks,
       God's Mother deigned to appear to me,
       And in a vision full of majesty
       Will'd me to leave my base vocation   80
       And free my country from calamity:
       Her aid she promis'd, and assur'd success.
       In complete glory she reveal'd herself;
       And, whereas I was black and swart before,
       With those clear rays which she infus'd on me   85
       That beauty am I blest with you may see.
       Ask me what question thou canst possible,
       And I will answer unpremeditated:
       My courage try by combat, if thou dar'st,
       And thou shalt find that I exceed my sex.   90

76. whilst] *edd.;* whilest *F.*   86. with] *This edn, conj. anon.* (*in Camb.*)*;* with,
which *F.*   90. my] *F;* thy *conj. anon.* (*in Camb.*).

71. *takes upon her*] assumes responsi-
bility or the initiative; cuts a figure
(Schmidt).

   bravely] finely, excellently; as Fr.
brave, or Sc. *braw.*

   at first dash] from the first, with a
suggestion of forwardness; cf. Intro.,
pp. xxxix-xl.

   73. *wit*] intelligence, mind.

   74. *our Lady gracious*] cf. 78, 'God's
Mother'; and 106.

   75. *estate*] state or condition of life.

   77. *parching heat*] cf. Hall, 112; and
2H6, I. i. 80.

   83. *complete*] accented on the first
syllable; cf. *Ham.,* I. iv. 52.

   85. *infus'd*] poured into, shed on.

   86. *beauty*] Hol., III. 600; Hall, however, mentions her 'foule face' (143).

   with] F 'which' is either a sophis-
ticating insertion, or a duplication of
the abbreviation 'w^th' in which 't'
could easily be misread as 'c'.

   87. *possible*] for the transposition, see
Abbott, 419. Plutarch 424: 'as they
could possible'.

   88. *unpremeditated*] extempore, without previous thought.

Resolve on this; thou shalt be fortunate
If thou receive me for thy warlike mate.

Cha. Thou hast astonish'd me with thy high terms.
Only this proof I'll of thy valour make—
In single combat thou shalt buckle with me;   95
And if thou vanquishest, thy words are true;
Otherwise I renounce all confidence.

Puc. I am prepar'd: here is my keen-edg'd sword,
Deck'd with five flower-de-luces on each side,
The which at Touraine, in Saint Katherine's Church,
Out of a great deal of old iron I chose forth.   101

Cha. Then come, o' God's name; I fear no woman.

Puc. And while I live I'll ne'er fly from a man.

Here they fight, and JOAN LA PUCELLE *overcomes.*

Cha. Stay, stay thy hands; thou art an Amazon,
And fightest with the sword of Deborah.   105

Puc. Christ's Mother helps me, else I were too weak.

Cha. Whoe'er helps thee, 'tis thou that must help me.
Impatiently I burn with thy desire;
My heart and hands thou hast at once subdu'd.
Excellent Pucelle, if thy name be so,   110
Let me thy servant and not sovereign be:

97. Otherwise I] *F; I otherwise conj. Seymour.*   99. five] *Steevens;* fine *F.*   100.
Church] *Pope;* Church-yard *F.*   101. great deal of] *F;* deal *Dyce.*   102. o'
God's name] *F* (a . . .); o' God's great name *conj. this edn.*

91. *Resolve on this*] rest assured that,
make up your mind that.
     92. *mate*] continues the succession of
suggestive terms in which Joan is constantly involved. Cf. Intro., xxxix–xl,
and 111, 113–15 below.
     93. *terms*] words, expressions.
     95. *buckle*] join in close fight
(Schmidt).
     96. *if . . . true*] a sort of ordeal by
combat.
     97. *confidence*] used objectively=your
confidence in me.
     99. *flower-de-luces*] fleurs-de-lis, or
lilies, in the arms of France.
     100. *church*] as in the chronicle-
sources. The F 'Church-yard' is probably due to misreading the final loop

of the 'h' or the 'he' of the MS. as the
abbreviation 'y^d'.
     101–2.] Omission of 'great', margi-
nal insertion, and erroneous restoration would explain the metrical irregularity of both lines.
     102. *o'*] of = in.
     104. *Amazon*] a fabulous race of
female warriors of the Steppes; cf.
Hippolyta in *MND.*
     105. *Deborah*] Judges, iv. 4–6; cf.
above, I. i. 20 ff. and n.
     108. *thy desire*] objective genitive =
desire of (=for) thee.
     110. *Excellent*] excelling, exception-
ally great.
     111. *servant*] in an amatory sense;
cf. 113–15, and 92 above.

'Tis the French Dauphin sueth to thee thus.

Puc. I must not yield to any rites of love,
　　For my profession's sacred from above:
　　When I have chased all thy foes from hence,　　115
　　Then will I think upon a recompense.

Cha. Meantime look gracious on thy prostrate thrall.

Reig. My lord, methinks, is very long in talk.

Alen. Doubtless he shrives this woman to her smock;
　　Else ne'er could he so long protract his speech.　　120

Reig. Shall we disturb him, since he keeps no mean?

Alen. He may mean more than we poor men do know:
　　These women are shrewd tempters with their
　　　　tongues.

Reig. My lord, where are you? What devise you on?
　　Shall we give over Orleans, or no?　　125

Puc. Why, no, I say: distrustful recreants!
　　Fight till the last gasp; I will be your guard.

Cha. What she says I'll confirm; we'll fight it out.

Puc. Assign'd am I to be the English scourge.
　　This night the siege assuredly I'll raise:　　130
　　Expect Saint Martin's summer, halcyon's days,
　　Since I have entered into these wars.
　　Glory is like a circle in the water,

---

113. rites] *Pope;* rights *F.*　　125. over] *Rowe;* o're *F.*　　127. I will] *Capell;*
Ile *F.*　　131. halcyon's] *F;* halcyon *F3+edd.*

114. *sacred*] pa. pple of 'sacre' = to
hallow, consecrate; cf. Hall, 160.

118 ff.] typical cynical asides; cf.
3H6, III. i.

119. *shrives*] hears confession and
grants absolution.

smock] under-garment, shift.

121. *mean*] measure, limit; note the
pun with 122.

123. *shrewd*] cunning, artful.

124. *where are you?*] what is your
drift? what are your intentions?

129. *the English scourge*] as Talbot
is the French; cf. I. iv. 41; II. iii.
14–16.

131. *Saint Martin's summer*] Indian
summer, in autumn, at the feast of St
Martin (11 Nov.)—'prosperity after
misfortune, like fair weather after

winter has begun' (Johnson).

halcyon's days] a period of calm. The
halcyon is identified with the kingfisher, supposed to breed in a nest on
the sea about the winter solstice; cf.
Ovid, *Metam.,* xi. 10 (end), 'Perque
dies placidos hyberno tempore septem
/ Incubat Halcyone pendentibus
aequore nidis. / Tum via tuta maris:
ventos custodit, & arcet / Aeolus
egressu, praestatque nepotibus ae-
quor.' Cf. Lyly, II. 488. 23.

133 ff.] The imagery may have been
suggested by the halcyon reference
above. 'It is . . . likely that when he
wrote he visualised either the mytho-
logical nest floating on the sea or a
kingfisher diving into a stream', Armstrong, 43, n.

Which never ceaseth to enlarge itself
Till by broad spreading it disperse to nought.   135
With Henry's death the English circle ends;
Dispersed are the glories it included.
Now am I like that proud insulting ship
Which Caesar and his fortune bare at once.

Cha.   Was Mahomet inspired with a dove?   140
Thou with an eagle art inspired then.
Helen, the mother of great Constantine,
Nor yet Saint Philip's daughters, were like thee.
Bright star of Venus, fall'n down on the earth,

143. Saint] *F* (S).

134. *enlarge*] broaden.
138. *proud insulting*] L. *insultatio* = a springing or leaping on, i.e. mocking, behaving insolently towards, exulting over; cf. IV. vii. 19.
138-9.] North's *Plutarch (Caesar)*, III. 429-30, 'he followed a daungerous determinacion, to imbarke unknowen in a litle pynnase of twelve ores onely, to passe over the sea againe unto Brundusium... there came a great wind... the encownter was marvailous daungerous... the Maister of the pynnase ... bad the Maryners to cast about againe ... but Caesar then taking him by the hand sayd unto him, Good fellow, be of good cheere, and forwardes hardily, feare not, for thou hast *Caesar and his fortune* with thee'. Hart also quotes Peele's *Farewell to the Generalls*, 1589, 'You bear, quoth he, Caesar and Caesar's fortune in your ships'. ' Cf. *2H4*, I. i. 23'.
140. *Mahomet ... dove*] McKerrow, *Nashe*, IV. 200, quotes *Strange things out of Seb. Munster*, 1574, fol. 63ᵛ, 'For he [Mahomet] accustomed and taught a Doue to be fedde, and fetch meate at his eares, the which Doue his most subtile and craftye maister called the holy Ghoste. He preached openly, and made his bragges like a most lying villen that this Doue did shew vnto him the most secrete counsel of God, as often as the simple fowle did flye

vnto his eares for nourishment.'
Elizabethan references are common, e.g. Nashe, *The Terrors of the Night* (c. 1593), i. 351, and *Lenten Stuffe* (1598), iii. 192; Scot, *Discoverie of Witchcraft*, 1584; Raleigh, *History of the World*, 1614; Henry Howard, *A Defensatiue* ... , 1583.
140, 141. *with*] by.
141. *eagle*] 'The holy Joan is compared ... to the apostle John', the eagle, his attribute, being 'the symbol of the highest inspiration' (Hart).
142. *Helen*] mother of the Emperor Constantine, reported to have been led by a vision (cf. Joan) to the discovery of the true Cross, buried on Mt Calvary. 'Two frescoes representing this legend adorned the Guild Chapel at Stratford in Shakespeare's time' (Brooke, from Ward, *Shakespeare's Town and Times*).
Constantine] the Emperor who made Christianity the official religion of the Roman Empire in 323 A.D.
143. *Saint Philip's daughters*] Acts, xxi. 9, 'four daughters, virgins, which did prophesy'.
144. *Venus*] note the amatory classical imagery among the Christian.
144-5. *fall'n down ... worship*] Acts, xix. 35, 'the citie of the Ephesians is a worshipper of the great goddesse Diana and of ... the image, which came down from Jupiter' (Carter).

How may I reverent worship thee enough?   145
Alen. Leave off delays, and let us raise the siege.
Reign. Woman, do what thou canst to save our honours;
 Drive them from Orleans, and be immortaliz'd.
Cha. Presently we'll try: come, let's away about it:
 No prophet will I trust if she prove false.   *Exeunt.* 150

[SCENE III.—*London. Before the Tower.*]

Enter [the Duke of] GLOUCESTER, *with his Serving-men[, in blue coats].*

Glou. I am come to survey the Tower this day;
 Since Henry's death, I fear, there is conveyance.
 Where be these warders that they wait not here?
 Open the gates; 'tis Gloucester that calls.
1 Ward. [*Within.*] Who's there that knocketh so imperiously?
1 Serv. It is the noble Duke of Gloucester.   6
2 Ward. [*Within.*] Whoe'er he be, you may not be let in.

---

145. reverent] *Dyce²;* reverently *F.*   148. Orleans] *F;* hence *Capell.*   and be]
F; be *Marshall.*   149. Presently we'll] *F;* Presently *Pope.*

Scene III
SCENE III] *Capell; not in F.*   London ... Tower.] *edd.; not in F.*   S.D.] *Capell +*
edd.; Enter Gloster, with his Seruing-men | F.   1. I am come ... Tower this day] *F;*
I am this day come ... Tower *Pope.*   5, 7, 9. S.D. *Within.*] *Malone; not in F.*
5. knocketh] *Theobald;* knocks *F.*   6. *1 Serv.*] *edd.; Glost. 1. Man. | F.*   7. you]
F; he *Capell.*

---

145. *reverent*] adjective for adverb, normalized in F.

148. *be immortaliz'd*] gain immortal fame.

Scene III

In contrast to the unity among the French, the first main dissension on the English side—between Winchester and Gloucester—breaks out again. See Hall, 131 ff.

The 'pebble' theme is imported from Fabyan (App. 1), and later duplicated, for effect, in III. i, where it is amalgamated with Richard Plantagenet's claim and the larger 'Roses' quarrel. The compression of historical events is maintained by the initial reference, as in I. i, to Henry's death, and by the free handling of chronology.

S.D. blue coats] with Winchester's livery of 'tawny coats', a useful element in the pageantry or spectacle.

2. *conveyance*] legal = transfer of property or real estate; here, sharp dealing, dishonesty; cf. *Wiv.,* I. iii. 32, '"Convey," the wise it call: "Steal!" foh; a fico for the phrase!'

5. *knocketh*] F 'knocks' is a typical sophistication; cf. *R3,* v. iii. 176 S.D.

1 Serv. Villains, answer you so the Lord Protector?

1 Ward. [*Within.*] The Lord protect him! so we answer him:
      We do no otherwise than we are will'd.   10

Glou. Who willed you, or whose will stands but mine?
      There's none Protector of the realm but I.
      Break up the gates, I'll be your warrantize.
      Shall I be flouted thus by dunghill grooms?

> *Gloucester's men rush at the Tower gates, and*
> *Woodville the Lieutenant speaks within.*

Wood. [*Within.*] What noise is this? What traitors have we
      here?   15

Glou. Lieutenant, is it you whose voice I hear?
      Open the gates; here's Gloucester that would enter.

Wood. [*Within.*] Have patience, noble Duke; I may not open;
      The Cardinal of Winchester forbids:
      From him I have express commandment   20
      That thou nor none of thine shall be let in.

Glou. Faint-hearted Woodville, prizest him 'fore me?
      Arrogant Winchester, that haughty prelate
      Whom Henry, our late sovereign, ne'er could brook!
      Thou art no friend to God, or to the King.   25
      Open the gates, or I'll shut thee out shortly.

Serving-men. Open the gates unto the Lord Protector;
      We'll burst them open, if that you come not quickly.

> *Enter to the Protector at the Tower gates* WINCHESTER *and*
> *his men in tawny coats.*

Win. How now, ambitious Humphrey! What means this?

8. *1 Serv.*] edd.; I. Man. / F.   15, 18. *Within.*] *Alexander; not in* F.   28. We'll]
Pope; Or wee'le F.   29. Humphrey] *Theobald; Vmpheir /* F.

8.] Cf. John, xviii. 22, where an
officer 'struck Jesus . . . saying, Answer-
est thou the high priest so?'

8–9. *Protector . . . protect*] The same
pun occurs in *2H6*, II. i. 54.

13. *Break up*] open by violence,
burst through; cf. Matt., xxiv. 43.

      warrantize] surety, pledge, guaran-
tee.

14. *dunghill*] a common Elizabethan
term of contempt.

19. *Cardinal*] He was Bishop of
Winchester, and Cardinal of St
Eusebius.

23–4. *Arrogant . . .*] Hall, 139; and
cf. v. i. 32–3.

24. *brook*] endure.

28. *We'll*] F 'Or' is probably a duplication of the previous syllable.

      S.D. tawny coats] the dress of sum-
moners or apparitors of an ecclesias-
tical court.

Glou. Peel'd priest, dost thou command me be shut out?   30
Win. I do, thou most usurping proditor,
   And not Protector, of the King or realm.
Glou. Stand back, thou manifest conspirator,
   Thou that contrived'st to murder our dead lord;
   Thou that giv'st whores indulgences to sin: 35
   I'll canvas thee in thy broad cardinal's hat,
   If thou proceed in this thy insolence.
Win. Nay, stand thou back; I will not budge a foot:
   This be Damascus, be thou cursed Cain,
   To slay thy brother Abel, if thou wilt.   40
Glou. I will not slay thee, but I'll drive thee back.
   Thy scarlet robes, as a child's bearing-cloth,
   I'll use to carry thee out of this place.
Win. Do what thou dar'st, I beard thee to thy face.
Glou. What! am I dar'd and bearded to my face?   45
   Draw, men, for all this privileged place—
   Blue coats to tawny. Priest, beware your beard;
   I mean to tug it, and to cuff you soundly.
   Under my feet I'll stamp thy cardinal's hat;
   In spite of Pope or dignities of church,   50

---

30. Peel'd] *edd.;* Piel'd *F.*   be] *Pope;* to be *F.*   47. tawny] *Pope;* Tawny
Coats *F.*   49. I'll] *F2;* I *F1.*

30. *Peel'd*] tonsured; having lost the
hair (cf. the disease references at 35
and 53).

be] F 'to' was probably inserted by
the scribe to fill the ellipsis; cf. I. vi. 12;
III. i. 119.

31. *proditor*] betrayer, traitor.

34. *contrived'st*] plotted; Hall, 131.

dead lord] i.e. Henry V.

35. *Thou . . . sin*] a reference to the
Southwark stews, under the control of
the Bishop of Winchester, who lived
near. Hart is probably right in regarding the 'usury' of *Meas.*, III. ii. 5, as
related to the 'indulgences' here, since
the Bishop received a revenue from
the various houses. One of these bore
the sign of the Cardinal's Hat. See
also 53 and n.

36. *canvas*] (*a*) toss in a canvas or
coarse sheet, with a probable allusion

to the Cardinal's Hat (35 and n.); (*b*)
examine or search out thoroughly, as
through a canvas sieve.

39. *Damascus . . . Cain*] cf. Mande-
ville, *Travels* (ed. Pollard, 1900), 81,
'In that place where Damascus was
founded Cain slew Abel'.

cursed Cain] Gen., iv. 8, 11.

42. *scarlet robes*] suggestive of the
whore of Babylon? Cf. 56; and Rev.,
xvii. 3–4.

bearing-cloth] christening robe; an
extension of the idea in 'canvas'?

44. *beard*] defy, insult.

46. *privileged*] having immunity,
from e.g. disorder, as a royal precinct;
cf. the Temple Garden, II. iv. 86.

47. *tawny*] F shows a typical scribal
repetition; see Intro., p. xx.

50. *dignities*] metonymy, for digni-
taries.

Here by the cheeks I'll drag thee up and down.
Win. Gloucester, thou'lt answer this before the Pope.
Glou. Winchester goose! I cry, 'A rope! a rope!'
Now beat them hence; why do you let them stay?
Thee I'll chase hence, thou wolf in sheep's array. 55
Out, tawny coats! Out, scarlet hypocrite!

Here GLOUCESTER's *men beat out the Cardinal's men, and enter
in the hurly-burly the Mayor of London and his Officers.*

May. Fie, lords! that you, being supreme magistrates,
Thus contumeliously should break the peace!
Glou. Peace, Mayor! thou know'st little of my wrongs:
Here's Beaufort, that regards nor God nor King, 60
Hath here distrain'd the Tower to his use.
Win. Here's Gloucester, a foe to citizens,
One that still motions war, and never peace,
O'ercharging your free purses with large fines;
That seeks to overthrow religion, 65
Because he is Protector of the realm,
And would have armour here out of the Tower,
To crown himself King and suppress the Prince.
Glou. I will not answer thee with words, but blows.

Here they skirmish again.

May. Nought rests for me in this tumultous strife 70
But to make open proclamation.
Come, officer, as loud as e'er thou canst. *Cry.*

52. thou'lt] *Pope;* thou wilt *F.*   60. Beaufort] *Capell; Beauford / F.*   72. canst.
Cry.] *This edn;* canst, cry: *F;* canst, / Cry. *edd.*

53. *Winchester goose*] a swelling in the
groin, the result of venereal disease
(cf. 35); one so affected.
A rope!] (a) a halter, (b) a parrot-cry
of abuse; cf. *Err.,* IV. iv. 39–40.
55. *wolf in sheep's array*] the type of
hypocrisy in Aesop, and Matt., vii. 15,
'Beware of false prophets, which come
to you in sheep's clothing but inwardly
they are ravening wolves'.
56. *scarlet*] see 42 and n.
S.D. hurly-burly] tumult, uproar.
57. *magistrates*] members of the exe-
cutive government of the country.
58. *contumeliously*] by slandering each
other.
61. *distrain'd*] seized, confiscated
(legal).
63. *still*] Elizabethan sense = always.
motions] proposes, moves.
68. *Prince*] L. *princeps* = ruler, king.
70. *rests*] Fr. *rester* = remains.
72 S.D. Cry.] The F S.D. 'cry' (cf.
II. i. 38) has been erroneously incorporated in the text; cf. e.g. *Cor.,* I. iv.
42, 'followes'.

Off. All manner of men, assembled here in arms this day,
　　against God's peace and the King's, we charge and
　　command you, in his Highness' name, to repair　　75
　　to your several dwelling-places; and not to wear,
　　handle, or use any sword, weapon, or dagger, hence-
　　forward, upon pain of death.
Glou. Cardinal, I'll be no breaker of the law;
　　But we shall meet and break our minds at large.　　80
Win. Gloucester, we will meet, to thy cost, be sure;
　　Thy heart-blood I will have for this day's work.
May. I'll call for clubs if you will not away.
　　This Cardinal's more haughty than the devil.
Glou. Mayor, farewell: thou dost but what thou may'st.　　85
Win. Abominable Gloucester, guard thy head,
　　For I intend to have it ere't be long.
　　　　　　　　Exeunt[, severally, Gloucester and Winchester,
　　　　　　　　　　　　　　　with their Serving-men].
May. See the coast clear'd, and then we will depart.
　　Good God, these nobles should such stomachs bear!
　　I myself fight not once in forty year.　　*Exeunt.*　　90

[SCENE IV.—*Orleans.*]

Enter the Master-Gunner of Orleans and his Boy.

M. Gun. Sirrah, thou know'st how Orleans is besieg'd,

73. *Off.*] *not in* F.　　87. ere't be] *Capell;* ere F.　　87. S.D.] *Capell+edd.; Exeunt. |*
F.　　89. these] F; that *Rowe.*

SCENE IV] *Capell; not in* F.　　*Orleans.*] *Camb.; not in* F.

80. *break*] reveal, disclose.
　at large] in full, at length.
　83. *call for clubs*] call out the ap-
prentices with their clubs—to quell
a riot, though often to take part in
one.
　84. *haughty . . . devil*] the pride of
Lucifer, the sin by which the angels
fell.
　86. *Abominable*] from the false deri-
vation 'ab+hominis' had the sense of
inhuman, unnatural.
　89. *stomachs*] angry tempers, haughty
spirit of resentment; cf. *H8*, IV. ii. 34,
'a man / Of an unbounded stomach'.
　90. *forty*] a round number.
　year] the normal Elizabethan plural.

The opposing sides are for the first

And how the English have the suburbs won.

Boy. Father, I know; and oft have shot at them,
    Howe'er unfortunate I miss'd my aim.

M. Gun. But now thou shalt not. Be thou rul'd by me: 5
    Chief master-gunner am I of this town;
    Something I must do to procure me grace.
    The Prince' espials have informed me
    How the English, in the suburbs close intrench'd,
    Wont, through a secret grate of iron bars   10
    In yonder tower, to overpeer the city,
    And thence discover how with most advantage
    They may vex us with shot or with assault.
    To intercept this inconvenience,
    A piece of ordnance 'gainst it I have plac'd   15
    And even these three days watch'd if I could see
      them.
    Now do thou watch, for I can stay no longer.
    If thou spy'st any, run and bring me word;
    And thou shalt find me at the Governor's.   *Exit.*

Boy. Father, I warrant you; take you no care;   20
    I'll never trouble you if I may spy them.   *Exit.*

---

8. Prince' espials] *This edn;* Princes espyals *F;* Princes 'spials *Pope.*   8–9. informed me / How the] *F;* inform'd me how / The *conj. this edn.*   10. Wont] *Steevens, conj. Tyrwhitt;* Went *F.*   13. They may vex us] *F;* Vex us they may *conj. this edn.*   16. watch'd] *This edn, conj. Vaughan;* haue I watcht, *F.*   16–17.] *This edn, conj. Vaughan;* And . . . watcht, / . . . watch, / . . . longer. *F.*

time brought together, and still another misfortune befalls the English, in the death of Salisbury. At the same time the heroic Talbot is introduced, with a condemnation of the cowardly Falstaff—a theme already touched as narrative in I. i.

The matter is from Hall, 144–5.

The Master-Gunner has probably placed his 'piece of ordnance' (15) at stage-level, but off-stage, and not 'on the walls' (Camb.). See Gaw, 37 ff., and Wilson, 129, 'no gun is seen by the audience'.

1. *sirrah*] a form used to inferiors.

4. *Howe'er*] although, notwithstanding that.

7. *grace*] honour.

8. *Prince'*] F seems to have normalized or been influenced by the following syllable. Cf. *Per.,* II, Gower 22, 'his prince' desire'.

espials] spies; occurs in Hall, 110, 114, etc.

10. *Wont*] F exemplifies a common *o/e* error; = are accustomed.

11. *tower*] turret or top in the theatre.

13. *vex*] trouble, harass.

15. *'gainst*] opposite, directed against.

16.] a typical scribal repetition in F of 'have I', itself probably inverted in 15.

20. *take you no care*] don't worry.

Enter SALISBURY *and* TALBOT *on the Turrets, with*
[SIR WILLIAM GLANSDALE, SIR THOMAS GARGRAVE, *and*]
Others.

Sal. Talbot, my life, my joy, again return'd!
  How wert thou handled, being prisoner?
  Or by what means gots thou to be releas'd?
  Discourse, I prithee, on this turret's top.   25
Tal. The Earl of Bedford had a prisoner,
  Call'd the brave Lord Ponton de Santrailles;
  For him I was exchang'd and ransomed.
  But with a baser man of arms by far
  Once in contempt they would have barter'd me: 30
  Which I disdaining scorn'd, and craved death
  Rather than I would be so vile-esteem'd.
  In fine, redeem'd I was as I desir'd.
  But O! the treacherous Falstaff wounds my heart,
  Whom with my bare fists I would execute   35
  If I now had him brought into my power.
Sal. Yet tell'st thou not how thou wert entertain'd.
Tal. With scoffs and scorns and contumelious taunts.
  In open market-place produc'd they me
  To be a public spectacle to all;   40
  Here, said they, is the Terror of the French,
  The scarecrow that affrights our children so.
  Then broke I from the officers that led me,
  And with my nails digg'd stones out of the ground

---

21. S.D.] *edd.; Enter Salisbury and Talbot on the Turrets, with others. | F.* 24. gots]
F (got's). 26. Earl] *F;* Duke *Theobald.* 27. Call'd] *F;* Called *Pope.*
Santrailles] *Capell;* Santrayle *| F.* 28. ransomed] *Pope;* ransom'd *F.* 32. vile-]
Pope+edd.; pil'd *F.* 34. Falstaff] *F, Wilson;* Fastolfe *Thecbald+edd.*

21. S.D. Turrets] see head-note and
n. to 11.

24. *gots*] Abbott, 340; a common
Elizabethan form, mainly for eu-
phony.

29. *baser*] of lower birth, or rank.
man of arms] soldier.

32. *vile-esteem'd*] held cheap; valued
at a low price (L. *estimare*).

33. *In fine*] to sum up; in short.

redeem'd] ransom'd, bought back
(L. *redimo*).

34. *treacherous Falstaff*] cf. I. i. 105 ff.;
III. ii. 104 ff.; IV. i. 9 ff.

37. *entertain'd*] received, treated.

38. *contumelious*] see I. iii. 58 n.

41. *Terror . . .*] Hall, 230, 'to the
French a very scourge and a daylie
terror', and 229, 'the terror and scourge
of the French people'.

To hurl at the beholders of my shame.   45
My grisly countenance made others fly;
None durst come near for fear of sudden death.
In iron walls they deem'd me not secure;
So great fear of my name 'mongst them were spread
That they suppos'd I could rend bars of steel   50
And spurn in pieces posts of adamant.
Wherefore a guard of chosen shot I had,
That walk'd about me every minute-while;
And if I did but stir out of my bed,
Ready they were to shoot me to the heart.   55

Enter the Boy with a linstock[, and exit].

Sal. I grieve to hear what torments you endur'd;
But we will be reveng'd sufficiently.
Now it is supper-time in Orleans:
Here, through this grate, I count each one
And view the Frenchmen how they fortify: 60
Let us look in; the sight will much delight thee.
Sir Thomas Gargrave, and Sir William Glansdale,
Let me have your express opinions
Where is best place to make our battery next.
Gar. I think at the North Gate, for there stands lords.   65
Glan. And I here, at the bulwark of the bridge.
Tal. For aught I see, this city must be famish'd,
Or with light skirmishes enfeebled.

---

49. fear . . . were] *F;* fear . . . was *Pope*.   55. S.D. *and exit*.] *This edn; not in F.*
59. grate] *F;* secret grate *Dyce*.   65. stands] *F;* stand *F2+edd.*   67. aught]
Theobald²; ought *F.*

46. *grisly*] grim, ghastly.
51. *adamant*] a legendary substance
of excessive hardness; cf. its doublet
'diamond'.
52. *shot*] gunners, marksmen.
53. *minute-while*] minute's space.
55. S.D.] 'The boy crosses the stage
with lighted linstock to warn the spectators what to expect' (Wilson). His
exit is missing.
linstock] a staff, or stock, about three
feet long, with a forked head to hold a
match or torch, of prepared lint, for

firing a gun; cf. *H5*, III, Chor. 55.
59. *grate*] cf. I. iv. 10. Hall has 'a
secret grate of iron bars'.
63. *express*] precise, considered.
64. *battery*] bombardment.
65. *stands*] cf. Abbott, 333, and
Franz, 672.
66. *bulwark*] manned fortification;
cf. Golding, *Ovid*, viii. 480–1, 'And
looke with what a violent brunt a
mightie Bullet goes / From engines
bent against a wall, or *bulwarks* full of
foes'.

Here they shoot, and SALISBURY [*and* GARGRAVE] *fall down.*

Sal. O Lord, have mercy on us, wretched sinners!
Gar. O Lord, have mercy on me, woeful man!   70
Tal. What chance is this that suddenly hath cross'd us?
          Speak, Salisbury; at least, if thou canst speak:
          How far'st thou, mirror of all martial men?
          One of thy eyes and thy cheek's side struck off!
          Accursed tower! accursed fatal hand   75
          That hath contriv'd this woeful tragedy!
          In thirteen battles Salisbury o'ercame;
          Henry the Fifth he first train'd to the wars;
          Whilst any trump did sound, or drum struck up,
          His sword did ne'er leave striking in the field.   80
          Yet liv'st thou, Salisbury? Though thy speech doth fail,
          One eye thou hast to look to heaven for grace;
          The sun with one eye vieweth all the world.
          Heaven, be thou gracious to none alive,
          If Salisbury want mercy at thy hands!   85
          Sir Thomas Gargrave, hast thou any life?
          Speak unto Talbot; nay, look up to him.
          Bear hence his body; I'll help to bury it.
                    [*Exeunt some with the body of Gargrave.*]

---

68. S.D.] *edd.; Here they shot, and | Salisbury falls downe. | F.*   72. canst] *Pope;*
canst, *F.*   85. want] *This edn;* wants *F.*   86, 87, 88.] *This edn, conj. Harold*
Brooks; 88, 86, 87 *F.*   88. I'll] *This edn;* I will *F.*   S.D.] *This edn; not in F.*

---

68. S.D.] 'They shoot' (not 'Boy
shoots') implies action in the tiring-
house (Wilson).

69–70.] 'The opening petition of the
Litany is: "O God the Father of heaven: have mercy upon us, miserable
sinners". The ordinary "Lord have
mercy upon us" occurs several times
in the Liturgy, but . . . was otherwise
well known' (Noble).

71. *chance*] unfortunate event, mishap.

73. *mirror*] example; in *The Mirror*
for Magistrates, Salisbury was indeed
selected as the example or mirror of
the 'valiant men' of Henry VI's reign
(142 ff.).

martial] warlike, fighting.

75. *fatal*] fraught with destiny.

76. *contriv'd*] devised, planned.

82–3. *One eye . . . world*] Ovid, *Metam.*,
xiii (Polyphemus), 851–3: 'Unum est
in media lumen mihi fronte; sed in-
star / Ingentis clypei. Quid? Non haec
omnia magnus / Sol videt e coelo? Soli
tamen unicus orbis'. Cf. Golding,
'*Vewes* not the Sun all things from heauen? Yit but one only eye / Hath hee'.

88.] transposed in F with 86 and 87,
probably by an omission and erroneous insertion of the scribe, who was
confused by the two bodies and the
interrupted address to Salisbury and
thought the direction must apply to
him. Salisbury's body, however, was
removed later, at 109.

Salisbury, cheer thy spirit with this comfort,
Thou shalt not die whiles——   90
He beckons with his hand and smiles on me,
As who should say, 'When I am dead and gone,
Remember to avenge me on the French.'
Plantagenet, I will; and, Nero-like,
Play on the lute, beholding the towns burn.   95
Wretched shall France be only in my name.

Here an alarum, and it thunders and lightens.

What stir is this? What tumult's in the heavens?
Whence cometh this alarum, and the noise?

Enter a Messenger.

Mess. My lord, my lord, the French have gather'd head:
The Dauphin, with one Joan de Pucelle join'd,   100
A holy prophetess new risen up,
Is come with a great power to raise the siege.

Here Salisbury lifteth himself up, and groans.

Tal. Hear, hear how dying Salisbury doth groan;
It irks his heart he cannot be reveng'd.
Frenchmen, I'll be a Salisbury to you.   105
Puzzel or Pucelle, dolphin or dogfish,
Your hearts I'll stamp out with my horse's heels
And make a quagmire of your mingled brains.

94. Nero-like] *Pope;* like thee *F1;* Nero like will *F2;* like thee, Nero *Malone.*   98.
the] *F;* this *Pope.*   100. de] *F;* la *edd.*   106. Puzzel or Pucelle] *F (Puzel or
Pussel).*

94. *Plantagenet*] Salisbury was a
Montacute, but also a descendant of
Edward III (Wilson).
  Nero-like] The F reading is probably
due to the omission of 'Nero', and consequent emendation, conjectural.
  Hart quotes Grafton's *Chronicle,* I.
61, 'He commaunded the City of
Rome to be set on fyre, and himself in
the meane season, with all semblant of
joy, sitting in an high Tower to beholde
the same, played upon the Harpe, and
sang the destruction of Troy'.

96. S.D. it thunders . . .] Hall,
148.
  99. *gather'd head*] raised an army,
drawn their forces together.
  102. *power*] army, fighting force.
  106. *Puzzel*] common drab, with a
probable play on 'pizzle'.
  Pucelle] maid; also harlot.
  dolphin] Some writers considered the
dolphin as the highest in the 'chain of
being' among the fishes; see Tillyard,
EWP., 27. The dogfish, by contrast,
was one of the lowest.

Convey we Salisbury into his tent,
And then try what these dastard Frenchmen dare.   110
Alarum. Exeunt [with the body of Salisbury].

[SCENE V.—*Before Orleans.*]

Here an alarum again, and TALBOT *pursueth the* DAUPHIN, *and
driveth him: then enter* JOAN LA PUCELLE, *driving Englishmen before her [, and exit after them]. Then enter* TALBOT.

Tal. Where is my strength, my valour, and my force?
Our English troops retire, I cannot stay them;
A woman clad in armour chaseth them.

*Enter [*LA*] PUCELLE.*

Here, here she comes. I'll have a bout with thee;
Devil or devil's dam, I'll conjure thee: 5
Blood will I draw on thee, thou art a witch,
And straightway give thy soul to him thou serv'st.
Puc. Come, come, 'tis only I that must disgrace thee.

109. we] *This edn, conj. Vaughan;* me *F.*   110. then] *This edn;* then wee'le *F.*
S.D.] *This edn; Alarum. Exeunt. / F.*

                          Scene v

SCENE V] *Capell + edd.; not in F.*   *Before Orleans.*] *Capell; not in F.*   S.D. *and
exit after them*] *Dyce; not in F.*   3. them] *F; men conj. Vaughan.*   6. art a] *F;
arrant conj. this edn.*

109. *we*] F has an m/w error, as in
Meas., v. i. 13. Talbot would not dele-
gate this pious duty. The metrical irregularity in 110 is due to consequent
emendation of the sense.

Scene v

With the intervention of Joan—
maid, heroine, and goddess to the
French, but witch and strumpet to the
English—the English fortunes continue downwards, in spite of all that
the great warrior Talbot can do. He
himself cannot prevail against her, his
men flee, and the besieged garrison of
Orleans is relieved.

Source—Hall, 143–6.
   4. *a bout with*] cf. III. ii. 56. The term
has here a bawdy implication, like
so many references to Joan; see *Sh.
Bawdy.*
   5. *Devil, or devil's dam*] 'the devil and
his dam' was proverbial, going back
to *Piers the Plowman* (Hart). Cf. *John*,
II. i. 127–8, 'as like / As . . . devil to his
dam'.
   conjure] control, constrain.
   6. *Blood . . .*] 'He that could draw
the witch's blood was free from her
power' (Johnson); cf. Giffard, *Dialogue concerning Witches* (Sh. Assoc.
Facs., 1931), sigs. B1^v, E3^v, E4.

Here they fight.

Tal. Heavens, can you suffer hell so to prevail?
　　My breast I'll burst with straining of my courage,   10
　　And from my shoulders crack my arms asunder,
　　But I will chastise this high-minded strumpet.

They fight again.

Puc. Talbot, farewell; thy hour is not yet come:
　　I must go victual Orleans forthwith.

A short alarum: then enter the town with soldiers.

　　O'ertake me if thou canst: I scorn thy strength.   15
　　Go, go, cheer up thy hunger-starved men;
　　Help Salisbury to make his testament:
　　This day is ours, as many more shall be.   *Exit.*
Tal. My thoughts are whirled like a potter's wheel;
　　I know not where I am, nor what I do: 20
　　A witch by fear, not force, like Hannibal,
　　Drives back our troops and conquers as she lists:
　　So bees with smoke, and doves with noisome stench,
　　Are from their hives and houses driven away.

16. hunger] *Rowe;* hungry *F.*

9.] cf. Matt., xvi. 18, 'And the gates of hell shall not prevayle against it'.

12. *But*] if I do not.
high-minded] arrogant, overweening (Schmidt).

13. *thy hour* . . .] cf. John, vii. 30, 'because his hour was not yet come' (Noble).

14. S.D.] 'Joan here goes from the lower to the upper stage, . . . lines 15–18 being spoken' thence (Brooke).

16. *hunger-starved*] cf. *3H6,* I. iv. 5. 'Starved' (Ger. *sterben*) means 'perished, dead'; the scribe, or compositor, 'improved' the sense. 'Hunger-starved is in Golding's *Ovid*' (Hart).

19. *whirled . . . wheel*] cf. Jer., xviii. 3 (Carter).

21. *Hannibal*] Livy, XXII. xvi–xvii; and North's *Plutarch,* v. 97, 'Annibal . . . commaunded his souldiers to bring forth two thowsand oxen which they had gotten in spoyle . . . and then tying torches or fire linckes unto their hornes, he appointed the nimblest men he had to light them, and to drive the oxen up the hill to the toppe of the mountaines. . . . the whole armie marched after them fayer and softly . . . the Romanes . . . were affrayed of this straunge sight, and . . . foorthwith forsooke their peeces and holdes.' Hannibal thus rescued his army from encirclement.

22. *lists*] pleases.

23. *smoke . . . stench*] possibly suggested by the Hannibal reference in 21 (Hart). A characteristic piece of Euphuism.

They call'd us, for our fierceness, English dogs;   25
Now like to whelps we crying run away.

A short alarum.

Hark, countrymen! either renew the fight,
Or tear the lions out of England's coat;
Renounce your style, give sheep in lions' stead:
Sheep run not half so treacherous from the wolf,   30
Or horse or oxen from the leopard,
As you fly from your oft-subdued slaves.

Alarum. Here another skirmish.

It will not be: retire into your trenches:
You all consented unto Salisbury's death,
For none would strike a stroke in his revenge.   35
Pucelle is enter'd into Orleans
In spite of us or aught that we could do.
O, would I were to die with Salisbury!
The shame hereof will make me hide my head.

Exit Talbot. Alarum; retreat.

29. style] *Marshall, conj. Dyce;* Soyle *F.*

26. *whelps*] young dogs.
28. *lions . . . England's coat*] cf. i. i. 81;
the three lions passant quartered with
the fleur-de-lis in the English coat of
arms.
29. *style*] F *Soyle* was due to a misreading which gave a plausible and
easier sense.
give] display as an armorial bearing;
cf. *Wiv.*, i. i. 16.
30. *treacherous*] The running away of

the English, like sheep, is treachery to
Talbot.
31. *leopard*] trisyllabic (?).
33. *It will not be*] It is useless.
34. *consented unto*] cf. i. i. 5; conspired
together to bring about.
35. *his*] objective genitive = in revenge of him.
39.] Carter compares Jer., xiv. 3,
'They were ashamed and confounded,
and covered their heads.'

[SCENE VI.—*Orleans*.]

Flourish. Enter on the walls, [LA] PUCELLE, CHARLES, REIGNIER,
ALENÇON, *and Soldiers*.

Puc. Advance our waving colours on the walls;
    Rescu'd is Orleans from the English.
    Thus Joan de Pucelle hath perform'd her word.
Cha. Divinest creature, Astraea's daughter,
    How shall I honour thee for this success?   5
    Thy promises are like Adonis' gardens,
    That one day bloom'd, and fruitful were the next.
    France, triumph in thy glorious prophetess!
    Recover'd is the town of Orleans:
    More blessed hap did ne'er befall our state.   10
Reig. Why ring not bells aloud throughout the town?
    Dauphin, command the citizens make bonfires
    And feast and banquet in the open streets
    To celebrate the joy that God hath given us.

Scene VI

SCENE VI] *Capell; not in F.*   *Orleans.*] *edd.; not in F.*   S.D.] *F (subst.).*
6. gardens] *Hanmer+edd.;* Garden *F.*   11. not bells] *This edn, conj. Steevens;* not
out the Bells *F.*

Act I concludes with the English
fortunes at their lowest ebb, and the
French triumphant in Orleans under
Joan's inspiration and in spite of
Talbot.

This climax is marked by a tableau
effect, balancing that of the funeral
of Henry V at the beginning. It was
'similar to those mounted upon actual
city gates at occasions of triumph. In
his speech praising Pucelle, the Dauphin incorporates such elements of the
street shows as Astraea, the garden, the
pyramid, and the assurance of ever-
lasting fame for the one honored. In
addition, further well known features
of the civic celebrations are ordered—
bonfires, pealing of bells, and feasting
in the streets' (Venezky). Cf., especially, S.D., 4 ff., and 21 ff.

    1. *Advance*] raise aloft; cf. *R3*, I. ii. 40.
    4. *creature*] trisyllabic.

Astraea] goddess of justice, who lived
among men in the Golden Age, but
who, with the increase of wickedness,
was forced to leave the earth in the
Iron Age, and was placed among the
stars; cf. Ovid, *Metam.*, I. iv: 'Victa
iacet pietas: et virgo caede madentes /
Ultima coelestum terras Astraea re-
liquit', the conclusion of which is
quoted in the original in *Tit.*, IV. iii. 4.

    6. *Adonis' gardens*] mythical gardens
(or garden) noted for fertility and
plenitude. See Pliny, *Nat. Hist.*, XIX. iv;
Spenser, *F.Q.*, III. vi. 29–42; Tillyard,
EWP., 14, 29.

    11.] The scribe characteristical-
ly repeated 'out the'; see Intro., p.
xx.

    For the celebrations, see head-note,
and cf. *2H6*, v. i. 3, and *1 Tamb.*,
1334–6.

    11–13.] Hall, 149 (not in Hol.).

Alen. All France will be replete with mirth and joy   15
　　When they shall hear how we have play'd the men.
Cha. 'Tis Joan, not we, by whom the day is won;
　　For which I will divide my crown with her,
　　And all the priests and friars in my realm
　　Shall in procession sing her endless praise.   20
　　A statelier pyramis to her I'll rear
　　Than Rhodope's of Memphis ever was;
　　In memory of her, when she is dead,
　　Her ashes, in an urn more precious
　　Than the rich jewel-coffer of Darius,   25
　　Transported shall be at high festivals
　　Before the kings and queens of France.
　　No longer on Saint Denis will we cry,
　　But Joan de Pucelle shall be France's saint.
　　Come in, and let us banquet royally   30
　　After this golden day of victory.   *Flourish. Exeunt.*

22. of] *Dyce, conj. Capell;* or *F.*   25. rich jewel-coffer] *This edn, conj. Steevens;* rich-iewel'd Coffer *F;* rich jewel'd coffer *Pope.*   27. kings] *F;* royal kings *conj. this edn.*

15. *replete with*] full of.

21–2. *pyramis . . . Rhodope of Memphis*] Rhodope was a Greek courtesan, who married a king of Memphis (in Egypt), and was reputed the builder of the third Pyramid; see Pliny, *Nat. Hist.,* xxxvi. xii. 1, and Greene, *Mamillia* (Gros. II. 270), 'they which came to *Memphis* thought they had seene nothing unlesse they had viewed the *Pyramides* built by Rhodope'.

25. *rich jewel-coffer of Darius*] cf. Puttenham, *Arte of English Poesie,* 31–2 (Arber), 'In what price the noble poemes of Homer were holden with Alexander the Great, insomuch as every night they were layd under his pillow, and by day were carried in *the rich jewel-cofer* of Darius, lately before vanquished by him in battaile'; and North's *Plutarch,* III. 333 (marginal note), 'Some thinke that this place should be ment of *the riche coffer,* that was found among king Darius *juells,* in the which Alexander would have all Homers works kept'.

26. *high*] of great importance, of greatest consequence.

28. *Saint Denis*] patron saint of Paris, or France.

ACT II

SCENE I.—[*Before Orleans.*]

Enter [, on the Walls,] a [French] Sergeant of a Band,
with two Sentinels.

Serg. Sirs, take your places and be vigilant;
　　If any noise or soldier you perceive
　　Near to the walls, by some apparent sign
　　Let us have knowledge at the court of guard.
1 Sent. Sergeant, you shall. [*Exit Serg.*] Thus are poor servitors,
　　When others sleep upon their quiet beds,　　　　　　　　6
　　Constrain'd to watch in darkness, rain, and cold.

Enter TALBOT, BEDFORD, BURGUNDY, [*and Forces,*]
with scaling-ladders.

ACT II

Scene I

ACT II SCENE I] *edd.; Actus Secundus. Scena Prima. | F.*　*Before Orleans.*]
Theobald; not in F.　S.D. *, on the Walls,*] *This edn; to the Gate | Capell; not in F.*
French] *Capell; not in F.*　5. *1 Sent.*] *edd.; Sent. | F.*　S.D. *Exit Serg.*] *edd.; not*
in F.　7. S.D. *Burgundy, and Forces*] *Capell; and Burgundy | F.*　*scaling-ladders.*]
This edn; scaling ladders: Their Drummes beating a Dead March. | F+edd.

　　This Act shows Talbot reversing the English fortunes with the capture of Orleans, paying honour to the body of Salisbury, and outwitting the Countess of Auvergne; by way of contrast, the Temple Garden scene introduces a new source of civil dissension, the quarrel of Somerset and York, to which is added York's claim for restoration to his blood, and his claim, through Mortimer, to the crown itself. This claim, repeated and expanded in *2 Henry VI*, is in fact the germ of the much larger dissension that runs throughout the rest of the tetra-logy and issues in the Wars of the Roses.

　　The material (Hall, 142–3) is adapted from the capture of Le Mans.

　　3. *apparent*] plain, clear.

　　4. *court of guard*] guard-room, or courtyard adjoining.

　　5. *servitors*] those who served in the wars, soldiers.

　　7. S.D.] see n. at II. ii. I.

　　Burgundy] With the murder of his father in 1419, he became an enemy of the Dauphin (Hall, 93). He is here introduced, unnecessarily, to prepare for his later part in the action.

Tal. Lord Regent, and redoubted Burgundy,
　　By whose approach the regions of Artois,
　　Walloon, and Picardy, are friends to us,　　　10
　　This happy night the Frenchmen are secure,
　　Having all day carous'd and banqueted,
　　Embrace we then this opportunity,
　　As fitting best to quittance their deceit,
　　Contriv'd by art and baleful sorcery.　　　15
Bed. Coward of France, how much he wrongs his fame,
　　Despairing of his own arm's fortitude,
　　To join with witches and the help of hell!
Bur. Traitors have never other company.
　　But what's that Pucelle whom they term so pure?　　20
Tal. A maid, they say.
Bed. 　　　　　　A maid! and be so martial!
Bur. Pray God she prove not masculine ere long,
　　If underneath the standard of the French
　　She carry armour as she hath begun.
Tal. Well, let them practise and converse with spirits;　　25
　　God is our fortress, in whose conquering name
　　Let us resolve to scale their flinty bulwarks.
Bed. Ascend, brave Talbot; we will follow thee.
Tal. Not all together; better far, I guess,
　　That we do make our entrance several ways,　　　30
　　That if it chance the one of us do fall,

29. all together] *Rowe;* altogether. *F.*　　31. fall] *This edn;* faile *F.*

9. *approach*] arrival, coming.
10. *Walloon*] the border country between the Netherlands (Belgium and Holland) and France.
11. *secure*] original L. sense = free from care; carelessly confident.
12. *carous'd and banqueted*] Hall, 143; 'banquet and carouse' is in *2 Tamb.*, 2490, 2787, and 2794.
14. *quittance*] requite, repay; common in Greene.
15. *Contriv'd*] planned, plotted.
art] short for 'art magic' (L. *ars magica*); magic.
16. *Coward of France*] the Dauphin.
fame] original sense of L. *fama* =

report, reputation; cf. II. iii. 68.
17. *fortitude*] strength (L. *fortitudo*).
22. *prove not masculine*] do not show the effect of relations with men.
23. *standard*] probably with a quibble (=penis' as in *LLL.*, IV. iii. 363; see *Sh. Bawdy*, 194.
24. *carry armour*] cf. *2H4*, II. iv. 47–50; further quibbling?
26. *fortress*] cf. 2 Sam., xxii. 2, 'The Lorde is my rocke and my fortresse', and Ps., xxxi. 3.
30. *several*] separate; cf. I. i. 71.
31. *fall*] in contrast to 'rise' (32). The same F error occurs in *2H6*, IV. ii. 33, and *3H6*, II. i. 190.

The other yet may rise against their force.
Bed. Agreed; I'll to yon corner.
Bur.   And I to this.
Tal. And here will Talbot mount, or make his grave.
Now, Salisbury, for thee and for the right   35
Of English Henry, shall this night appear
How much in duty I am bound to both.
Sent. Arm! arm! the enemy doth make assault.
                    Cry, 'Saint George!' 'A Talbot!'
                    [*The English scale the walls, and exeunt.*]

*The French leap over the walls in their shirts. Enter,
several ways* [*the*] *Bastard* [*of* ORLEANS], ALENÇON,
REIGNIER, *half ready and half unready.*

Alen. How now, my lords? What, all unready so?
Bast. Unready! Ay, and glad we 'scap'd so well.   40
Reig. 'Twas time, I trow, to wake and leave our beds,
Hearing alarums at our chamber-doors.
Alen. Of all exploits since first I follow'd arms
Ne'er heard I of a warlike enterprise
More venturous or desperate than this.   45
Bast. I think this Talbot be a fiend of hell.
Reig. If not of hell, the heavens, sure, favour him.
Alen. Here cometh Charles: I marvel how he sped.

Enter CHARLES *and* LA PUCELLE.

Bast. Tut! holy Joan was his defensive guard.
Cha. Is this thy cunning, thou deceitful dame?   50
Didst thou at first, to flatter us withal,

38. S.D. *Cry . . . exeunt.*] *This edn; Cry, S. George, A Talbot. | F; The English, scaling
the Walls, Cry St George! A Talbot! | Theobald.   over*] F (*ore*).   *the Bastard of
Orleans*] *edd.; Bastard | F.   48. S.D. *La Pucelle*] *edd.; Ioane | F.*

38. S.D. The French . . . shirts]
authorial S.D.; from Hall, 143.
     Reignier] introduced here, unhis-
torically, in preparation for the
Margaret–Suffolk scenes in Act v.
     ready] dressed.
     41. *I trow*] I am sure, I dare say.
     47. *favour*] look on him with a friend-
ly favour or countenance, befriend.

48. *sped*] fared.
     49. *holy*] probably with a quibble;
cf. *Sh. Bawdy*, 128.
     defensive] serving to protect, defend-
ing.
     50. *cunning*] knowledge or skill, here
specifically used of magic.
     51. *flatter*] encourage with (false)
hopes.

Make us partakers of a little gain,
That now our loss might be ten times so much?

Puc. Wherefore is Charles impatient with his friend?
At all times will you have my power alike?   55
Sleeping or waking, must I still prevail,
Or will you blame and lay the fault on me?
Improvident soldiers! had your watch been good
This sudden mischief never could have fallen.

Cha. Duke of Alençon, this was your default,   60
That, being captain of the watch to-night,
Did look no better to that weighty charge.

Alen. Had all your quarters been as safely kept
As that whereof I had the government,
We had not been thus shamefully surpris'd.   65

Bast. Mine was secure.

Reig.   And so was mine, my lord.

Cha. And for myself, most part of all this night,
Within her quarter and mine own precinct
I was employ'd in passing to and fro
About relieving of the sentinels.   70
Then how or which way should they first break in?

Puc. Question, my lords, no further of the case,
How or which way; 'tis sure they found some place
But weakly guarded, where the breach was made.
And now there rests no other shift but this: 75
To gather our soldiers, scatter'd and dispers'd,
And lay new platforms to endamage them.

*Alarum. Enter an [English] Soldier, crying, 'A Talbot!
A Talbot!' They fly, leaving their clothes behind.*

54, 72. *Puc.*] *edd.*; Ioane. / F.   77. them.] *Capell*; them. / Exeunt. / F.   77. S.D.
an English] *Capell*; a / F.

withal] with this, therewith.
54. *impatient*] angry.
56. *prevail*] be victorious.
58. *Improvident*] wanting foresight
(L. *pro*+*videre*) and care (Schmidt).
59. *mischief*] the original sense, misfortune or calamity.
fallen] befallen, happened.
61. *to-night*] last night.

63. *quarters ... kept*] parts of the camp
... guarded.
68. *precinct*] area under his control.
70. *About*] engaged in, concerned
with.
74. *But*] only.
75. *rests*] remains (Fr. *rester*).
shift] resource, device.
77. *platforms*] plans; Hart quotes

Sold. I'll be so bold to take what they have left.
  The cry of 'Talbot' serves me for a sword;
  For I have loaden me with many spoils,   80
  Using no other weapon but his name.   *Exit.*

[SCENE II.—*Orleans. Within the Town.*]

Enter TALBOT, BEDFORD, BURGUNDY [, *a Captain, and*
Others].

Bed. The day begins to break, and night is fled,
  Whose pitchy mantle over-veil'd the earth.
  Here sound retreat and cease our hot pursuit.

Retreat [*sounded*].

Tal. Bring forth the body of old Salisbury,
  And here advance it in the market-place,   5
  The middle centre of this cursed town.

[*Dead March. Enter with the body of Salisbury.*]

Scene II

SCENE II] *Capell; not in F.*   *Orleans. Within the Town.*] *Pope; not in F.*   S.D. *a*
Captain, and Others] *Capell; not in F.*   3. S.D.] *Capell; Retreat. | F.*   6. S.D.]
This edn; not in F.

Cotgrave for the meaning, 'plot, modell' (ground-plan).
  S.D.] based on the terror caused by Talbot's name, Hall, 230.

Scene II

The last scene is continued, Salisbury's burial is put in hand, and Talbot is invited to visit the Countess of Auvergne.
  The historical source is Hall, 145; the invitation is fictitious, but probably suggested by the Robin Hood cycle.
  S.D. Dead March] see collation, and Intro., p. xvii. This direction belongs here, if anywhere, and is probably a prompter's note for the funeral of Salisbury (4 ff.), but inadvertently placed against the identical entry at II. i. 7, which could have caught the eye in the same opening of the MS. It is not clear from the F text that the body was actually brought on. It may well have been, and made an exit through the centre back (cf. 'middle centre', 6); the absence of S.DD. for the pageant being comparable to the instances of Henry's funeral at I. i. 45, and Gargrave's removal at I. iv. 87.
  2. *pitchy mantle*] cf. Spenser, *F.Q.*, I. v. 20.
  3. *retreat*] signal recalling a pursuing force.
  5. *advance*] raise aloft on a bier or platform.
  6. *middle centre*] cf. *F.Q.*, v. v. 57.

Now have I paid my vow unto his soul;
For every drop of blood was drawn from him
There hath at least five Frenchmen died to-night.
And that hereafter ages may behold   10
What ruin happen'd in revenge of him,
Within their chiefest temple I'll erect
A tomb, wherein his corpse shall be interr'd;
Upon the which, that every one may read,
Shall be engrav'd the sack of Orleans,   15
The treacherous manner of his mournful death,
And what a terror he had been to France. [*Exit Funeral.*]
But, lords, in all our bloody massacre,
I muse we met not with the Dauphin's Grace,
His new-come champion, virtuous Joan of Aire,   20
Nor any of his false confederates.
Bed. 'Tis thought, Lord Talbot, when the fight began,
Rous'd on the sudden from their drowsy beds,
They did amongst the troops of armed men
Leap o'er the walls for refuge in the field.   25
Bur. Myself, as far as I could well discern
For smoke and dusky vapours of the night,
Am sure I scar'd the Dauphin and his trull,
When arm in arm they both came swiftly running,
Like to a pair of loving turtle-doves   30
That could not live asunder day or night.
After that things are set in order here,
We'll follow them with all the power we have.

Enter a Messenger.

17. S.D.] *This edn; not in* F.   20. Aire] *This edn;* Acre F; Arc Rowe+edd

7. *my vow*] sc. of vengeance; cf. I. iv. 94, 104 ff.

8. *was*] For the omission of the rel. pron., see Abbott, 244.

9. *hath*] see Abbott, 334, 335.

11. *ruin*] death and destruction.

12 ff.] Salisbury was buried in England; Hall, 145.

16. *mournful*] causing sorrow or grief; *OED.* 3.

17. *a terror*] Hall, 144; cf. I. iv. 42.

19. *muse*] wonder.

20. *champion*] defendant; one who fights for another.

virtuous] typically ironical.

Aire] F *Acre* probably represents an i,'c misreading: cf. 'Aire' at v. iv. 49, and Hol., III. 600/2, 'Are'.

32. *things*] the ordering of the captured city and the funeral of Salisbury.

33. *power*] armed strength, forces.

Mess. All hail, my lords! Which of this princely train
  Call ye the warlike Talbot, for his acts   35
  So much applauded through the realm of France?
Tal. Here is the Talbot: who would speak with him?
Mess. The virtuous lady, Countess of Auvergne,
  With modesty admiring thy renown,
  By me entreats, great lord, thou would'st vouchsafe 40
  To visit her poor castle where she lies,
  That she may boast she hath beheld the man
  Whose glory fills the world with loud report.
Bur. Is it even so? Nay, then I see our wars
  Will turn unto a peaceful comic sport,   45
  When ladies crave to be encounter'd with.
  You may not, my lord, despise her gentle suit.
Tal. Ne'er trust me then; for when a world of men
  Could not prevail with all their oratory,
  Yet hath a woman's kindness over-rul'd;   50
  And therefore tell her I return great thanks
  And in submission will attend on her.
  Will not your honours bear me company?
Bed. No, truly, it is more than manners will;
  And I have heard it said unbidden guests   55
  Are often welcomest when they are gone.
Tal. Well then, alone, since there's no remedy,
  I mean to prove this lady's courtesy.
  Come hither, Captain. *Whispers.* You perceive my
   mind?
Cap. I do, my Lord, and mean accordingly. *Exeunt.* 60

---

38. Auvergne] *F* (Ouergne). 54. it is] *Malone;* 'tis *F.* 59. S.D. *Whispers.*]
as *Johnson; after line 59 | F.* 59. mind?] *Dyce;* minde. *F.*

---

35. *acts*] deeds, things done (L. *actus*).

36. *applauded*] praised (L. *laus*).

37. *would*] wishes to.

41. *lies*] lives, dwells.

43. *report*] (*a*) commendation, with a suggestion of (*b*) resounding noise.

45. *comic*] ending happily, as in a comedy; causing mirth.

46. *encounter'd with*] (*a*) met; (*b*) made love to.

47. *gentle*] well bred, courteous.

48. *a world*] a great number.

49. *oratory*] eloquence.

50. *over-rul'd*] prevailed.

52. *attend on*] wait on, visit.

54. *manners*] i.e. good manners.

55–6. *unbidden guests . . .*] proverbial.

58. *prove*] try, test (L. *probare*).

59. *perceive my mind*] understand my intention.

60. *mean*] sc. to act.

[SCENE III.—*Auvergne. The Countess's Castle.*]

Enter [*the*] COUNTESS [*and her Porter*].

Count. Porter, remember what I gave in charge;
    And when you have done so, bring the keys to me.
Port. Madam, I will.   *Exit.*
Count. The plot is laid; if all things fall out right,
    I shall as famous be by this exploit,   5
    As Scythian Tomyris by Cyrus' death.
    Great is the rumour of this dreadful knight,
    And his achievements of no less account.
    Fain would mine eyes be witness with mine ears
    To give their censure of these rare reports.   10

Enter Messenger and TALBOT.

Mess. According as your ladyship desir'd,
    By message crav'd, so is Lord Talbot come.
Count. And he is welcome. What! is this the man?
Mess. Madam, it is.
Count.   Is this the Scourge of France?

Scene III

SCENE III] *Capell; not in* F.   *Auvergne . . . Castle.*] *Camb.; The Countess of Auvergne's Castle. | Pope; Auvergne. Court of the Castle. | Capell.*   S.D.] *edd.; Enter Countesse. | F.*   11.] *This edn;* Madame, according . . . desir'd *F;* Madam . . . ladyship *Pope.*

1. *gave in charge*] commanded.

6. *Tomyris . . . Cyrus*] cf. *3H6*, I. iv. 114 (Wilson), and Cooper, *Thesaurus,* (Cyrus). 'At the last beeyng insaciable in couetyng countreyes, he was slaine by Tomyris, Queene of Scithia, with 200000 Persians'. He had captured and put to death her son, in revenge for whom she had his head cut off and thrown into a wine-skin of human blood (he having been blood-thirsty). Cf. *Mirror,* I. 321.

7–10.] Cf. 2 Chron., ix. 6, 'Howbeit I believed not their report, untill I came and mine eyes had seene it: and beholde, the one halfe of thy greate wisdome was not tolde me: for thou exceedest the fame that I heard'; and 67 below. Shakespeare seems to have had in mind the Queen of Sheba and Solomon.

7. *rumour*] talk or report.

dreadful] the original literal meaning =causing dread.

10. *censure*] opinion, not necessarily unfavourable (L. *censeo*); cf. *R3*, II. ii. 144, 'To give your censures in this business'.

11.] F 'Madam' seems the superfluous element; and could have originated from an expansion of a MS. 'M.' for the Messenger or from 14.

Is this the Talbot, so much fear'd abroad   15
That with his name the mothers still their babes?
I see report is fabulous and false:
I thought I should have seen some Hercules,
A second Hector, for his grim aspect
And large proportion of his strong-knit limbs.   20
Alas, this is a child, a silly dwarf!
It cannot be this weak and writhled shrimp
Should strike such terror to his enemies.

Tal. Madam, I have been bold to trouble you;
But since your ladyship is not at leisure,   25
I'll sort some other time to visit you. [*Going.*]

Count. What means he now? Go ask him whither he goes.

Mess. Stay, my Lord Talbot, for my lady craves
To know the cause of your abrupt departure.

Tal. Marry, for that she's in a wrong belief,   30
I go to certify her Talbot's here.

Enter Porter with keys.

Count. If thou be he, then art thou prisoner.

Tal. Prisoner! To whom?

Count.   To me, blood-thirsty lord;
And for that cause I train'd thee to my house.
Long time thy shadow hath been thrall to me,   35
For in my gallery thy picture hangs;
But now the substance shall endure the like,

---

15. abroad] *edd.;* abroad? *F.*   26. S.D. *Going.*] *Capell; not in F.*   27. goes.]
Pope; goes? *F.*   29. departure.] *edd.;* departure? *F.*

15. *abroad*] everywhere, round about.
16.] cf. II. i. 79 ff., and Hall, 230;
and IV. ii. 16.
19. *Hector*] cf. Hall, 227, 'Thys English Hector'.
   for] because of, on account of.
   aspect] usual Elizabethan accent, on the second syllable.
21. *silly*] poor, feeble, frail.
22. *writhled shrimp*] small wrinkled and twisted man. The statement is without historical authority; cf. *N.Q.*, XII (1885), 502. It seems likely that the same actor played Talbot and later

Richard of Gloucester (Richard III).
26. *sort*] arrange, choose.
33. *blood-thirsty*] i.e. like Cyrus; see 6 above and n.
34. *train'd*] drew (Fr. *trainer*), decoyed, allured; cf. Madden, 205 n., where it is used of a falcon.
35. *shadow*] image or portrait, contrasted with the reality or substance (37). The idea is similar to that of witches practising on a wax representation in order to harm the person represented.
   thrall] slave, enslaved.

And I will chain these legs and arms of thine,
That hast by tyranny these many years
Wasted our country, slain our citizens,   40
And sent our sons and husbands captivate.

Tal. Ha, ha, ha!

Count. Laughest thou, wretch? Thy mirth shall turn to moan.

Tal. I laugh to see your ladyship so fond
To think that you have aught but Talbot's shadow   45
Whereon to practise your severity.

Count. Why, art not thou the man?

Tal.   I am indeed.

Count. Then have I substance too.

Tal. No, no, I am but shadow of myself:
You are deceiv'd, my substance is not here;   50
For what you see is but the smallest part
And least proportion of humanity:
I tell you, madam, were the whole frame here,
It is of such a spacious lofty pitch
Your roof were not sufficient to contain't.   55

Count. This is a riddling merchant for the nonce;
He will be here, and yet he is not here:
How can these contrarieties agree?

Tal. That will I show you presently.

Winds his horn; drums strike up; a peal of ordnance.
Enter Soldiers.

---

47. Why,] *edd.;* Why? *F.*   59. That] *F;* That, madam *conj. Steevens;* Lady that *Keightley.*

39. *tyranny*] cruelty, pitiless violence.

41. *captivate*] pa. pple = captured, made prisoner; cf. v. iii. 107.

43. *moan*] grief, lamentation.

44. *fond*] foolish (the commonest Elizabethan sense).

52. *proportion*] portion, part, *OED.* 1. Talbot alludes partly to his own size, but also to his own insignificance compared with the body of men who constitute his power or substance.

humanity] mankind.

53, 54. *frame . . . pitch*] 'apt at once to a building and to the human body' (Wilson).

56. *merchant*] contemptuous=fellow; cf. *Rom.*, II. iv. 153, 'saucy merchant', and modern 'chap', from 'chapman'.

for the nonce] as the occasion requires; here almost a tag with no special meaning.

58. *contrarieties*] contradictions. K. Muir, *N.Q.*, cxcviii (1953), 240, suggests a reference to William Averell's 'A Mervailous Combat of Contrarieties'.

59. *presently*] usual Elizabethan sense =immediately.

Winds his horn] typical Robin Hood. ordnance] artillery, which 'prob-

How say you, madam? Are you now persuaded   60
That Talbot is but shadow of himself?
These are his substance, sinews, arms, and strength,
With which he yoketh your rebellious necks,
Razeth your cities, and subverts your towns,
And in a moment makes them desolate.   65

Count. Victorious Talbot, pardon my abuse;
I find thou art no less than fame hath bruited,
And more than may be gather'd by thy shape.
Let my presumption not provoke thy wrath,
For I am sorry that with reverence   70
I did not entertain thee as thou art.

Tal. Be not dismay'd, fair lady, nor misconster
The mind of Talbot as you did mistake
The outward composition of his body.
What you have done hath not offended me;   75
Nor other satisfaction do I crave
But only, with your patience, that we may
Taste of your wine and see what cates you have,
For soldiers' stomachs always serve them well.

Count. With all my heart, and think me honoured   80
To feast so great a warrior in my house.   *Exeunt.*

ably suggests that the gates are blown in' (Wilson).

64. *subverts*] destroys, overthrows.

66. *abuse*] common Elizabethan sense = deception, delusion.

67. *fame*] report, rumour (L. *fama*); and cf. 7–10 above and n.

bruited] proclaimed with noise (cf. Fr. *bruit*), announced loudly.

69. *provoke*] L. sense = call forth.

71. *entertain*] receive = common Elizabethan sense; cf. *Err.*, III. i. 120.

72. *misconster*] misconstrue.

73. *mistake*] literally = take or understand wrongly.

74. *composition*] constitution.

77. *patience*] leave, permission, sufferance (L. *patior*).

78. *cates*] delicacies, dainties.

79. *stomachs*] appetites, with a possible allusion to the other sense of courage.

[SCENE IV.—*London. The Temple Garden.*]

Enter [the Earls of] SOMERSET, SUFFOLK, [*and*] WARWICK*;*
RICHARD PLANTAGENET, [VERNON,] *and* [*an*]*other* [*Lawyer*].

Plan. Great lords and gentlemen, what means this silence?
Dare no man answer in a case of truth?
Suff. Within the Temple Hall we were too loud;
The garden here is more convenient.
Plan. Then say at once if I maintain'd the truth;   5
Or else was wrangling Somerset in th' error?
Suff. Faith, I have been a truant in the law
And never yet could frame my will to it;
And therefore frame the law unto my will.
Som. Judge you, my Lord of Warwick, then, between us.   10
War. Between two hawks, which flies the higher pitch;
Between two dogs, which hath the deeper mouth;

Scene IV

SCENE IV] *Capell; not in* F.   London.... Garden.] *Pope; not in* F.   S.D.] *Capell;*
Enter Richard Plantagenet, Warwick, Somerset, Poole, and others. | F.   1, etc. *Plan.*]
Rowe; Yorke. | F.   6. th' error] F; error *Hudson, conj. Dyce.*

The scene is fictitious, but constructed round the York–Lancaster 'intestine division' and the claim to the throne of Richard Plantagenet. This theme is shortly to be woven into the main structure by his reinstatement in his father's title (III. i), after Mortimer's transfer to him of the claim (II. v). The material incorporated here, and later elaborated in *2H6*, II. ii, is from Hall, 2, 21.

'Shakespeare brilliantly imagines the quarrel of the roses to have started among a group of young aristocrats, studying law in the Temple' (Brooke); cf. 7; II. v. 19, 45 ff. The scene is crammed with legal terminology. Venezky mentions the 'mannered dialogue, patterned movements, symbolical properties and political import pronounced by a commentator'.

S.D. Temple] one of the Inns of Court, or buildings, in London, belonging to the four legal societies which

have the exclusive right of admitting persons to practise at the bar.

2. *case of truth*] While this is, as Wilson says, left undefined, it is clear that the question at issue was one affecting Plantagenet's reinstatement or the succession to the crown, or both combined. Such questions were best left undefined in that period, in view of the powers of the censor, the Master of the Revels.

3. *were*] should have been (Wilson).

6. *Or else*] possibly = in other words; or is it 'heads I win; tails you lose' (Brooke)?

6. *wrangling*] (*a*) quarrelling, (*b*) in formal disputation; cf. senior wrangler.

7. *a truant*] neglectful of my duty; cf. *1H4*, v. i. 94.

8. *frame*] adapt.

11. *pitch*] greatest height; cf. *2H6*, II. i. 6, 12.

12. *mouth*] voice, bark.

Between two blades, which bears the better temper;
Between two horses, which doth bear him best;
Between two girls, which hath the merriest eye—   15
I have perhaps some shallow spirit of judgment;
But in these nice sharp quillets of the law,
Good faith, I am no wiser than a daw.

Plan. Tut, tut, here is a mannerly forbearance:
The truth appears so naked on my side   20
That any purblind eye may find it out.

Som. And on my side it is so well apparell'd,
So clear, so shining, and so evident,
That it will glimmer through a blind man's eye.

Plan. Since you are tongue-tied and so loath to speak,   25
In dumb significants proclaim your thoughts:
Let him that is a true-born gentleman
And stands upon the honour of his birth,
If he suppose that I have pleaded truth,
From off this brier pluck a white rose with me.   30

Som. Let him that is no coward nor no flatterer,
But dare maintain the party of the truth,
Pluck a red rose from off this thorn with me.

War. I love no colours; and without all colour
Of base insinuating flattery   35
I pluck this white rose with Plantagenet.

Suff. I pluck this red rose with young Somerset,
And say withal I think he held the right.

Ver. Stay, lords and gentlemen, and pluck no more
Till you conclude that he upon whose side   40

---

14. *bear him*] behave, carry himself.
17. *nice*] fine.
sharp] subtle, acute.
quillets] fine or subtle distinctions.
18. *no wiser than a daw*] proverbial; cf. *Cor.*, IV. v. 44.
20. *truth . . . naked*] cf. the naked truth.
21. *purblind*] partially blind.
22. *apparell'd*] in contrast to 'naked' above.
23. *evident*] in its primary L. sense = able to be seen, obvious, indubitable.
24. *blind man's eye*] going one better than 'purblind eye' above; cf. Eras-

mus, *Adagia*, s.v. perspicuitas, 'vel caeco appareat'.
26. *significants*] signs, symbols; in dumb show.
28. *stands upon*] insists on, is particular about.
29. *pleaded*] in the legal sense = put forward an argument of.
32. *party*] legal = side, in a case.
34. *colours*] a pun on the legal sense = support, corroborative evidence; military ensigns; and hues.
colour] semblance.
38. *withal*] besides, at the same time.
40 ff. *conclude . . . opinion . . . objected*

The fewest roses from the tree are cropp'd
Shall yield the other in the right opinion.
Som. Good Master Vernon, it is well objected:
If I have fewest, I subscribe in silence.
Plan. And I.　　　　　　　　　　　　　　　45
Ver. Then for the truth and plainness of the case,
I pluck this pale and maiden blossom here,
Giving my verdict on the white rose side.
Som. Prick not your finger as you pluck it off,
Lest, bleeding, you do paint the white rose red,　50
And fall on my side so against your will.
Ver. If I, my lord, for my opinion bleed,
Opinion shall be surgeon to my hurt
And keep me on the side where still I am.
Som. Well, well, come on: who else?　　　　55
Law. Unless my study and my books be false, [*To Somerset.*]
The argument you held was wrong in law;
In sign whereof I pluck a white rose too.
Plan. Now, Somerset, where is your argument?
Som. Here in my scabbard, meditating that　　60
Shall dye your white rose in a bloody red.
Plan. Meantime your cheeks do counterfeit our roses;
For pale they look with fear, as witnessing
The truth on our side.
Som.　　　　　　　　No, Plantagenet,
'Tis not for fear, but anger that thy cheeks　　65
Blush for pure shame to counterfeit our roses,
And yet thy tongue will not confess thy error.
Plan. Hath not thy rose a canker, Somerset?

---

41. from the tree are cropp'd] *This edn;* are cropt from the Tree *F+edd.*　56.
S.D. *To Somerset.*] *Rowe; not in F.*　57. law] *This edn; conj. anon. (in Camb.) ;* you *F.*
60. scabbard, meditating] *edd.;* Scabbard, meditating, *F.*

..*subscribe* ... *verdict* ...] note the succession of legal terms.

42. *yield*] grant.

44. *subscribe*] agree, concur; literally, to sign at the foot of a document.

53. *Opinion*] reputation; punning on 52.

54. *still*] Elizabethan sense=always; cf. 104, 130.

57. *wrong in law*] as opposed to wrong in fact. They are discussing 'a question in the law' (IV. i. 95). The F *you* probably arose from confusion of *y* and *L;* cf. Yet/Let, III. ii. 117.

60, 61.] For omission of the rel. pron., see Abbott, 244.

62. *counterfeit*] imitate.

65. *that*] caused by the fact that.

68. *canker*] (*a*) worm that feeds in the

Som. Hath not thy rose a thorn, Plantagenet?

Plan. Ay, sharp and piercing, to maintain his truth;   70
    Whiles thy consuming canker eats his falsehood.

Som. Well, I'll find friends to wear my bleeding roses,
    That shall maintain what I have said is true,
    Where false Plantagenet dare not be seen.

Plan. Now, by this maiden blossom in my hand,   75
    I scorn thee and thy fashion, peevish boy.

Suff. Turn not thy scorns this way, Plantagenet.

Plan. Proud Pole, I will, and scorn both him and thee.

Suff. I'll turn my part thereof into thy throat.

Som. Away, away, good William de la Pole!   80
    We grace the yeoman by conversing with him.

War. Now, by God's will, thou wrong'st him, Somerset;
    His grandfather was Lionel Duke of Clarence,
    Third son to the third Edward, King of England:
    Spring crestless yeomen from so deep a root?   85

Plan. He bears him on the place's privilege,
    Or durst not for his craven heart say thus.

Som. By Him that made me, I'll maintain my words
    On any plot of ground in Christendom.
    Was not thy father, Richard Earl of Cambridge,   90

---

72. roses] *F;* rose *Dyce²*.   76. fashion] *F;* passion *Pope;* faction *Theobald.*
78, etc. Pole] *F(Poole).*

bud; (*b*) the dog-rose, *OED.*, 5; cf.
1H4, I. iii. 176.

70. *his*] the normal Elizabethan
form = its.

76. *fashion*] the fashion he is starting,
of wearing a red rose.

  peevish] silly, senseless.

78. *Pole*] Suffolk's family name; cf.
2H6, IV. i. 70.

81. *grace*] (*a*) favour, (*b*) ennoble (by
the title of 'his Grace').

  the yeoman] cf. 90–1, 95; the execution of Plantagenet's father, the Earl
of Cambridge, for treason (*H5*, II. ii.
66–181), meant the forfeiture to the
crown of all his lands and titles; and
hence the loss of these to his heirs.

83–4. *grandfather*] actually his great-
great-grandfather; see App. II, and cf.
Hall, 2; II. v. 63 ff., and *2H6*, II. ii.

85. *crestless*] (*a*) not bearing a heral-
dic crest or arms; ignoble; (*b*) without
a top (referring to the genealogical tree
implied in 'root'); (*c*) coward, by association with 'crest-fallen' (of a cock)—
an association extended in 'craven'
below. Cf. *Shr.*, II. i. 222 ff., 'What is
your *crest*? a coxcomb? . . . you crow
too like a *craven*'.

86.] 'he shapes his conduct to the
liberty the place affords him: he pre-
sumes on the privilege of the place'
(Schmidt).

  privilege] legal: 'The Temple, being
(originally) a religious house, was an
asylum' (Johnson). But, as a law-
court, it was privileged in its own
right.

87. *craven*] used of a cock that is 'not
game'. Cf. 'crestless' at 85 above.

For treason headed in our late king's days?
And by his treason stand'st not thou attainted,
Corrupted, and exempt from ancient gentry?
His trespass yet lives guilty in thy blood;
And, till thou be restor'd, thou art a yeoman. 95
Plan. My father was attached, not attainted,
Condemn'd to die for treason, but no traitor;
And that I'll prove on better men than Somerset,
Were growing time once ripen'd to my will.
For your partaker Pole, and you yourself, 100
I'll note you in my book of memory,
To scourge you for this apprehension:
Look to it well, and say you are well warn'd.
Som. Ah, thou shalt find us ready for thee still;
And know us by these colours for thy foes, 105
For these my friends in spite of thee shall wear.
Plan. And, by my soul, this pale and angry rose,
As cognizance of my blood-drinking hate,
Will I for ever, and my faction, wear,
Until it wither with me to my grave, 110
Or flourish to the height of my degree.
Suff. Go forward, and be chok'd with thy ambition!

91. headed] *Pope;* executed *F.* 102. this apprehension] *F;* misapprehension *conj. Vaughan;* this reprehension *Theobald.*

91. *headed*] see Intro., p. xix. The metre, and the scribe's attempt to sophisticate an unpleasant expression, seem to justify Pope's emendation. Hall (128) says Cambridge was 'beheded'.

92, 96. *attainted*] His blood, like his father's, was 'tainted' by the accusation of treason.

93. *Corrupted*] = tainted, as 92.
exempt] excluded, debarred.

96. *attached, not attainted*] arrested, not convicted of treason by bill of attainder. There was no bill, the Earl having been executed by the King's direct order. Plantagenet was 'restored to his blood' (cf. III. i. 159 ff.) without any formal reinstatement.

98. *on*] by duel with.

99.] foreshadowing York's rise in *2* and *3H6*; cf. 110–11.

100. *partaker*] part-taker, supporter.

101. *note*] (*a*) take a note of; (*b*) brand, stigmatize, as in *Cæs.,* IV. iii. 2 (L. *nota*=brand).

102. *apprehension*] conception, opinion.

104, 130. *still*] Elizabethan sense= always.

108. *cognizance*] badge, distinguishing mark; from the device or emblem worn by the retainers.
blood-drinking] bloodthirsty.

110. *to my grave*] looks forward, ironically, to *3H6,* as 'the height of my degree' does to his acceptance as heir by Henry VI.

111. *flourish*] (*a*) blossom, (*b*) succeed.

And so farewell until I meet thee next.   *Exit.*
Som. Have with thee, Pole. Farewell, ambitious Richard.
                                                           Exit.
Plan. How I am brav'd and must perforce endure it!   115
War. This blot that they object against your house
  Shall be wip'd out in the next Parliament,
  Call'd for the truce of Winchester and Gloucester;
  And if thou be not then created York,
  I will not live to be accounted Warwick.   120
  Meantime, in signal of my love to thee,
  Against proud Somerset and William Pole,
  Will I upon thy party wear this rose.
  And here I prophesy: this brawl to-day,
  Grown to this faction in the Temple Garden,   125
  Shall send between the Red Rose and the White
  A thousand souls to death and deadly night.
Plan. Good Master Vernon, I am bound to you,
  That you on my behalf would pluck a flower.
Ver. In your behalf still will I wear the same.   130
Law. And so will I.
Plan. Thanks, gentlemen.
  Come, let us four to dinner. I dare say
  This quarrel will drink blood another day.   *Exeunt.*

---

117. wip'd] *F2* (wip't); whipt *F1*. 127. A] *F;* Ten *conj. this edn (Collier MS.).*
132. gentlemen] *This edn; conj. anon.;* gentle. *F1;* gentle sir *F2+edd.*

114. *Have with thee*] I'll go along with you.
115. *brav'd*] defied, insulted.
116. *object*] urge, cast up.
121. *signal*] sign, token.
123. *party*] side.

124–7.] cf. *3H6*, II. v. 97 ff., especially, 'Wither one rose, and let the other flourish: / If you contend, a thousand lives must wither.'
133. *four*] a mess (of lawyers etc.); cf. *LLL.*, IV. iii. 207.

[SCENE V.—*The Tower of London.*]

Enter MORTIMER, *brought in a chair, and Gaolers.*

Mor. Kind keepers of my weak decaying age,
     Let dying Mortimer here rest himself.
     Even like a man new haled from the rack,
     So fare my limbs with long imprisonment;
     And these grey locks, the pursuivants of Death,   5
     Nestor-like aged in an age of care,
     Argue the end of Edmund Mortimer.
     These eyes, like lamps whose wasting oil is spent,
     Wax dim, as drawing to their exigent;
     Weak shoulders, overborne with burdening grief,   10
     And pithless arms, like to a wither'd vine

Scene v

SCENE V] *Capell; not in* F.   *The Tower of London.*] *Camb.; A Room in the Tower. |
Capell; not in* F.   S.D.] F (... *Iaylors.*).   3. rack] *Pope; Wrack* F.   5. Death]
This edn; death F.   11. like to] F; look like *conj. Vaughan;* are like *conj. this
edn.*

The scene continues and develops Plantagenet's claim to the crown. The theme is basic to the tetralogy, though not to *1 Henry VI*, and is more fully repeated as part of the plot in *2 Henry VI*, II. ii.

The material is from Hall, 2, 21, 27, 28, 128. Shakespeare follows Hall in errors about Mortimer's imprisonment (28) and age (128) (having perhaps—see Boswell-Stone, 219, n.—confused him with his cousin Sir John Mortimer), as he does in *1 Henry IV*, I. iii. 145–6, and *2 Henry VI*, II. ii. 38 ff.; and further confuses him with his uncle Sir Edmund Mortimer (cf. 74–5 and n.).

The scene may be compared with that of the dying Gaunt in *Richard II*, and that of the persecution of Katherine in *Henry VIII*.

S.D. in a chair] cf. Hall, 128, 'long tyme had been restrained ... and ... waxed lame'. Actually Mortimer died aged 32.

1. *keepers*] gaolers. Mortimer was 'kepte in the courte vnder ... a keper' (Hall, 28).

4. *limbs*] cf. 'lame', n. to S D. above.

5. *pursuivants*] the heralds that proclaim the approach of 'that fell sergeant', Death.

6. *Nestor*] a type of old age (Hart); cf. North, *Plutarch*, 'And thus he lived as Nestor, in manner three ages of man'.

7. *Argue*] prove, show.

8–9. *eyes ... lamps ... dim*] cf. 1 Sam., iii. 2, 'Eli ... his eyes began to waxe dimme that he could not see and yet the light of God went out'. The Genevan marginal Note explains 'the lampes which burnt in the night' (Carter). Compare *Err.*, v. i. 312–13, 'Yet hath my night of life some memory, / My wasting lamps some fading glimmer left'; and *R2*, I. iii. 221–4.

9. *exigent*] end, extremity; cf. *Ant.*, IV. xiv. 63.

11.] A verb is necessary, 'like' itself

That droops his sapless branches to the ground.
Yet are these feet, whose strengthless stay is numb,
Unable to support this lump of clay,
Swift-winged with desire to get a grave,   15
As witting I no other comfort have.
But tell me, keeper, will my nephew come?
1 Keep. Richard Plantagenet, my lord, will come:
We sent unto the Temple, unto his chamber,
And answer was return'd that he will come.   20
Mor. Enough: my soul shall then be satisfied.
Poor gentleman! his wrong doth equal mine.
Since Henry Monmouth first began to reign,
Before whose glory I was great in arms,
This loathsome sequestration have I had;   25
And even since then hath Richard been obscur'd,
Depriv'd of honour and inheritance.
But now the arbitrator of despairs,
Just Death, kind umpire of men's miseries,
With sweet enlargement doth dismiss me hence.   30
I would his troubles likewise were expir'd,
That so he might recover what was lost.

Enter RICHARD [PLANTAGENET].

1 Keep. My lord, your loving nephew now is come.
Mor. Richard Plantagenet, my friend, is come?

18, 33, etc. *1 Keep.*] *edd.; Keeper. | F.*   32. S.D.] *edd.; Enter Richard. | F.*   34. is]
This edn; is he F.

will not do, and the simplest explanation is that of omission and subsequent
conjectural emendation; though it is
impossible to be certain what was
omitted.
    13. *feet . . . stay*] cf. *2H6*, ii. iii. 25,
'My stay, my guide, and lantern to my
feet' and 'lamps' above. The imagery
is from Ps., lxxi. 5; xviii. 1; cxix. 105.
    numb] paralysed.
    16. *As witting*] as if they knew.
    17. *nephew*] see head-note; 86 below;
and App. II.
    19. *the Temple . . .*] cf. the fiction
of Plantagenet as a law-student in
ii. iv.

21. *soul . . . satisfied*] cf. Isa., liii. 11,
'He shall see of the travaile of his soule,
and shall be satisfied' (Carter).
    22. *his wrong*] the wrong done to
him; cf. ii. iv. 90–5.
    23. *Henry Monmouth*] Henry V, Earl
of Monmouth; cf. *H5*, iv. vii.
    25. *sequestration*] (*a*) isolation, seclu-
sion; (*b*) legal = loss of property,
rights, etc.
    28, 29. *arbitrator . . . umpire*] continu-
ing the legal phraseology. Cf. *Rom.*, iv.
i. 63.
    30. *enlargement*] setting at large, free-
dom.
    31. *expir'd*] ended, like his own life

Plan. Ay, noble uncle, thus ignobly us'd,   35
    Your nephew, late despised Richard, comes.
Mor. Direct mine arms I may embrace his neck
    And in his bosom spend my latter gasp.
    O, tell me when my lips do touch his cheeks,
    That I may kindly give one fainting kiss.   40
    And now declare, sweet stem from York's great stock,
    Why did'st thou say of late thou wert despis'd?
Plan. First, lean thine aged back against mine arm,
    And, in that ease, I'll tell thee my disease.
    This day, in argument upon a case,   45
    Some words there grew 'twixt Somerset and me;
    Among which terms he us'd his lavish tongue
    And did upbraid me with my father's death;
    Which obloquy set bars before my tongue,
    Else with the like I had requited him.   50
    Therefore, good uncle, for my father's sake,
    In honour of a true Plantagenet,
    And for alliance' sake, declare the cause
    My father, Earl of Cambridge, lost his head.
Mor. That cause, fair nephew, that imprison'd me   55
    And hath detain'd me all my flowering youth
    Within a loathsome dungeon, there to pine,
    Was cursed instrument of his decease.
Plan. Discover more at large what cause that was,
    For I am ignorant and cannot guess.   60
Mor. I will, if that my fading breath permit
    And death approach not ere my tale be done.
    Henry the Fourth, grandfather to this king,

---

35. *Plan.*] *edd.; Rich.* / F (*throughout*).   53. alliance'] *This edn; Alliance F.*
61. fading] F; failing *Hudson, conj. S. Walker.*

35. *ignobly*] lit. = contrary to his
nobility or rank.
  36. *late*] lately (Mason).
  38. *latter*] latest; cf. 'latter days'.
  40. *kindly*] (*a*) to one of my kin or
family; (*b*) affectionately.
  41. *stem . . . stock*] a standard genealogical metaphor in these plays.
  44. *disease*] (*a*) un-ease; (*b*) distress.
  45. *case*] see II. iv. 2 and n.

47. *lavish tongue*] unrestrained expression or language—a standard
Elizabethan dramatic cliché.
  53. *alliance'*] kinship's.
  56. *flowering*] flourishing, vigorous.
  59. *Discover*] uncover, reveal.
  at large] in full, fully.
  63 ff.] Hall, 2; as in *2H6*, II. ii. 10 ff.
App. III shows how recollection of
this passage affected the report of *2H5*.

Depos'd his nephew Richard, Edward's son,
The first-begotten, and the lawful heir   65
Of Edward king, the third of that descent;
During whose reign the Percies of the north,
Finding his usurpation most unjust,
Endeavour'd my advancement to the throne.
The reason mov'd these warlike lords to this   70
Was, for that—young King Richard thus remov'd,
Leaving no heir begotten of his body—
I was the next by birth and parentage;
For by my mother I derived am
From Lionel Duke of Clarence, the third son   75
To King Edward the Third; whereas he
From John of Gaunt doth bring his pedigree
Being but fourth of that heroic line.
But mark: as in this haughty great attempt
They laboured to plant the rightful heir,   80
I lost my liberty, and they their lives.
Long after this, when Henry the Fifth,
Succeeding his father Bolingbroke, did reign,
Thy father, Earl of Cambridge then, deriv'd
From famous Edmund Langley, Duke of York,   85
Marrying my sister, that thy mother was,
Again, in pity of my hard distress,
Levied an army, weening to redeem
And have install'd me in the diadem;
But, as the rest, so fell that noble earl,   90
And was beheaded. Thus the Mortimers,
In whom the title rested, were suppress'd.
Plan. Of which, my lord, your honour is the last.

71. King] *F2; not in F.*   76. To King Edward the Third] *F;* Unto the third
King Edward *conj. this edn.*   84. Cambridge then,] *This edn;* Cambridge,
then *F.*

64. *nephew*] cousin—a common
Elizabethan use.
67. *the Percies*] Hall, 23 ff., 28, and
head-note above.
69. *advancement*] elevation.
74. *mother*] cf. head-note; suggesting
Hall, 28 rather than 2, and confusing
Mortimer with his uncle Sir John. He
himself should have said grandmother.

79. *haughty*] high-pitched (Fr. *haut*).
84–91.] cf. *H5*, II. ii. Though there
is no levying of an army, there is no
inconsistency as Malone thought,
since, as Hart says, the *Chronic*
'implies a force' in order to 'deliuer
the kyng a liue into the handes of his
enemies, or els to murther him' (Hall,
60–1).

Mor. True; and thou seest that I no issue have,
  And that my fainting words do warrant death.   95
  Thou art my heir; the rest I wish thee gather:
  But yet be wary in thy studious care.
Plan. Thy grave admonishments prevail with me;
  But yet methinks my father's execution
  Was nothing less than bloody tyranny.   100
Mor. With silence, nephew, be thou politic;
  Strong-fixed is the house of Lancaster,
  And like a mountain, not to be remov'd.
  But now thy uncle is removing hence,
  As princes do their courts when they are cloy'd   105
  With long continuance in a settled place.
Plan. O uncle, would some part of my young years
  Might but redeem the passing of your age!
Mor. Thou dost then wrong me, as that slaughterer doth,
  Which giveth many wounds when one will kill.   110
  Mourn not, except thou sorrow for my good;
  Only give order for my funeral.
  And so farewell; and fair befall thy hopes,
  And prosperous be thy life in peace and war!   *Dies.*
Plan. And peace, no war, befall thy parting soul!   115
  In prison hast thou spent a pilgrimage,
  And like a hermit overpass'd thy days.
  Well, I will lock his counsel in my breast;

---

102. Strong-fixed] *Theobald;* Strong fixed *F.*   108. passing] *This edn;* passage *F.*
113. befall] *Theobald;* be all *F.*

95. *warrant*] certify, guarantee.
96. *gather*] infer; or collect (his inheritance).
98. *admonishments*] warnings (L. *monere*).
99. *methinks*] it seems to me.
100. *tyranny*] cruelty.
101. *politic*] prudent.
103. *mountain . . . remov'd*] Ps., cxxv. 1, 'even as the mount Sion: which may not be removed' (Noble); cf. Isa., liv. 10.
106. *settled*] rooted, firm.
108. *redeem*] ransom, buy back (from death).
  passing] F 'passage' is corrupted by

'age', as 'steal' (F send), I. i. 176 was affected by 'intend'.
112. *give order*] make the arrangements.
113. *fair befall*] cf. 115, where the word is echoed. The 'f' has obviously fallen out at some stage of setting or printing. There are five other examples of the phrase in Shakespeare, but none of 'fair be all'.
114. *prosperous . . . war*] long-range irony, especially in view of York's ignominious death in *3H6*.
116. *pilgrimage*] a common Biblical metaphor; cf. e.g. Gen., xlvii. 9; Ps., cxix. 54, cxxvi. 1; etc.

And what I do imagine, let that rest.
Keepers, convey him hence; and I myself   120
Will see his burial better than his life.

Exeunt [Gaolers, bearing out the body of Mortimer].

Here dies the dusky torch of Mortimer,
Chok'd with ambition of the meaner sort;
And for those wrongs, those bitter injuries,
Which Somerset hath offer'd to my house,   125
I doubt not but with honour to redress;
And therefore haste I to the Parliament,
Either to be restored to my blood,
Or make mine ill th' advantage of my good.   *Exit.*

---

121. S.D.] *Capell; Exit. | F.*   129. mine] *This edn;* my *F.*   ill] *Theobald;*
will *F.*

119. *imagine*] a play on the normal
phrase for treason, to 'imagine' the
king's death.

rest] leave that alone; no matter.

122. *dusky*] referring to (*a*) his near
blindness, (*b*) the darkness of death.

123. *the meaner sort*] those whose
claim to the crown, and whose rank,
were inferior to his own.

124. *for*] as for.

128. *blood*] rank due to his blood
or descent, and its privileges, *OED.*,
13.

129. *Or . . . good*] 'Or make my injuries an instrument for attaining my
ambition' (Brooke).

mine ill] F 'my will' is not merely
a sophistication of 'my' for 'mine', but
a misreading of 'ne' as 'w', with the
spelling 'myne'.

ACT III

SCENE I.—[*London. The Parliament House.*]

Flourish. Enter KING, EXETER, GLOUCESTER, WINCHESTER,
WARWICK, SOMERSET, SUFFOLK, RICHARD PLANTAGENET.
GLOUCESTER *offers to put up a bill;* WINCHESTER *snatches it,
tears it.*

Win. Com'st thou with deep-premeditated lines,
    With written pamphlets studiously devis'd,
    Humphrey of Gloucester? If thou canst accuse
    Or aught intend'st to lay unto my charge,
    Do it without invention, suddenly;   5
    As I with sudden and extemporal speech
    Purpose to answer what thou canst object.
Glou. Presumptuous priest, this place commands my
      patience,
    Or thou shouldst find thou hast dishonour'd me.

ACT III

Scene I

ACT III SCENE I] *F* (*Actus Tertius. Scena Prima.*).   *London.*] *Cambridge* + *edd.*
The . . . House.] *Capell* + *edd.*   1. deep-premeditated] *Dyce, S. Walker conj.;* deepe
premeditated *F.*   2, 3. devis'd, / Humphrey of Gloucester?] *Cambridge;*
deuis'd? / *Humfrey* of Gloster, *F.*

The quarrel of Winchester and
Gloucester is continued from I. iii. Two
sets of accusations (Hall, 130 and 197)
against Winchester are here combined.
Civil dissension now spreads from the
nobles to the people in the 'pebble'
incident, drawn from Fabyan, 596.
Shakespeare transfers the scene from
Leicester to London (77), and inter-
weaves Plantagenet's claim to his inheritance from the preceding scenes.
Exeter concludes with a choric soliloquy of impending disaster. For the in-

terruptions of ceremony, see Intro., pp.
lii–liii; Tillyard, *Sh. Hist. Plays,* 140,
compares *Tit.,* I. i. 244 ff.

S.D. put up a bill] bring forward or
present a list of accusations.

1. *lines*] prepared writing; Hart
compares 'marriage lines'.

2. *pamphlets*] written compositions
(Hart).

5. *invention*] plan, previous search for
subject-matter.

suddenly] extempore.

7. *object*] urge against (me).

Think not, although in writing I preferr'd   10
The manner of thy vile outrageous crimes,
That therefore I have forg'd, or am not able
Verbatim to rehearse my method penn'd.
No, prelate; such is thy audacious wickedness,
Thy lewd, pestiferous, and dissentious pranks,   15
As very infants prattle of thy pride.
Thou art a most pernicious usurer,
Froward by nature, enemy to peace;
Lascivious, wanton, more than well beseems
A man of thy profession and degree;   20
And for thy treachery, what's more manifest,
In that thou laid'st a trap to take my life,
As well at London Bridge as at the Tower?
Beside, I fear me, if thy thoughts were sifted,
The King, thy sovereign, is not quite exempt   25
From envious malice of thy swelling heart.
Win. Gloucester, I do defy thee. Lords, vouchsafe
To give me hearing what I shall reply.
If covetous, ambitious, or perverse,

---

13. my method penn'd] *This edn;* the Methode of my Penne F.   21, 23.
manifest, / . . . Tower?] *This edn;* manifest? / . . . Tower. *F.*   29. If] *This edn,*
Vaughan conj.; If I were *F.*

---

10. *preferr'd*] L. sense = brought
forward.

11. *vile outrageous*] cf. *1 Tamb.*, 545.

13. *rehearse*] give an account of,
narrate.

my method penn'd] 'my' may have
been misplaced in printing, and the
rest supplied by conjecture; or 'penn'd'
misread as 'penne' by scribe or compositor, with consequent 'correction'.
Cf. *LLL.*, v. ii. 402 (cf. 147, 305), 'O,
never will I trust to speeches penn'd';
and *Lyly*, i. 271, 'An Oration . . . either
penned, either premeditated'.

method] in logic, the arrangement of
matter for delivery; a summary of
contents (*OED.*, 4); cf. *Tw. N.*, I.
v. 230.

14 ff.] Carter compares 1 Tim., iii. 2,
where the qualifications of a bishop are
the opposite of Winchester's.

14, 16. *such . . . As*] see Abbott, 109.

15. *lewd*] Elizabethan sense =
wicked, vile.

pestiferous] pernicious; deadly; 'that
bringeth death and destruction'
(Cooper).

pranks] mischievous tricks (Schmidt),
implying malice (Wilson).

17. *usurer*] Winchester's wealth derived from his use of a Papal Bull, and
from the 'usury' (cf. *Meas.*, III. ii. 7) or
revenue from the stews in Southwark;
see I. iii. 23–4 and 35; and Hall, 139,
211. The same theme is introduced in
his death-scene, *2H6*, III. iii.

22. *trap*] Hall, 131; the third article
of Gloucester's accusations; the fourth
occurs below, 25–6.

26. *envious*] full of ill-will or malice.

28. *me*] redundant object, common
in Shakespeare; cf. Abbott, 414.

29.] 'I were' has probably been
added by the scribe.

As he will have me, how am I so poor? 30
Or how haps it I seek not to advance
Or raise myself, but keep my wonted calling?
And for dissension, who preferreth peace
More than I do?—except I be provok'd.
No, my good lords, it is not that offends; 35
It is not that that hath incens'd the Duke;
It is because no one should sway but he,
No one but he should be about the King;
And that engenders thunder in his breast
And makes him roar these accusations forth. 40
But he shall know I am as good—
Glou.   As good!
Thou bastard of my grandfather!
Win. Ay, lordly sir; for what are you, I pray,
But one imperious in another's throne?
Glou. Am I not Protector, saucy priest? 45
Win. And am not I a prelate of the church?
Glou. Yes, as an outlaw in a castle keeps,
And useth it—to patronage his theft.
Win. Unreverent Gloucester!
Glou.   Thou art reverend
Touching thy spiritual function, not thy life. 50

31. it] *F;* that *conj. this edn.*   32. myself, ... calling?] *Cambridge;* my selfe? ...
Calling. *F.*   41. good—] *F2;* good. *F.*   45. Protector] *F;* Lord Protector
Keightley, conj. S. Walker.   49. reverend] *F3;* reuerent *F.*

29 ff. *covetous, ambitious, ... poor*] 'the ryche Cardinall' begs the question and equivocates characteristically. Hall, 210, says, 'His couetous[ness] insaciable . . . made hym bothe to forget God, hys Prynce and hym selfe. . . "I thought my self able to be equale with kinges, and so thought to encrease my treasure in hoope to haue worne a tryple Croune"'.

31. *it*] = 'that'? Both were written 'yᵗ'.

advance] raise.

34. *except . . .*] another characteristic reservation.

35. *that*] For the omission of the relative, see Abbott, 244.

42. *bastard*] Winchester was an illegitimate son of John of Gaunt by Catherine Swynford, whom Gaunt afterwards married (Malone). See App. II; and cf. *2H6*, II. i. 41. Such aspersions were the recognized practice in vituperative rhetoric; cf. Baldwin, II. 331 ff., and *3H6*, I. iv. 19 ff.

44. *imperious*] imperial, acting like a king.

45. *saucy*] insolent.

47. *keeps*] dwells for defence.

48. *patronage*] uphold, defend; cf. Cooper, *patronus* = defender.

49. *reverend*] with a pun on 'reverent'; the two forms were in fact not distinguished.

Win. Rome shall remedy this.
Glou.   Roam thither then.
War. [*to Win.*] My lord, it were your duty to forbear.
Som. Ay, so the bishop be not overborne.
    Methinks my lord should be religious,
    And know the office that belongs to such.   55
War. Methinks his lordship should be humbler;
    It fitteth not a prelate so to plead.
Som. Yes, when his holy state is touch'd so near.
War. State holy or unhallow'd, what of that?
    Is not his Grace Protector to the King?   60
Plan. [*Aside.*] Plantagenet, I see, must hold his tongue,
    Lest it be said, 'Speak, sirrah, when you should;
    Must your bold verdict enter talk with lords?'
    Else would I have a fling at Winchester.
K. Hen. Uncles of Gloucester and of Winchester,   65
    The special watchmen of our English weal,

---

51. *Glou.*] Hanmer, Capell; Warw. / F.   52–5. Warw. [*to Win.*] My lord ... such.]
This edn, after Hanmer; My Lord ... *Som.* I, see ... such. *F; Som.* My lord ... *War.*
Ay, see ... *Som.* Methinks my lord ... such. *Theobald; War.* (*to Win.*) My lord ...
Som. I'll see ... such. *Hanmer; Som.* (*to Glo.*) My lord ... *War.* Ay, see ... *Som.*
Methinks ... such. *Capell.*   53. so] *Sisson;* see *F.*   61. S.D. *Aside.*] *Hanmer;*
not in *F.*   65. *K. Hen.*] *F* (*King.*) *throughout.*

    51. *remedy*] with the accent possibly on the second syllable; cf. 16th-century *remeady, remede.*

    Rome . . . Roam] a common pun in Shakespeare; cf. *John,* III. i. 180; *Cæs.,* I. ii. 156.

    51–5.] The F distribution of speeches is generally agreed to be faulty. The simplest explanation is that *Glou.* was omitted at 51, 'Roam....', and *Warw.* raised into its place. The error is most probably scribal.

    The balancing halves of 51 obviously conclude the dialogue of Gloucester and Winchester. Their adherents, Warwick and Somerset, then take over.

    53. *so*] F 'see' is an easy misreading of 'soe'. The ironical 'see' is quite out of place here; Somerset is defending the bishop, Winchester. It would be even more uncharacteristic of the straightforward Warwick.

    overborne] cf. v. ii. 60; over-ruled, subdued.

    54. *my lord*] Gloucester.

    55. *office*] L. *officium* = duty, honour due.

    such] people in Winchester's 'holy state'.

    56. *his lordship*] Winchester.

    58. *touch'd so near*] affected so closely or seriously.

    holy state] 'ecclesiastical status' (Wilson).

    63. *verdict*] statement on the truth of a case where the law is admitted (Blackstone); truth-telling; a reference, of course, to his claim to reinstatement in his inheritance.

    enter talk] engage in discussion; cf. Greene, *Defence of Conny-catching* (ed. Harrison), 55.

    64. *fling*] an attack in words.

    66. *weal*] well-being, common good, as in 'commonweal'.

I would prevail, if prayers might prevail,
To join your hearts in love and amity.
O, what a scandal is it to our crown
That two such noble peers as ye should jar!   70
Believe me, lords, my tender years can tell
Civil dissension is a viperous worm
That gnaws the bowels of the commonwealth.

A noise within, 'Down with the tawny-coats!'

What tumult's this?
War.   An uproar, I dare warrant,
Begun through malice of the Bishop's men.   75

A noise again, 'Stones! Stones!'
Enter Mayor.

May. O, my good lords, and virtuous Henry,
Pity the city of London, pity us!
The Bishop and the Duke of Gloucester's men,
Forbidden late to carry any weapon,
Have fill'd their pockets full of pebble stones   80
And, banding themselves in contrary parts,
Do pelt so fast at one another's pate
That many have their giddy brains knock'd out:
Our windows are broke down in every street,
And we for fear compell'd to shut our shops.   85

Enter [Servingmen] in skirmish with bloody pates.

74. What] *edd.; King.* What *F.*   80. pebble] *F* (peeble).   82. pate] *F;* pates
Pope.   85. S.D. *Servingmen*] *edd.; not in F.*

68. *love and amity*] Henry quotes, characteristically, from the Prayer Book.

70. *jar*] disagree.

72. *civil dissension*] Henry goes to the root of the trouble, but, as the following lines show, is powerless to affect the course of events, except superficially.

72–3. *viperous worm . . . gnaws the bowels*] a reference to Aesop's snake in the bosom (cf. *2H6*, III. i. 343–4). Hart compares Sylvester's *Du Bartas*, 'Or, like our own (late) York and Lancaster, / Ambitious broachers of that

Viper war, / Which did the womb of their own Dam devour, . . .'

74. *uproar*] disturbance.

78. *Bishop*] i.e. Bishop's; cf. *R2*, II. iii. 62, 'Shall be your love and labour's recompense'.

78 ff.] The incident is from Fabyan, 596; see App. I (*c*).

79. *late*] adjective for adverb; see Abbott, 23.

81. *contrary parts*] opposing parties. 'Contrary' is accented, here, on the second syllable.

83. *giddy*] wild with fury (Vaughan).

K. Hen. We charge you, on allegiance to ourself,
      To hold your slaughtering hands and keep the peace.
      Pray, uncle Gloucester, mitigate this strife.
1 Serv. Nay, if we be forbidden stones, we'll fall to it with
      our teeth.   90
2 Serv. Do what ye dare, we are as resolute.

Skirmish again.

Glou. You of my household, leave this peevish broil,
      And set this unaccustom'd fight aside.
3 Serv. My lord, we know your Grace to be a man
      Just and upright, and, for your royal birth,   95
      Inferior to none but to his Majesty;
      And ere that we will suffer such a prince,
      So kind a father of the commonweal,
      To be disgraced by an inkhorn mate,
      We and our wives and children all will fight   100
      And have our bodies slaughter'd by thy foes.
1 Serv. Ay, and the very parings of our nails
      Shall pitch a field when we are dead.   *Begin again.*
Glou.   Stay, stay, I say!
      And if you love me, as you say you do,
      Let me persuade you to forbear awhile.   105
K. Hen. O, how this discord doth afflict my soul!
      Can you, my Lord of Winchester, behold
      My sighs and tears, and will not once relent?
      Who should be pitiful, if you be not?
      Or who should study to prefer a peace   110
      If holy churchmen take delight in broils?

93. fight] *F;* sight *conj. Vaughan.*

92. *peevish*] foolish.
93. *unaccustom'd*] strange, unusual,
with possibly a suggestion of being
'contra bonos mores', contrary to good
manners or customs.
97. *suffer*] allow.
prince] in both the usual Elizabethan
senses, sovereign ruler (as Protector),
and member of the royal family.
99. *disgraced*] (*a*) insulted; (*b*) treated without proper respect for his
'Grace'.

inkhorn mate] low pedant (Brooke);
bookish fellow (Hart).
103. *pitch a field*] implying the presence of stakes, as distinct from a 'plain
field' (Hart).
106. *discord*] The servants now repeat the jars of their masters (I. i. 44).
110. *prefer*] literal L. sense = bring
forward, offer.
111. *holy churchmen . . .*] cf. I. i. 33;
I. iii. 19 and n.; III. i. 127–8 and n.;
and *2H6*, II. i. 24–6.

War. My Lord Protector, yield; yield, Winchester;
        Except you mean with obstinate repulse
        To slay your sovereign and destroy the realm.
        You see what mischief, and what murder too,   115
        Hath been enacted through your enmity;
        Then be at peace, except ye thirst for blood.
Win. He shall submit, or I will never yield.
Glou. Compassion on the King commands me stoop,
        Or I would see his heart out, ere the priest   120
        Should ever get that privilege of me.
War. Behold, my Lord of Winchester, the Duke
        Hath banish'd moody discontented fury,
        As by his smoothed brows it doth appear:
        Why look you still so stern and tragical?   125
Glou. Here, Winchester, I offer thee my hand.
K. Hen. Fie, uncle Beaufort! I have heard you preach
        That malice was a great and grievous sin;
        And will you not maintain the thing you teach,
        But prove a chief offender in the same?   130
War. Sweet King! The Bishop hath a kindly gird.
        For shame, my Lord of Winchester, relent!
        What, shall a child instruct you what to do?
Win. Well, Duke of Gloucester, I will yield to thee;
        Love for thy love and hand for hand I give.   135
Glou. [*Aside.*] Ay, but, I fear me, with a hollow heart.—
        See here, my friends and loving countrymen,

---

112. My Lord Protector, yield] *Pope;* Yeeld my Lord Protector *F.*   129, 130.
teach, /...same?] *Pope;* teach? /...same. *F.*   136. S.D. *Aside.*] *Collier; not in F.*

112.] F ruins both the verse and the chiasmus by reverting to the normal prose order. This is frequent in this play, and is probably the work of the scribe.

113. *repulse*] rejection (of a request).
115. *mischief*] harm.
116. *enacted*] accomplished, performed.
121. *privilege*] advantage, in having his opponent make the first move.
123. *moody*] angry.
127–9. *preach ... malice ... teach*] cf. 111 above and n.; and *2H6*, II. i. 24–6,

'*Tantaene animis coelestibus irae?* / Churchmen so hot? Good uncle, can you dote, / To hide such malice with such holiness?' Noble compares Rom., ii. 21–3, 'Thou therefore which teachest another, teachest thou not thyselfe? Thou preachest a man shoulde not steale, yet stealest thou?'

131. *hath a kindly gird*] has been given (by the king) a reproof proper to his fault, since based on the principles of the religion he purports to practise—a reproof in kind. There is also probably the suggestion of kindness.

This token serveth for a flag of truce
Betwixt ourselves and all our followers:
So help me God, as I dissemble not!   140

Win. [*Aside.*] So help me God, as I intend it not!

K. Hen. O loving uncle, kind Duke of Gloucester,
How joyful am I made by this contract!
Away, my masters! trouble us no more,
But join in friendship, as your lords have done.   145

3 Serv. Content; I'll to the surgeon's.

1 Serv. And so will I.

2 Serv. And I will see what physic the tavern affords.

Exeunt [*Servingmen, Mayor, etc.*].

War. Accept this scroll, most gracious sovereign,
Which in the right of Richard Plantagenet   150
We do exhibit to your Majesty.

Glou. Well urg'd, my Lord of Warwick; for, sweet prince,
And if your Grace mark every circumstance,
You have great reason to do Richard right,
Especially for those occasions   155
At Eltham Place I told your Majesty.

K. Hen. And those occasions, uncle, were of force;
Therefore, my loving lords, our pleasure is
That Richard be restored to his blood.

War. Let Richard be restored to his blood;   160
So shall his father's wrongs be recompens'd.

Win. As will the rest, so willeth Winchester.

K. Hen. If Richard will be true, not that alone
But all the whole inheritance I give
That doth belong unto the house of York,   165
From whence you spring by lineal descent.

141. S.D. *Aside.*] *Pope; not in F.*   142. kind] *F; and kind Collier².*   148. S.D.]
Capell; Exeunt. | F.   156. Eltham] *F* (Eltam).   163. alone] *F2+edd.;* all
alone *F.*

138. *This token*] the handshake.

141. *as I intend it not*] possibly ambiguous = as I don't intend to dissemble.
If so, the *Aside* is unnecessary.

143. *contract*] most commonly accented on the second syllable.

144. *masters*] familiar condescend-
ing term for the servants, or 'tawny-
coats'.

151. *exhibit*] the technical term for
'submit for consideration' (Wilson).

155. *occasions*] reasons, circum-
stances. The relative pronoun is under-
stood.

159. *restored to his blood*] reinstated in
his father's forfeited titles; cf. II. v. 128,
and Hall, 138.

161. *recompens'd*] compensated.

Plan. Thy humble servant vows obedience
　　And humble service till the point of death.

K. Hen. Stoop then and set your knee against my foot;
　　And in reguerdon of that duty done　　　　　　170
　　I girt thee with the valiant sword of York:
　　Rise, Richard, like a true Plantagenet,
　　And rise created princely Duke of York.

Plan. And so thrive Richard as thy foes may fall!
　　And as my duty springs, so perish they　　　　175
　　That grudge one thought against your Majesty!

All. Welcome, high Prince, the mighty Duke of York!

Som. [*Aside.*] Perish, base Prince, ignoble Duke of York!

Glou. Now will it best avail your Majesty
　　To cross the seas and to be crown'd in France.　180
　　The presence of a king engenders love
　　Amongst his subjects and his loyal friends,
　　As it disanimates his enemies.

K. Hen. When Gloucester says the word, King Henry goes;
　　For friendly counsel cuts off many foes.　　　185

Glou. Your ships already are in readiness.

　　　　　　Sennet. Flourish. Exeunt all but Exeter.

Exe. Ay, we may march in England, or in France,
　　Not seeing what is likely to ensue.
　　This late dissension grown betwixt the peers
　　Burns under feigned ashes of forg'd love,　　　190
　　And will at last break out into a flame;

---

168. humble] *F;* faithful *Pope.*　　178. S.D. *Aside.*] *Rowe; not in F.*　　186. S.D. *Exeunt all but*] *F* (*Exeunt. Manet*).

---

168. *humble*] probably a scribal or compositorial repetition, from 167.

168, 170. *service . . . duty*] feudal terms, from a vassal to his superior.

170. *reguerdon*] ample reward (Hart).

171. *girt*] old form of 'gird'.

173. *princely*] of the royal blood; cf. 97 above and n.

174–6.] forward-looking dramatic irony. Plantagenet was to claim the crown, and his son, Edward IV, to take it, from Henry.

176. *grudge one thought*] have one grudging, or envious, thought;

think resentfully; cf. IV. i. 141.

180. *crown'd in France*] in 1431; Hall, 160–1.

183. *disanimates*] disheartens, discourages; cf. Cooper, *animare* = to give courage or boldness to.

186. *already . . . readiness*] note the word-play.

190. *Burns . . . ashes*] cf. Horace, *Odes,* II. i. 7–8, 'ignes / Suppositos cineri doloso', which likewise refers to civil war; see Malone, XXIII. 87. Baldwin, *Sm. Latine,* II. 534, notes that the 'setting and sentiment are similar'.

As fester'd members rot but by degree
Till bones and flesh and sinews fall away,
So will this base and envious discord breed.
And now I fear that fatal prophecy   195
Which in the time of Henry nam'd the Fifth
Was in the mouth of every sucking babe:
That Henry born at Monmouth should win all,
And Henry born at Windsor should lose all:
Which is so plain that Exeter doth wish   200
His days may finish ere that hapless time.   *Exit.*

SCENE II. [—*France. Before Rouen.*]

Enter [La] Pucelle *disguised, with four Soldiers
with sacks upon their backs.*

Puc. These are the city gates, the gates of Rouen,
    Through which our policy must make a breach.

192. degree] *F; degrees Rowe.*   199. should lose] *F2+edd.; loose F.*

Scene II

SCENE II] *F (Scæna Secunda.).*   *France. Before Rouen.*] *Cambridge; not in F;*
Change to Roan in France. | Pope.

194. *breed*] increase of itself, multiply.

195. *prophecy*] Hall, 108.

197. *in the mouth of every sucking babe*] cf. Ps., viii. 2 in Sternhold and Hopkins, 'Euen by the mouthes of sucking babes, / thou wilt confound thy foes, / For in these babes thy might is sene / thy graces they disclose.'

Scene II

The fortunes of war, by which Rouen is (fictitiously) 'lost and recover'd in a day', are used to expand the parts of Joan, witch and courtesan, and of the heroic Talbot who is contrasted once again with the coward Falstaff. Similar liberties are taken with the age and death (Hall, 178) of the heroic Bedford just as he has seen the overthrow of the subtle-witted French. Burgundy is shown for the last time as an ally of England on the eve of his defection to the French.

The French capture of Rouen is adapted from the taking of the castle of Cornill (Hall, 197, but more probably Fabyan, 615). The burning cresset is from the capture of Le Mans (Hall, 142), already used in substance for the capture of Orleans (ii. i). A similar incident is described at the capture of Pontelarche (Hall, 211).

S.D. four] Fabyan, 615: Hall and Holinshed say six, and omit the speaking of French. Fabyan's marginal note says, 'four soldiers dressed as husbandmen, carrying sacks, and speaking French'.

2. *policy*] stratagem, craft; cf. iii. iii. 12.

Take heed, be wary how you place your words;
Talk like the vulgar sort of market men
That come to gather money for their corn.   5
If we have entrance, as I hope we shall,
And that we find the slothful watch but weak,
I'll by a sign give notice to our friends,
That Charles the Dauphin may encounter them.

1 Sold. Our sacks shall be a mean to sack the city,   10
And we be lords and rulers over Rouen;
Therefore we'll knock.   *Knock.*

Watch. [*Within.*] Qui la?

Puc. Paysans, la pauvre gens de France:
Poor market folks that come to sell their corn.   15

Watch. [*Opens the gate.*] Enter, go in; the market bell is rung.

Puc. Now, Rouen, I'll shake thy bulwarks to the ground.

Exeunt.

Enter CHARLES, [*the*] *Bastard* [*of* ORLEANS], ALENÇON
[, REIGNIER, *and Forces*].

Cha. Saint Denis bless this happy stratagem,
And once again we'll sleep secure in Rouen.

Bast. Here enter'd Pucelle and her practisants;   20

---

10. *1 Sold.*] Capell (*1. S.*); *Souldier.* | F.   13. S.D. *Within*] Capell; *not in* F.
13. Qui la?] F (*Che la.*); Qui est la? *Malone*.   14. Paysans ... France] F
(*Peasauns la pouure gens de Fraunce*); Paysans, pauvre gens ... France, *Rowe*.
16. S.D. *Opens the gate.*] Hart; *Guard open.* | *Capell*; *not in* F.   17. S.D. *the Bastard
of Orleans*] Cambridge; *Bastard* | F.   *Reignier*] *edd.*; *not in* F.   *and Forces*]
Capell; *not in* F.

3. *place*] arrange, dispose (Wilson, from *OED.*, 1b).

4. *vulgar*] of the common people (L. *vulgus*), used without disparagement.

market men] men who come to market; marketing people.

6, 7. *If ... And that ...*] Abbott, 285, 'the Elizabethan habit of omitting [the purely conjunctional "that"] at the beginning of a sentence, where the construction is obvious, and then inserting it to connect a more distant clause with the conjunction on which the clause depends.'

10. *sacks ... sack*] a characteristic pun; cf. *1H4*, v. iii. 51–2.

mean] alternative form of 'means'.

11. *be*] = shall be.

13. *Qui la?*] the F omission of 'va' may represent pidgin French. Nashe has the forms 'Cheuela', i. 359. 24, and 'Queuela', ii. 229. 12.

14. *gens*] folk; a contemporary French form.

17. S.D. *Reignier*] see Intro., p. xvii.

18. *Saint Denis*] see I. vi. 28 and n.

19. *secure*] original L. sense = free from care.

20. *practisants*] 'Practice ... was treachery and perhaps in the softer sense stratagem. Practisants are therefore confederates in stratagems' (Johnson).

Now she is there, how will she specify
Here is the best and safest passage in?

Reig. By thrusting out a torch from yonder tower,
Which once discern'd shows that her meaning is:
No way to that, for weakness, which she enter'd.   25

Enter [LA] PUCELLE *on the top, thrusting out a torch burning.*

Puc. Behold, this is the happy wedding torch
That joineth Rouen unto her countrymen,
But burning fatal to the Talbonites.   *Exit.*

Bast. See, noble Charles, the beacon of our friend,
The burning torch, in yonder turret stands.   30

Cha. Now shine it like a comet of revenge,
A prophet to the fall of all our foes!

Reig. Defer no time, delays have dangerous ends;
Enter and cry 'The Dauphin!' presently,
And then do execution on the watch.   [*Exeunt.*] 35

An Alarum. [*Enter*] TALBOT *in an excursion.*

Tal. France, thou shalt rue this treason with thy tears,
If Talbot but survive thy treachery.
Pucelle, that witch, that damned sorceress,
Hath wrought this hellish mischief unawares,
That hardly we escap'd the pride of France.   *Exit.* 40

21. specify] *Rowe;* specifie? *F.*   22. Here] *F;* Where *Rowe.*   28. Talbonites] *F;*
Talbotites *Theobald.*   30. torch,] *This edn;* Torch *F.*   35. S.D. *Exeunt.*]
Alarum. | *F;* Alarum. Exeunt. | *edd.*   *Enter*] *Capell; not in F.*

22. *Here*] the F reading is confirmed
by 24-5.
23. *tower*] Hall says 'steeple'; the reference here is probably to the theatre
tower or 'top' (25 S.D.) from which
the flag was flown to show that a play
was on; see *W.S.,* I. 293, Adams, 303,
and Hodges, 32-3. It was also referred
to as the 'turret', I. iv. 11, 21. S.D., 25.
25. *No way to that, for weakness*] no
way compares in weakness with that
(to = in comparison with).
28. *Talbonites*] 'a derivative formed
from a Latinized form of Talbot's
name Talbo-onis, though Talbottus is
the form used by Camden' (Brooke).

F has the less likely form, and is thus
probably correct.
31. *shine it*] may it shine; the imagery
is continued from I. i. 2 (see Intro.,
pp. lv-lvi).
32. *prophet*] i.e. omen; cf. I. i. 1 ff.
33. *delays* . . .] proverbial; Tilley,
145. Gascoigne has 'Omnis mora
trahit periculum'.
34. *presently*] Elizabethan sense—
immediately.
39. *mischief*] harm, disaster.
unawares] by surprise; on us, who
were taken unawares.
40. *hardly*] with difficulty.
pride] power and arrogance (Hart);

An alarum: excursions. BEDFORD, *brought in sick in a chair.*
Enter TALBOT *and* BURGUNDY *without: within,* [LA] PUGELLE,
CHARLES, BASTARD, [ALENÇON,] *and* REIGNIER, *on the walls.*

Puc. Good morrow, gallants! Want ye corn for bread?
  I think the Duke of Burgundy will fast
  Before he'll buy again at such a rate.
  'Twas full of darnel: do you like the taste?
Bur. Scoff on, vile fiend and shameless courtezan!   45
  I trust ere long to choke thee with thine own,
  And make thee curse the harvest of that corn.
Cha. Your Grace may starve, perhaps, before that time.
Bed. O, let no words, but deeds, revenge this treason!
Puc. What will you do, good grey-beard? Break a lance 50
  And run a tilt at Death within a chair?
Tal. Foul fiend of France and hag of all despite,
  Encompass'd with thy lustful paramours,
  Becomes it thee to taunt his valiant age
  And twit with cowardice a man half dead?   55
  Damsel, I'll have a bout with you again,
  Or else let Talbot perish with this shame.
Puc. Are ye so hot? Yet, Pucelle, hold thy peace;

40. S.D. *Alençon] Collier; not in F.* 50–1.] *as Pope;* What . . . gray-beard?
. . . Death, / . . . Chayre. *F.* 51. a tilt] *F* (a-Tilt). 57. this] *F;* his *Rowe.*
58. hot?] *Pope;* hot, Sir : *F.*

the phrase was a favourite of Marlowe's, e.g. 'the pride of Asia'. Cf. IV.
vi. 15, 'the pride of Gallia'.

 S.D. excursions] the passage across
the stage of small bodies of soldiers in
simulation of a battle.

 Bedford] Hall, 178, for the death of
Bedford, four years after the burning
of Joan.

 Alençon] see Intro., p. xvii.

 44. *darnel*] tares, cockle; note the
continuation of the imagery from the
parable of the Sower in 'choke' (46),
and 'harvest . . . corn' (47). The word
was used of 'any injurious weed, but
properly Lolium' (Hart). Steevens
suggested that, since darnel affected
the eyes (Ovid, *Fasti*, I. 691), 'Pucelle
means to intimate that the corn she
carried had produced the same effect

on the guards of Rouen, otherwise
they would have seen through her dis-
guise'.

 48. *starve*] die; cf. Ger. *sterben.*

 52. *hag*] witch; cf. *Mac.*, IV. i. 48, etc.
of all despite] full of spite or malice;
all-malignant (Wilson).

 55. *with cowardice*] 'in a cowardly
manner', not 'to blame him for his
cowardice'.

 56. *a bout*] cf. I. v. 4; the sense is
equivocal, like so many remarks applied to Joan; cf. 'hot', 58; and see *Sh.
Bawdy*, 78.

 58.] The first part of the F line is
certainly corrupt. The 'sir' is probably
intrusive; possibly a misreading of a
question mark as 'S^r'.

 hot] (*a*) hot-tempered; (*b*) passion-
ate, lustful; *Sh. Bawdy*, 130.

If Talbot do but thunder, rain will follow.

The English whisper together in council.

God speed the parliament! Who shall be the Speaker?   60
Tal. Dare ye come forth and meet us in the field?
Puc. Belike your lordship takes us then for fools,
     To try if that our own be ours or no.
Tal. I speak not to that railing Hecate,
     But unto thee, Alençon, and the rest;   65
     Will ye, like soldiers, come and fight it out?
Alen. Signior, no.
Tal. Signior, hang! Base muleteers of France!
     Like peasant foot-boys do they keep the walls,
     And dare not take up arms like gentlemen.   70
Puc. Captains, away, let's get us from the walls,
     For Talbot means no goodness by his looks.
     God b'uy, my lord; we came to tell you but
     That we are here.   *Exeunt from the walls.*
Tal. And there will we be too, ere it be long,   75
     Or else reproach be Talbot's greatest fame!
     Vow, Burgundy, by honour of thy house,
     Prick'd on by public wrongs sustain'd in France,
     Either to get the town again or die;
     And I, as sure as English Henry lives,   80
     And as his father here was conqueror,
     As sure as in this late-betrayed town
     Great Coeur-de-lion's heart was buried—

---

59. S.D. *The English*] F (*They*).   68. muleteers] *Rowe;* Muleters F.   71.
Captains, away] *Rowe;* Away Captaines F.   73. b'uy] *F;* be wi' you *Rowe.*
to tell you but] *This edn;* but to tell you *F.*   83. Coeur-de-lion] F (Cordelion).

60. *Speaker*] (*a*) spokesman; (*b*) pre-
sident or chairman of the parliament.
64. *Hecate*] 'The ancients thought of
Hecate first as a moon-goddess, then
as a divinity of the infernal regions,
and, lastly, as a natural development
of these two ideas, as patroness of
witches' (Baldwin, II. 437).
68. *Base*] of low birth, in contrast to
'gentlemen' (70).
71. *Captains, away,*] F has a typical
scribal normalization of an inversion.

72. *goodness*] good.
73. *to tell you but*] probably another
normalization of word-order; but the
short line following may indicate deeper corruption.
78. *Prick'd on*] goaded, instigated.
public wrongs] See App. I (Hall, 147
etc.).
83. *Coeur-de-lion*] Richard Cœur-de-
Lion; cf. *John*, I. i. 54. Richard 'willed
his heart to be conueied vnto Rouen,
and there buried; in testimonie of the

      So sure I swear to get the town or die.
Bur. My vows are equal partners with thy vows.   85
Tal. But, ere we go, regard this dying prince,
      The valiant Duke of Bedford. Come, my lord,
      We will bestow you in some better place,
      Fitter for sickness and for crazy age.
Bed. Lord Talbot, do not so dishonour me;   90
      Here will I sit, before the walls of Rouen,
      And will be partner of your weal or woe.
Bur. Courageous Bedford, let us now persuade you.
Bed. Not to be gone from hence; for once I read
      That stout Pendragon in his litter sick   95
      Came to the field and vanquished his foes.
      Methinks I should revive the soldiers' hearts,
      Because I ever found them as myself.
Tal. Undaunted spirit in a dying breast!
      Then be it so: heavens keep old Bedford safe!   100
      And now no more ado, brave Burgundy,
      But gather we our forces out of hand,
      And set upon our boasting enemy.
                    Exeunt [all but Bedford and attendants].

          An alarum: excursions. Enter Sir JOHN FALSTAFF
                    and a Captain.

Cap. Whither away, John Falstaff, in such haste?
Fal. Whither away? To save myself by flight: 105
      We are like to have the overthrow again.
Cap. What! Will you fly, and leave Lord Talbot?

103. S.D.] *Cambridge, after Capell; Exit. | F.*   Falstaff] *F, Wilson (throughout);
Fastolfe| Theobald+edd.*   104. John] *This edn; Sir Iohn | F.*

loue which he had euer borne vnto
that citie for the stedfast faith and tried
loialtie at all times found in the citizens
there' (Hol., III. 1. 11).

    86. *regard*] (*a*) observe; (*b*) tend.
    89. *crazy*] decrepit, broken down.
    95–7. *Pendragon . . .*] Hol., *Hist Scot.*,
99. 1. 97, says that Uther Pendragon's
brother 'euen sicke as he was, caused
himselfe to be caried forth in a litter;
with whose presence his people were

so incouraged, that, incountring
with the Saxons, they wan the victorie'.
    97. *Methinks*] it seems to me.
    103. S.D. Falstaff] Hall, 149 ff. This
is still another duplication of Falstaff's
cowardice at Patay; cf. I. i. 105; I. iv.
34; and IV. i. 9 ff.
    104. *John*] the F 'Sir', which is extra-
metrical, may be attributed to the
scribe's habit of 'recollection'.

Fal.   Ay,
    All the Talbots in the world, to save my life.   *Exit.*
Cap. Cowardly knight! ill fortune follow thee!   *Exit.*

> *Retreat: excursions.* [LA] PUCELLE, ALENÇON *and*
>   CHARLES *fly.*

Bed. Now, quiet soul, depart when heaven please,   110
    For I have seen our enemies' overthrow.
    What is the trust or strength of foolish man?
    They that of late were daring with their scoffs
    Are glad and fain by flight to save themselves.
>   *Bedford dies, and is carried in by two in his chair.*

> *An alarum. Enter* TALBOT, BURGUNDY, *and the rest.*

Tal. Lost, and recover'd in a day again!   115
    This is a double honour, Burgundy:
    Let heavens have glory for this victory!
Bur. Warlike and martial Talbot, Burgundy
    Enshrines thee in his heart, and there erects
    Thy noble deeds as valour's monuments.   120
Tal. Thanks, gentle Duke. But where is Pucelle now?
    I think her old familiar is asleep.
    Now where's the Bastard's braves, and Charles his gleeks?
    What, all amort? Rouen hangs her head for grief
    That such a valiant company are fled.   125

107–8. Ay, / All . . . life.] *as Hanmer; as one line* / F.   114. glad] *F;* fled *conj.*
Vaughan.   117. Let] *Dyce²;* Yet *F.*   123. gleeks] *F* (glikes).

110–11.] cf. Luke, ii. 29 ff., 'Lord,   fain to save his life by flight.
now lettest thou thy servant depart in   *fain*] well pleased; cf. *2H6,* II. i. 8.
peace. . . For mine eyes have seen thy   117.] cf. *H5,* IV. viii. 111, after Agin-
salvation'.   court; a form of the *Te Deum.* For the
    112.] cf. Jer., xvii. 5, 'Cursed be the   F error, see Intro., p. xxii.
man that putteth his trust in man, and   121. *gentle*] noble.
that taketh flesh for his arme' (Noble).   122. *familiar*] attendant spirit = the
    114. *glad*] Vaughan says that the F   devil.
line is 'insufferable: what is "fain" but   123. *braves*] boasts or brags, so typi-
"glad"?' The line rightly means,   cal of the French.
'They have not only fled, but are well   *gleeks*] scoffs.
pleased to have fled'.   124. *amort*] downcast, dispirited; cf.
    fain . . . themselves] cf. *An Homily*   *Shr.,* IV. iii. 36, 'What, sweeting! all
against . . . Rebellion, 'David . . . was   amort?'

Now will we take some order in the town.
Placing therein some expert officers,
And then depart to Paris to the King,
For there young Henry with his nobles lie.
Bur. What wills Lord Talbot pleaseth Burgundy.   130
Tal. But yet, before we go, let's not forget
The noble Duke of Bedford, late deceas'd,
But see his exequies fulfill'd in Rouen:
A braver soldier never couched lance,
A gentler heart did never sway in court;   135
But kings and mightiest potentates must die,
For that's the end of human misery.   *Exeunt.*

SCENE III. [—*The plains near Rouen.*]

Enter CHARLES, [*the*] *Bastard* [*of* ORLEANS], ALENÇON,
[LA] PUCELLE[, *and Forces*].

Puc. Dismay not, Princes, at this accident,
Nor grieve that Rouen is so recovered:
Care is no cure, but rather corrosive,

Scene III

SCENE III] *F* (*Scæna Tertia.*).   *The . . . Rouen.*] *Capell* + *edd.; not in F.*   S.D.
the Bastard of Orleans] *edd.; Bastard* | *F.*   *La Pucelle*] *F* (*Pucell*).   *and Forces*]
Capell; not in F.

126. *take some order*] make some arrangements or necessary dispositions.
127. *expert*] experienced, proved, tried (L. *expertus*).
133. *exequies*] funeral rites.

Scene III

The Duke of Burgundy's alienation from the English was a process spread over a very long period, and is traced in at least six separate passages in Hall (147, 154, 160, 167–8, 173–4, 176). It was made possible by the extinction of the desire to avenge the murder of his father by the French king (Hall, 194), and was fed by resentment at the Duke of Bedford's treatment of him over

Orleans (Hall, 147), and at the release by the English of the Duke of Orleans. The persuasions of Charles are unhistorical. All this has been telescoped and transferred to a single feat of persuasion by Joan, whose part and powers it serves to amplify.

1. *Dismay*] occasionally used intransitively; *OED.*, 3.
accident] unforeseen happening.
3. *Care is no cure*] proverbial; cf. *LLL.*, v. ii. 28, 'past cure, past care'. Cf. Greene, *Pandosto*, 'in things past cure, care is a corrosive' (Hazlitt, *Shakespeare's Library*, Part I, vol. IV, p. 44); and Tilley, 133.
corrosive] acting like a sharp or bitter

For things that are not to be remedied.
Let frantic Talbot triumph for a while   5
And like a peacock sweep along his tail;
We'll pull his plumes and take away his train,
If Dauphin and the rest will be but rul'd.

Cha. We have been guided by thee hitherto,
And of thy cunning had no diffidence;   10
One sudden foil shall never breed distrust.

Bast. Search out thy wit for secret policies,
And we will make thee famous through the world.

Alen. We'll set thy statue in some holy place,
And have thee reverenc'd like a blessed saint.   15
Employ thee, then, sweet virgin, for our good.

Puc. Then thus it must be; this doth Joan devise:
By fair persuasions, mix'd with sugar'd words,
We will entice the Duke of Burgundy
To leave the Talbot and to follow us.   20

Cha. Ay, marry, sweeting, if we could do that,
France were no place for Henry's warriors;
Nor should that nation boast it so with us,
But be extirped from our provinces.

Alen. For ever should they be expuls'd from France,   25
And not have title of an earldom here.

Puc. Your honours shall perceive how I will work
To bring this matter to the wished end.

medicine. The sense is probably that of aggravating a disease, but may include a suggestion of purging or cleansing something incurable, like an ulcer; see *OED.*, A. 4.

5, 6. *frantic . . . peacock*] common imagery for a proud general and his forces; cf. *3H6*, v. i. 76, 'Where George of Clarence *sweeps* along'; *Troil.*, III. iii. 251–2. 'The peacock . . . has anger and lunacy imagery associated' with it (Armstrong, 85).

8. *be . . . rul'd*] take advice, follow instructions.

10. *cunning*] skill, with special reference to sorcery and magic; cf. II. i. 50.

diffidence] lack of confidence; distrust.

11. *foil*] defeat; cf. 'to foil'.

12. *wit*] intelligence.

secret policies] plans or stratagems intended to deceive and destroy, being secret from the enemy.

18. *sugar'd*] sweet; a common Elizabethan adjective when sugar was still a rarity, e.g. *2H6*, III. ii. 45; *R3*, III. i. 13; *FQ.*, III. vi. 25.

21. *sweeting*] maintains the amorous approach to Joan by Charles.

24. *extirped*] extirpated; a common Elizabethan form; cf. e.g. *F.Q.*, I. x. 25; *Meas.*, III. ii. 110.

25. *expuls'd*] alternative form of 'expelled'.

26. *title*] legal sense = ownership, dominion over.

Drum sounds afar off.

Hark! by the sound of drum you may perceive
Their powers are marching unto Paris-ward.   30

Here sound an English march.

There goes the Talbot, with his colours spread,
And all the troops of English after him.

French march.

Now in the rearward comes the Duke and his:
Fortune in favour makes him lag behind.
Summon a parley; we will talk with him.   35

Trumpets sound a parley.

Cha. A parley with the Duke of Burgundy!

[*Enter* BURGUNDY.]

Bur. Who craves a parley with the Burgundy?
Puc. The princely Charles of France, thy countryman.
Bur. What say'st thou, Charles? for I am marching hence.
Cha. Speak, Pucelle, and enchant him with thy words.   40
Puc. Brave Burgundy, undoubted hope of France,
      Stay, let thy humble handmaid speak to thee.
Bur. Speak on, but be not over-tedious.
Puc. Look on thy country, look on fertile France,

30. S.D.] *F; Here . . . march. Enter, and pass over at a distance, Talbot and his forces.* |
Capell+edd.   32. S.D.] *F; French march. Enter the Duke of Burgundy and forces.* |
Capell+edd.   36. S.D.] *This edn; not in F.*

30. *unto Paris-ward*] a normal Elizabethan tmesis—to-ward Paris. It sur-
vives in 'to windward'.
    S.D.] Editors make the English (and
Burgundians, 32) enter here and pass
over the stage. This is superfluous, and
improbable with the available cast;
they are merely described as they pass
within sight, but off-stage. Then Burgundy enters alone, after the *parley*.
    32. S.D. French March] very slow,
with time for lagging; cf. Dekker,
Seven Deadly Sins, 'He comes but slowly

as if hee trodde a French March'
(Hart).
    34. *in favour*] favourably disposed to
the French, who wished to talk to him
separately.
    40. *enchant*] a further suggestion of
the witch; cf. 'bewitch'd' (58).
    42. *thy humble handmaid*] cf. 1 Sam.,
xxv. 24, 'I pray thee, let thine hand-
maide speake to thee', from the story
of Abigail and Nabal (Noble).
    44. *Look on*] in the Biblical sense of
'look with pity on' (Wilson).

And see the cities and the towns defac'd 45
By wasting ruin of the cruel foe;
As looks the mother on her lowly babe
When death doth close his tender dying eyes,
See, see the pining malady of France;
Behold the wounds, the most unnatural wounds 50
Which thou thyself hast given her woeful breast.
O, turn thy edged sword another way;
Strike those that hurt, and hurt not those that help!
One drop of blood drawn from thy country's bosom
Should grieve thee more than streams of foreign gore. 55
Return thee therefore with a flood of tears,
And wash away thy country's stained spots.

Bur. [*Aside.*] Either she hath bewitch'd me with her words,
Or nature makes me suddenly relent.

Puc. Besides, all French and France exclaims on thee, 60
Doubting thy birth and lawful progeny.
Who join'st thou with but with a lordly nation
That will not trust thee but for profit's sake?
When Talbot hath set footing once in France,
And fashion'd thee that instrument of ill, 65
Who then but English Henry will be lord,
And thou be thrust out like a fugitive?
Call we to mind, and mark but this for proof:
Was not the Duke of Orleans thy foe?

---

48. tender dying] *Pope;* tender-dying *F.*   58, 78. S.D. *Aside.*] *This edn; not in F.*

---

45. *defac'd*] disfigured.

48. *tender dying*] dying young, in its tender years (his = its).

49. *pining*] causing to waste away.

malady of France] perhaps an oblique reference to venereal disease—the French evil; cf. *H5,* v. i. 87; and see *Sh. Bawdy,* 150.

50. *unnatural*] against natural kinship; against his own country.

57. *stained*] transferred epithet; the spots are stains on the reputation of his country.

59. *nature*] i.e. human nature; kinship and affection.

60. *exclaims on*] accuses loudly.

61. *doubting thy birth*] the obverse of

the standard text-book aspersions used in 'vituperation', as in York's attack on Margaret, *3H6,* I. iv. 119 ff. The historical facts are not relevant.

progeny] lineage, descent: *OED.,* 5; cf. v. iv. 38.

62 ff.] Hall, 176; referring to Burgundy's discovery that the English alliance curtailed his own power.

67. *fugitive*] (*a*) a deserter, or runaway to the other party (Hart); (*b*) a runaway slave, with no standing or rights.

69. *Orleans*] captured in 1415, and released by the English in 1440 (five years after Burgundy abandoned the English alliance). It was enough

And was he not in England prisoner? 70
But when they heard he was thine enemy
They set him free without his ransom paid,
In spite of Burgundy and all his friends.
See then, thou fight'st against thy countrymen,
And join'st with them will be thy slaughter-men. 75
Come, come, return; return, thou wandering lord;
Charles and the rest will take thee in their arms.
Bur. [*Aside.*] I am vanquished; these haughty words of hers
Have batter'd me like roaring cannon-shot
And made me almost yield upon my knees.— 80
Forgive me, country, and sweet countrymen!
And, lords, accept this hearty kind embrace.
My forces and my power of men are yours.
So farewell, Talbot; I'll no longer trust thee, 84
Puc. Done like a Frenchman! [*Aside.*] —turn and turn again.
Cha. Welcome, brave Duke! thy friendship makes us fresh.
Bast. And doth beget new courage in our breasts.
Alen. Pucelle hath bravely play'd her part in this,
And doth deserve a coronet of gold.
Cha. Now let us on, my lords, and join our powers, 90
And seek how we may prejudice the foe.   *Exeunt.*

85. S.D. *Aside.*] *Dyce; Capell (after Puc.); not in* F.

that he was an enemy of Burgundy.

72. *without his ransom paid*] L. construction=without paying his ransom; cf. I. i. 157, and see Abbott, 418.

75. *slaughter-men*] murderers; cf. *3H6*, I. iv. 169; *Tit.*, IV. iv. 58; etc.

76. *wandering*] the sense of L. *errare*; cf. Hall, 176, 'return to the path from which . . . he had straied and *erred*'.

78. *haughty*] high, lofty.

83. *power*] force, army.

85. *turn . . .*] an 'appeal to the audience' (Brooke); probably out of character for Joan, but representing the standard view of the French character; cf. 'a fickle, wavering nation' at IV. i. 138.

86. *makes . . . fresh*] invigorates (Wilson).

88. *bravely*] (*c*) courageously; (*b*) handsomely (Fr. *brave*).

91. *prejudice*] injure; *OED*. I. i.

SCENE IV. [—*Paris. The Palace.*]

Enter the KING, GLOUCESTER, WINCHESTER, YORK, SUFFOLK,
SOMERSET, WARWICK, EXETER: [VERNON *and* BASSET.]
To them, with his soldiers, TALBOT.

Tal. My gracious Prince, and honourable peers,
Hearing of your arrival in this realm,
I have awhile given truce unto my wars
To do my duty to my sovereign:
In sign whereof, this arm, that hath reclaim'd   5
To your obedience fifty fortresses,
Twelve cities, and seven walled towns of strength,
Beside five hundred prisoners of esteem,
Lets fall his sword before your Highness' feet;
And with submissive loyalty of heart   10
Ascribes the glory of his conquest got
First to my God, and next unto your Grace.   [*Kneels.*]
K. Hen. Is this the Talbot, uncle Gloucester,
That hath so long been resident in France?
Glou. Yes, if it please your Majesty, my liege.   15
K. Hen. Welcome, brave captain and victorious lord!

Scene IV

SCENE IV] (*Scœna Quarta.*).   Paris.] *Pope; not in* F.   *The Palace.*] *edd., after*
Capell; not in F.   S.D. *Vernon and Basset*] *Capell*+*edd.; not in* F.   12. S.D.]
edd.; not in F.   13. the] *Capell;* the Lord *F;* the fam'd *Rowe.*

The scene is almost entirely fictitious, and the usual liberties are taken with chronology. Henry was crowned in Paris in 1431; Talbot knighted in 1442.

The Vernon–Basset incident keeps alive the underlying 'Roses' quarrel and the fundamental internal division among the English.

S.D. Vernon, Basset] (Sir John) Vernon is mentioned in Hall, 229; (Peter) Basset as Henry V's Chamberlain (113). Both are fictiously attached to the contention of the nobles.

4. *duty*] in the feudal sense—homage; cf. III. i. 170. 'Talbot's speech in its reference to the places of God, the king, and himself in their due degrees carries with it the whole context of Hooker and the great Homily of obedience' (Tillyard, *EWP.*, 12).

5. *reclaim'd*] called back to obedience; also used as a legal term for reducing wild animals to domestication, *OED.*, I. 3.

6–8.] Hall, 170–1, lists a succession of towns, but gives no catalogue of numbers.

9, 11. *his*] its, referring to 'this arm'.

11. *Ascribes the glory . . .*] cf. Henry V after Agincourt; Ps., cxv. 1; and the Lord's Prayer, 'thine is the . . . glory'.

13. *the Talbot*] cf. II. iii. 15.

When I was young, as yet I am not old,
I do remember how my father said
A stouter champion never handled sword.
Long since we were resolved of your truth,   20
Your faithful service, and your toil in war;
Yet never have you tasted our reward,
Or been reguerdon'd with so much as thanks,
Because till now we never saw your face.
Therefore stand up; and for these good deserts   25
We here create you Earl of Shrewsbury;
And in our coronation take your place.

Sennet. Flourish. Exeunt all but Vernon and Basset.

Ver. Now, sir, to you that were so hot at sea,
Disgracing of these colours that I wear
In honour of my noble Lord of York,   30
Dar'st thou maintain the former words thou spak'st?
Bas. Yes, sir, as well as you dare patronage
The envious barking of your saucy tongue
Against my lord the Duke of Somerset.
Ver. Sirrah, thy lord I honour as he is.   35
Bas. Why, what is he? As good a man as York!
Ver. Hark ye, not so: in witness take ye that.   *Strikes him.*
Bas. Villain, thou knowest the law of arms is such
That whoso draws a sword, 'tis present death,
Or else this blow should broach thy dearest blood.   40
But I'll unto his Majesty, and crave

27. S.D. *Exeunt all but*] F (*Exeunt. Manet*).

17–18.] 'one of Shakespeare's pur-
poseful tamperings with dramatic
time. There is an advantage in making
the King appear older than he really
was without reminding the reader [or
spectator] that the whole long time
from infancy to maturity has elapsed
since the play began' (Brooke).
19. *champion*] warrior.
20. *resolved*] convinced; cf. *3H6*, II.
ii. 124.
22. *our*] the royal 'we'; cf. 24
23. *reguerdon'd*] rewarded.
28. *hot*] hot-tempered, angry.
32. *patronage*] defend; cf. III. i. 48.

33. *envious*] malicious, spiteful.
saucy] insolent.
35. *Sirrah*] contemptuous form of
'sir'.
37. *in witness*] The legal phraseology
of the lawyer's quarrel is continued,
the testing clause of wills and other
legal documents began 'In witness
whereof'.
38. *the law of arms*] Reed quotes
Blackstone, *Commentaries*, IV. 124, 'By
the ancient law . . . fighting in the
king's palace . . . was punished with
death'.
39. *present*] immediate.

I may have liberty to venge this wrong;
When thou shalt see I'll meet thee to thy cost.
Ver. Well, miscreant, I'll be there as soon as you;
And, after, meet you sooner than you would.   *Exeunt.*   45

ACT IV

SCENE I. [—*Paris. The Palace.*]

Enter [the] KING, GLOUCESTER, WINCHESTER, YORK,
SUFFOLK, SOMERSET, WARWICK, TALBOT, EXETER,
[the] GOVERNOR *[of Paris, and Others].*

Glou. Lord Bishop, set the crown upon his head.
Win. God save King Henry, of that name the sixth!
Glou. Now, Governor of Paris, take your oath,

[*Governor kneels.*]

That you elect no other king but him;

ACT IV

Scene 1

ACT IV SCENE I] F (*Actus Quartus. Scena Prima.*).
The Palace.] *Cambridge; not in F; A hall of state.* | *Capell.*
Exeter . . . Paris,] *Pope* (*subst.*)*; and Governor Exeter.* | *F.*
not in F.　　3. S.D.] *Capell; not in F.*

Paris.] *Pope; not in F.*
S.D. *the King*] F (*King*).
and Others.] *Cambridge;*

This Act, largely prepared in III. iii–
iv, is a remarkable tight unity, considering the scattered chronicle material. While devoted mainly to Talbot, it draws together many separate
threads. Talbot's heroism (and his
son's), which now reaches its climax,
is linked to the exposure of Falstaff's
cowardice. Falstaff is associated, by
the letter device, with the defection of
Burgundy, which Talbot is sent to
punish.

Against the single-minded patriotism of Talbot is shown the jarring discord of York and Somerset and their
followers. Henry remains ineffectual
in his simple adoption of the red rose,
and his equally simple promotion of
York to be Regent of France, and com-
mander of the infantry, while Somerset has the horse. Their jealousy, given
free scope by the impotence of Henry,
ensures the ruin of Talbot, while Lucy
and Exeter can only comment on the
inevitable disaster to him and to England.

To attain this unified effect, considerable liberties have been taken
with events and chronology. For example, it was Bedford who tore the
Garter from Falstaff; Vernon and
Basset are unhistorical here; Gloucester was in England, etc.; cf. Boswell-
Stone, 228.

The scene, like I. i and III. i, pre-
sents a twice-interrupted ceremony,
symbolic of the disintegration of
order.

1. *Bishop*] He was 'Henry bishop of
Winchester, and Cardinal of S. Eusebius' (Hall, 152).

2. *of that name the sixth*] a common
tag, in e.g. Hall, *Mirror*, etc.

4. *elect*] L. sense = choose, accept.

Esteem none friends but such as are his friends,   5
And none your foes but such as shall pretend
Malicious practices against his state:
This shall ye do, so help you righteous God!

[Exeunt Governor and his Train.]

Enter [Sir John] Falstaff.

Fal. My gracious sovereign, as I rode from Calais,
    To haste unto your coronation,   10
    A letter was deliver'd to my hands,
    Writ to your Grace from th' Duke of Burgundy.
Tal. Shame to the Duke of Burgundy and thee!
    I vow'd, base knight, when I did meet thee next,
    To tear the Garter from thy craven's leg, *[Plucks it off.]* 15
    Which I have done, because unworthily
    Thou wast installed in that high degree.
    Pardon me, princely Henry, and the rest:
    This dastard, at the battle of Patay,
    When but in all I was six thousand strong,   20
    And that the French were almost ten to one,
    Before we met or that a stroke was given,
    Like to a trusty squire did run away;
    In which assault we lost twelve hundred men;
    Myself and divers gentlemen beside   25
    Were there surpris'd and taken prisoners.
    Then judge, great lords, if I have done amiss,
    Or whether that such cowards ought to wear
    This ornament of knighthood, yea or no?

---

8. S.D. *Exeunt . . . Train.*] *Capell; not in F.*   *Falstaff*] *F, Dover Wilson; Fastolfe |
Theobald+edd.   14. thee] *F* (the).   15. S.D. *Plucks it off.*] *Capell; not in F.*
19. Patay] *Malone, conj. Capell; Poictiers | F.*

6. *pretend*] design, intend, purpose; cf. *Mac.*, II. iv. 24, 'What good could they pretend?'

9 ff.] Falstaff's treachery has already appeared at I. i. 105 ff.; I. iv. 34 ff.; III. ii. 104 ff.

14. *I vow'd*] Shakespeare transferred this incident from Bedford (dead in III. ii), in the interests of unity, and possibly on the hint (Hall, 150) that

Bedford restored the Garter 'against the mynd of the lorde Talbot'.

15, 19. *craven, dastard*] the exact opposite of the military virtues for which the Order of the Garter was awarded.

19. *Patay*] F has a scribal error.

22. *Before . . . or that*] see Abbott, 285, which compares the French use of 'que' instead of repeating 'si', 'quand', etc.

Glou. To say the truth, this fact was infamous, 30
    And ill-beseeming any common man,
    Much more a knight, a captain, and a leader.
Tal. When first this Order was ordain'd, my lords,
    Knights of the Garter were of noble birth,
    Valiant and virtuous, full of haughty courage, 35
    Such as were grown to credit by the wars;
    Not fearing death nor shrinking for distress,
    But always resolute in most extremes.
    He then that is not furnish'd in this sort
    Doth but usurp the sacred name of knight, 40
    Profaning this most honourable Order,
    And should, if I were worthy to be judge,
    Be quite degraded, like a hedge-born swain
    That doth presume to boast of gentle blood.
K. Hen. Stain to thy countrymen, thou hear'st thy doom! 45
    Be packing, therefore, thou that wast a knight;
    Henceforth we banish thee on pain of death.

    [*Exit Falstaff.*]

    And now, my Lord Protector, view the letter
    Sent from our uncle, Duke of Burgundy.
Glou. What means his Grace, that he hath chang'd his style?
    No more but plain and bluntly 'To the King'! 51
    Hath he forgot he is his sovereign?
    Or doth this churlish superscription

---

47. S.D.] *edd.; not in F.*   48. my] *edd.; not in F.*

30. *fact*] deed (L. *factum* = thing done), especially evil.

31. *common man*] one of the common people, without rank.

32. *captain*] leader, chief.

35. *haughty*] lofty, high.
courage] spirit, disposition.

36. *were grown to credit*] had risen to honourable reputation.

37. *for*] in face of; on account of.
distress] hardship; difficulty.

38. *most extremes*] greatest extremities.

39. *furnish'd in this sort*] so endowed (Brooke).

43. *degraded*] reduced in rank or degree.

hedge-born swain] person of very low birth; cf. *Mac.*, IV. i. 31; *2H6*, IV. ii. 52, where Cade was 'born under a hedge'. 'Swain' has no trace of the later poetic diction.

44. *gentle*] noble.

46. *Be packing*] be off—a rude dismissal.

47.] Wilson compares *2H4*, v. v. 64 (to Falstaff, *i.e.* Oldcastle), 'I banish thee on pain of death'.

48. *view*] see, in a wider sense than now.

50. *style*] designation, form of address.

53. *churlish*] rude, blunt.
superscription] address of a letter.

Pretend some alteration in good-will?
What's here? [*Reads.*] 'I have, upon especial cause,   55
Mov'd with compassion of my country's wrack,
Together with the pitiful complaints
Of such as your oppression feeds upon,
Forsaken your pernicious faction
And join'd with Charles, the rightful King of France.'
O monstrous treachery! Can this be so—   61
That in alliance, amity, and oaths,
There should be found such false dissembling guile?

K. Hen. What! doth my uncle Burgundy revolt?

Glou. He doth, my lord, and is become your foe.   65

K. Hen. Is that the worst this letter doth contain?

Glou. It is the worst, and all, my lord, he writes.

K. Hen. Why then Lord Talbot there shall talk with him
And give him chastisement for this abuse.
My lord, how say you, are you not content?   70

Tal. Content, my liege! Yes, but that I am prevented,
I should have begg'd I might have been employ'd.

K. Hen. Then gather strength and march unto him straight;
Let him perceive how ill we brook his treason,
And what offence it is to flout his friends.   75

Tal. I go, my lord, in heart desiring still
You may behold confusion of your foes.   [*Exit.*]

Enter VERNON *and* BASSET.

Ver. Grant me the combat, gracious sovereign.

Bas. And me, my lord, grant me the combat too.

---

54. Pretend] *F;* Portend *Rowe*³.   55. S.D. Reads.] *Rowe; not in F.*   55–60. 'I
have . . . France.'] *F (ital.).*   70. My lord, how say you, are] *Pope;* How say
you (my Lord) are *F.*   77. S.D.] *Rowe; not in F.*

---

54. *Pretend*] indicate, intend; cf. 6
above.
56. *wrack*] wreck, ruin.
64. *revolt*] rebel, with the idea of
turning from one side to the other; cf.
Joan's comment at III. iii. 85, 'turn,
and turn again'.
69. *abuse*] common Elizabethan
sense = deception.
71. *prevented*] anticipated (L. *pre* +

venire]; cf. Liturgy, 'Prevent us, O
Lord, in all our doings' (Steevens).
73. *strength*] military forces.
74. *brook*] endure, suffer.
75. *offence*] harm, wrong.
flout] mock.
76. *still*] always.
77. *confusion*] destruction.
78. *the combat*] permission to fight a
duel.

York. This is my servant: hear him, noble Prince.   80
Som. And this is mine: sweet Henry, favour him.
K. Hen. Be patient, lords, and give them leave to speak.
    Say, gentlemen, what makes you thus exclaim,
    And wherefore crave you combat, or with whom?
Ver. With him, my lord, for he hath done me wrong.   85
Bas. And I with him, for he hath done me wrong.
K. Hen. What is that wrong whereof you both complain?
    First let me know, and then I'll answer you.
Bas. Crossing the sea from England into France,
    This fellow here, with envious carping tongue,   90
    Upbraided me about the rose I wear,
    Saying the sanguine colour of the leaves
    Did represent my master's blushing cheeks
    When stubbornly he did repugn the truth
    About a certain question in the law,   95
    Argu'd betwixt the Duke of York and him;
    With other vile and ignominious terms:
    In confutation of which rude approach,
    And in defence of my lord's worthiness,
    I crave the benefit of law of arms.   100
Ver. And that is my petition, noble lord;
    For though he seem with forged quaint conceit
    To set a gloss upon his bold intent,
    Yet know, my lord, I was provok'd by him,
    And he first took exceptions at this badge,   105
    Pronouncing that the paleness of this flower
    Bewray'd the faintness of my master's heart.
York. Will not this malice, Somerset, be left?

---

80. *servant*] follower, retainer.

83. *exclaim*] shout or cry out.

90. *envious*] malicious.

92. *sanguine*] in the literal sense—blood-red.

leaves] petals—a popular use, *OED.*, I. 2.

94. *repugn*] reject, repel, oppose. The legal sense persists in 'repugnant'.

95. *a certain question*] cf. II. iv and II. v. 45 ff.; the question of succession, involving the attainder of York's father; cf. 'worthiness' (99).

98. *confutation*] legal term—refutation.

rude] unlearned, ignorant; not necessarily unmannerly.

100. *benefit*] privilege (legal).

102. *quaint conceit*] artful invention of fancy.

103. *set a gloss upon*] give a fair outward appearance to.

105. *took exceptions at*] disapproved of; found fault with.

107. *Bewray'd*] alternative form of 'betrayed'.

Som. Your private grudge, my Lord of York, will out,
    Though ne'er so cunningly you smother it.   110
K. Hen. Good Lord, what madness rules in brainsick men,
    When for so slight and frivolous a cause
    Such factious emulations shall arise!
    Good cousins both, of York and Somerset,
    Quiet yourselves, I pray, and be at peace.   115
York. Let this dissension first be tried by fight,
    And then your Highness shall command a peace.
Som. The quarrel toucheth none but us alone;
    Betwixt ourselves let us decide it then.
York. There is my pledge; accept it, Somerset.   120
Ver. Nay, let it rest where it began at first.
Bas. Confirm it so, mine honourable lord.
Glou. Confirm it so! Confounded be your strife!
    And perish ye, with your audacious prate!
    Presumptuous vassals, are you not asham'd   125
    With this immodest clamorous outrage
    To trouble and disturb the King and us?
    And you, my lords, methinks you do not well
    To bear with their perverse objections,
    Much less to take occasion from their mouths   130
    To raise a mutiny betwixt yourselves:
    Let me persuade you take a better course.
Exe. It grieves his Highness; good my lords, be friends.
K. Hen. Come hither, you that would be combatants:
    Henceforth I charge you, as you love our favour,   135
    Quite to forget this quarrel, and the cause.
    And you, my lords, remember where we are:
    In France, amongst a fickle wavering nation;

---

109. *grudge*] enmity.

110. *cunningly*] cleverly.

111. *brainsick*] foolish.

112. *frivolous*] legal—of no material significance.

113. *emulations*] jealous rivalries.

114. *cousins*] used loosely, of near relatives.

118. *toucheth*] concerns.

120. *pledge*] gage (in a duel), usually a glove thrown down.

121. *rest*] remain (Fr. *rester*).

123. *Confounded*] destroyed, wiped out.

126. *immodest*] not modest; arrogant.

128. *methinks*] it seems to me.

129. *objections*] accusations or criminal charges that they throw (L. *obiicere*) in one another's teeth.

131. *mutiny*] strife, riot.

138. *a fickle wavering nation*] cf. Hall, 116, 'The Parisians whiche euer like the wethercocke be variable and inconstant'.

If they perceive dissension in our looks,
And that within ourselves we disagree,   140
How will their grudging stomachs be provok'd
To wilful disobedience, and rebel!
Beside, what infamy will there arise
When foreign princes shall be certified
That for a toy, a thing of no regard,   145
King Henry's peers and chief nobility
Destroy'd themselves, and lost the realm of France!
O, think upon the conquest of my father,
My tender years, and let us not forgo
That for a trifle that was bought with blood!   150
Let me be umpire in this doubtful strife.
I see no reason if I wear this rose, [*Putting on a red rose.*]
That any one should therefore be suspicious
I more incline to Somerset than York:
Both are my kinsmen, and I love them both;   155
As well may they upbraid me with my crown
Because, forsooth, the King of Scots is crown'd.
But your discretions better can persuade
Than I am able to instruct or teach;
And therefore, as we hither came in peace,   160
So let us still continue peace and love.
Cousin of York, we institute your Grace
To be our Regent in the parts of France:
And, good my Lord of Somerset, unite

152. S.D.] *Johnson; not in F.*   163. the] *This edn; these F.*

139–42.] Note the explicit union of the two themes—English dissension and French revolt.

141. *grudging stomachs*] resentful tempers or pride.

provok'd] quibbling on the medical sense, with 'within', 'stomachs', and 'rebel' (Wilson).

142. *wilful disobedience, and rebel*] a reference to the Homily; cf. III. iv. 4, and n.

143. *infamy*] ill report or reputation (L. *infamia*).

144. *certified*] made certain (L. *certiorem facere*); informed.

145. *toy*] trifle.

regard] consequence, importance.

149. *forgo*] forfeit, lose.

150. *That*] demonstrative pronoun, object of 'forgo'.

151. *doubtful*] of which the result is doubtful.

154. *incline to*] lean towards the side of; favour.

161. *still*] always.

162 ff.] Hall, 179, for York's Regency. It was characteristic of Henry's lack of worldly wisdom to expect York to 'unite' his forces with Somerset's.

163. *the parts*] cf. *2H6*, I. i. 67; the regions, *OED.*, III. 13. The scribe or compositor probably sophisticated.

Your troops of horsemen with his bands of foot;   165
And like true subjects, sons of your progenitors,
Go cheerfully together and digest
Your angry choler on your enemies.
Ourself, my Lord Protector, and the rest,
After some respite will return to Calais;   170
From thence to England, where I hope ere long
To be presented by your victories
With Charles, Alençon, and that traiterous rout.

Flourish. Exeunt all but York, Warwick,
Exeter [and] Vernon.

War. My Lord of York, I promise you the King
Prettily, methought, did play the orator.   175
York. And so he did; but yet I like it not,
In that he wears the badge of Somerset.
War. Tush, that was but his fancy; blame him not;
I dare presume, sweet Prince, he thought no harm.
York. And if I wist he did—but let it rest;   180
Other affairs must now be managed. *Exeunt all but Exeter.*
Exe. Well didst thou, Richard, to suppress thy voice;
For, had the passions of thy heart burst out,
I fear we should have seen decipher'd there
More rancorous spite, more furious raging broils,   185
Than yet can be imagin'd or suppos'd.
But howsoe'er, no simple man that sees
This jarring discord of nobility,
This shouldering of each other in the Court,
This factious bandying of their favourites,   190

---

173. S.D. *Flourish.*] *edd.*; *F (after 181).*   *and*] *edd.*; *not in F.*   180. wist] *Capell;*
wish *F.*   181. S.D. *Exeunt all but*] *edd.*; *Exeunt. Flourish. Manet | F.*

167–8 *digest.* | *Your . . . choler*] distri-
bute, disperse, dissipate your anger.
170. *respite*] interval.
173. *rout*] disorderly assembly or
company; rabble.
S.D.] The F *Flourish,* which marks
a royal exit, belongs after 181; see
Intro., p. xvii.
175. *methought*] it seemed to me.
180.] York follows Mortimer's advice (II. v. 101; cf. 118–19) to be silent
and politic.

And if I wist] If I knew for certain.
Cf. *Ant.,* I. iii. 11, for the same misprint
in F.
183. *passions*] sorrowful or powerful
emotions.
184. *decipher'd*] discovered, disclosed.
187. *simple*] the opposite of 'gentle'
=ordinary, common.
188. *jarring discord*] a musical metaphor used also at III. i. 106, 194.
190. *bandying*] contending in words.
favourites] favourers, supporters.

But sees it doth presage some ill event.
'Tis much when sceptres are in children's hands;
But more when envy breeds unkind division:
There comes the ruin, there begins confusion.   *Exit.*

[SCENE II.—] *Before Bordeaux.*

Enter TALBOT, *with trump and drum.*

Tal.   Go to the gates of Bordeaux, trumpeter;
Summon their general unto the wall.

[*Trumpet*] *sounds. Enter General* [*and Others*] *aloft.*

English John Talbot, captains, calls you forth,
Servant in arms to Harry King of England;
And thus he would: Open your city gates,   5
Be humble to us, call my sovereign yours
And do him homage as obedient subjects,
And I'll withdraw me and my bloody power;
But if you frown upon this proffer'd peace,
You tempt the fury of my three attendants,   10

---

191. sees] *This edn, conj. H. Brooks;* that *F;* at *conj. Vaughan.*

Scene II

SCENE II] *Capell; not in F.*   S.D. *Before . . . drum.*] *F* (*Enter Talbot with Trumpe and Drumme, before Burdeaux.*).   2. S.D. *Trumpet sounds.*] *F* (*Sounds.*).   *and Others*] *Malone; not in F.*   3. calls] *F* (call).

191. *sees*] The F makes no sense as it stands, possibly owing to a slip in repeating the necessary link from 187: of the phrase 'sees that', 'sees' should have been repeated, but 'that' was repeated instead.

event] result, outcome (L. *eventus*).

192. *much*] serious, wonderful.

192.] cf. *2H6*, I. i. 246, 'Nor hold the sceptre in his childish fist'; and 'Woe to that Land that's govern'd by a Childe', *R3*, II. iii. 11.

193. *envy*] enmity, malice.

unkind] unnatural; against the law of 'kind' or natural relation.

division] disunity.

194. *confusion*] chaos, destruction.

Scene II

These events are of 1451, i.e. in the middle of those of *2H6*, and twenty years after the burning of Joan. The inhabitants of Gascony, and especially of Bordeaux, appealed to England for help if they were to remain loyal.

2. S.D. *aloft*] i.e. in the gallery or upper stage.

3. *captains*] chiefs, leaders.

5. *would*] wishes, desires; Abbott, 329.

8. *bloody*] able or liable to cause bloodshed.

10 ff. three attendants] Hall, 85 (Henry V, after the siege of Rouen), speaks of war's 'iii handmaides . . .

Lean Famine, quartering Steel, and climbing Fire,
Who in a moment even with the earth
Shall lay your stately and air-braving towers,
If you forsake the offer of their love.
Gen. Thou ominous and fearful owl of death,   15
Our nation's terror and their bloody scourge!
The period of thy tyranny approacheth.
On us thou canst not enter but by death;
For, I protest, we are well fortified,
And strong enough to issue out and fight.   20
If thou retire, the Dauphin, well appointed,
Stands with the snares of war to tangle thee;
On either hand thee there are squadrons pitch'd
To wall thee from the liberty of flight;
And no way canst thou turn thee for redress   25
But Death doth front thee with apparent spoil,
And pale Destruction meets thee in the face.
Ten thousand French have ta'en the sacrament
To rive their dangerous artillery

---

14. their] *F;* our *Hanmer;* his *conj. Dover Wilson.*   15. *Gen.*] *F (Cap.).*   29. rive]
F; rove *Dover Wilson, conj. Hart.*

---

bloud, fyre and famine'; cf. Hall, 165
(Henry VI, 1431–2), 'nothing was
spared, by the crueltie of Mars: whiche
by fire, bloud, or famyne, might be
catched or destroied'; cf. *H5*, 1 Prol.,
5–8, 'Then should the warlike Harry
. . . / Assume the port of *Mars*, and at
his heeles / . . . should Famine, Sword,
and Fire, / Crouch for employment'.
   11. *quartering*] Elizabethan practice
after hanging, and often in war.
   12–13. *even . . . lay*] level; cf. Luke,
xix. 44, 'lay thee even with the
ground'.
   13. *air-braving*] defying the heavens.
   14. *forsake*] refuse, decline.
   15. *owl of death*] cf. *R3*, IV. iv. 509;
F.Q., I. v. 30, 'The messenger of death,
the ghastly owle'; cf. Ovid, *Metam.*,
x. 521–2.
   16. *terror . . . scourge*] cf. I. ii. 129; I. iv.
41; II. iii. 14–16; and Virgil, *Aeneid*,
viii. 703, 'sanguineo . . . flagello', used
of Bellona, goddess of war.

17. *period*] end.
   21. *appointed*] equipped.
   23. *pitch'd*] set in battle order.
   25. *redress*] aid, relief.
   26. *front*] face (L. *frons* = forehead).
   apparent spoil] destruction in sight
(Hart).
   spoil] capture of the quarry, in hunt-
ing, and division of rewards to the
hounds, (hence) slaughter, massacre
(Onions); cf. snares (22), and the
'deer' simile below (45 ff.).
   27. *pale Destruction*] cf. Death, 26;
and Rev., vi. 8, 'a pale horse . . . Death
. . . to kill with sword, and with hunger,
and with death'.
   28. *ta'en the sacrament*] a way of making
a solemn public asseveration (Hart).
   29. *rive*] 'means only to *fire* their artillery. To *rive* is to *burst*; and a cannon,
when fired, has so much the appearance of bursting, that, in the language
of poetry, it may be well said to burst'
(Mason).

Upon no Christian soul but English Talbot.　　　30
Lo, there thou stand'st a breathing valiant man
Of an invincible unconquer'd spirit:
This is the latest glory of thy praise,
That I, thy enemy, due thee withal;
For ere the glass, that now begins to run,　　　35
Finish the process of his sandy hour,
These eyes, that see thee now well coloured,
Shall see thee wither'd, bloody, pale and dead.

Drum afar off.

Hark! hark! the Dauphin's drum, a warning bell,
Sings heavy music to thy timorous soul,　　　40
And mine shall ring thy dire departure out.

Exeunt [General, etc.].

Tal. He fables not; I hear the enemy.
　　Out, some light horsemen, and peruse their wings.
　　O, negligent and heedless discipline!
　　How are we park'd and bounded in a pale—　　　45
　　A little herd of England's timorous deer,
　　Maz'd with a yelping kennel of French curs!
　　If we be English deer, be then in blood;
　　Not rascal-like to fall down with a pinch,
　　But rather, moody-mad and desperate stags,　　　50
　　Turn on the bloody hounds with heads of steel

---

41. S.D.] *Malone; Exit. | F.*　　50. moody-mad and] *Capell;* moodie mad: And *F.*

34. *due*] endue, grace.

35. *glass*] the sandy hour-glass, *Mer. V.*, I. i. 25.

39. *warning-bell*] a bell for giving alarms of fire or invasion, *OED.*, 12.

40. *heavy*] serious, solemn (L. *gravis*).

41. *departure*] death.

43. *peruse*] reconnoitre.

wings] flanks of the enemy forces.

44. *discipline*] training in, or handling of, military affairs.

45 ff. *park'd . . . pale . . . deer*] the imagery was possibly suggested by 'snare' (22), 'spoil' (26), 'bloody, pale' (38); and is expanded through word-play on 'blood', 'pale', 'colour(s)', and 'deer'.

45. *park'd . . . pale*] enclosed, as in a park, or fenced and 'paled' circumference; cf. Hall, 229, 'a subtile labirynth, in the which he and hys people were enclosed'.

47. *Maz'd*] bewildered, confused; cf. 'labirynth' in n. above.

48. *in blood*] in perfect condition or vigour; cf. *LLL.*, IV. ii. 4.

49. *rascal*] (*a*) a lean, worthless deer; (*b*) a rogue, worthless character.

pinch] a slight bite (of a dog); cf. *3H6*, II. i. 16; a recognized huntsman's term, like those above.

50. *moody-mad*] furious with anger.

51. *heads of steel*] i.e. horns like spears or swords.

And make the cowards stand aloof at bay:
Sell every man his life as dear as mine,
And they shall find dear deer of us, my friends.
God and Saint George, Talbot and England's right,   55
Prosper our colours in this dangerous fight!   [*Exeunt.*]

[SCENE III.—*Plains in Gascony.*]

Enter a Messenger that meets YORK. *Enter* YORK *with trumpet,
and many Soldiers.*

York. Are not the speedy scouts return'd again
     That dogg'd the mighty army of the Dauphin?
Mess. They are return'd, my lord, and give it out
     That he is march'd to Bordeaux with his power
     To fight with Talbot; as he march'd along,   5
     By your espials were discovered
     Two mightier troops than that the Dauphin led,
     Which join'd with him and made their march for
          Bordeaux.   [*Exit.*]
York. A plague upon that villain Somerset
     That thus delays my promised supply   10
     Of horsemen that were levied for this siege!
     Renowned Talbot doth expect my aid,

56. S.D. *Exeunt.*] *edd.; not in* F.

Scene III

SCENE III] *Capell; not in* F.   *Plains in Gascony.*] *Capell; not in* F.   5. Talbot;
as . . . along,] *F2; Talbot* as . . . along. F.   8. S.D. *Exit.*] *This edn; not in* F.

56. *colours*] sums up the imagery of 'blood', 'pale', and the implied idea of colour.

Scene III

This scene, which properly includes sc. iii and sc. iv, but which F and editors treat as two, is really a carefully symmetrical study of the desertion of Talbot by the rivals York and Somerset, interviewed in turn by the messenger Lucy, who here assumes Exeter's rôle as chorus. The interviews are fictitious, and introduced for structure and unity, and to emphasize

the internal dissension of the English. They are interleaved between Talbot's peril and his fate.

S.D. *many*] indefinite, suggesting the author's hand; cf. the F lack of an *Exit.* for the messenger at 8.

3. *give it out*] assert, declare.

4. *power*] army, forces.

6. *espials*] spies.

9. *that villain Somerset*] Henry's co-operative arrangement (IV. i. 162–8) has resulted only in greater enmity between Somerset and York.

10. *supply*] aid, reinforcements.

And I am louted by a traitor villain
And cannot help the noble chevalier.
God comfort him in this necessity!　　15
If he miscarry, farewell wars in France.

Enter [Sir WILLIAM LUCY].

Lucy. Thou princely leader of our English strength,
　　Never so needful on the earth of France,
　　Spur to the rescue of the noble Talbot,
　　Who now is girdled with a waist of iron,　　20
　　And hemm'd about with grim destruction.
　　To Bordeaux, warlike Duke! to Bordeaux, York!
　　Else farewell, Talbot, France, and England's honour.
York. O God, that Somerset, who in proud heart
　　Doth stop my cornets, were in Talbot's place!　　25
　　So should we save a valiant gentleman
　　By forfeiting a traitor and a coward.
　　Mad ire and wrathful fury makes me weep
　　That thus we die while remiss traitors sleep.
Lucy. O, send some succour to the distress'd lord!　　30
York. He dies, we lose; I break my warlike word;
　　We mourn, France smiles; we lose, they daily get—
　　All long of this vile traitor Somerset.
Lucy. Then God take mercy on brave Talbot's soul,
　　And on his son, young John, who two hours since　　35

16. S.D.] *Theobald; Enter another Messenger. | F.*　　17. *Lucy.*] *Theobald; 2 Mes. | F.*
20. waist] *F* (waste).　　30. *Lucy.*] *Theobald (throughout); Mes. | F.*

13. *louted*] generally explained as 'mocked', 'made a lout or fool of'; but Hilda M. Hulme, *English Studies*, XXXIX (April 1958), 51–2, suggests that it means equally, if not primarily, 'delayed', confirming from 'delay' (46), 'sleeping neglection' (49), etc. = 'sneaking inactivity'. But Hall, 8, has 'left, lowted, and forsaken'.

　　traitor] cf. 27, 29, 33; ironical, coming from the newly reinstated York.

　　16. *miscarry*] come to harm or destruction.

　　S.D.] see Intro., p. xvii. The substitution for Lucy of a Messenger is indicated by the address to Lucy by name at 43; cf. also below at iv. S.D., 10, and 12.

　　20. *girdled . . . waist*] cf. *John*, II. i. 217; *Ado*, IV. i. 150. The pun on waste, waist is very common.

　　25. *cornets*] companies of cavalry—from the standard, which was originally a horn-shaped pennon, attached to a lance (Rothery, 68).

　　28. *makes*] for the singular form after two singular subjects, see Abbott, 336.

　　29. *remiss*] negligent, careless.

　　30. *distress'd*] in difficulties.

　　33. *long of*] on account of; cf. 46.

　　35. *who*] for *whom*; see Abbott, 274.

I met in travel toward his warlike father.
This seven years did not Talbot see his son;
And now they meet where both their lives are done.

York. Alas, what joy shall noble Talbot have
To bid his young son welcome to his grave?   40
Away, vexation almost stops my breath,
That sunder'd friends greet in the hour of death.
Lucy, farewell; no more my fortune can
But curse the cause I cannot aid the man.
Maine, Blois, Poictiers, and Tours, are won away,   45
Long all of Somerset and his delay.

Exit [York, with his Soldiers].

Lucy. Thus, while the vulture of sedition
Feeds in the bosom of such great commanders,
Sleeping neglection doth betray to loss
The conquest of our scarce-cold conqueror,   50
That ever-living man of memory,
Henry the Fifth. Whiles they each other cross,
Lives, honours, lands, and all, hurry to loss.

[SCENE IV.—*The same.*]

Enter SOMERSET, *with his Army* [, *a Captain of* TALBOT'S
with him].

Som. It is too late; I cannot send them now:

---

46. S.D.] *Hart, Collier; Exit | F.*   49. loss] *Pope;* losse: *F.*

[*Scene* IV]

SCENE IV] *Capell + edd.; Scene iii continued | conj. this edn.*

---

37. *seven*] a round figure for a long period, to emphasize the coming tragedy of separation.

41. *vexation*] much stronger than now=affliction, anguish.

42. *in the hour of death*] from the Litany; cf. iv. 18 below.

43. *can*] absolute use = is able to do.

44. *the cause*] him who is the cause that.

47–8. *vulture . . . | Feeds*] a metaphor from Prometheus and Tityus; cf. III. i. 72; typical Tudor imagery for civil dissension.

50–2.] Henry V and his exploits are a constant point of reference in this and other history plays. They contrast with the civil wars and the loss of France a time when England was united and victorious; cf. I. i. I ff.

51. *ever-living man of memory*] transferred epithet=man of ever-living memory.

[*Scene* IV]

S.D.] see Intro., p. xvii. Lucy does not leave the stage and return at II, but remains on stage, aside. The fol-

This expedition was by York and Talbot
Too rashly plotted: all our general force
Might with a sally of the very town
Be buckled with: the over-daring Talbot   5
Hath sullied all his gloss of former honour
By this unheedful, desperate, wild adventure:
York set him on to fight and die in shame
That, Talbot dead, great York might bear the name.

Cap. Here is Sir William Lucy, who with me   10
Set from our o'ermatch'd forces forth for aid.

Som. How now, Sir William! whither were you sent?

Lucy. Whither, my lord! From bought and sold Lord
        Talbot,
Who, ring'd about with bold adversity,
Cries out for noble York and Somerset   15
To beat assailing Death from his weak legions;
And whiles the honourable captain there
Drops bloody sweat from his war-wearied limbs,
And, in advantage lingering, looks for rescue,
You, his false hopes, the trust of England's honour,   20

---

11. aid.] *F, Dover Wilson;* aid. / *Enter Sir William Lucy.* / *Theobald+edd.*   18.
legions] *Rowe;* Regions *F.*

---

lowing lines of Somerset (1–9) are
intended to balance those of York at
iii. 9–16.

4. *the very town*] 'the mere garrison,
unsupported by the relieving armies'
(Brooke).

5. *buckled with*] encountered, tackled.

6. *sullied . . . gloss*] a frequent Shakespearean 'clothes' metaphor, no doubt
suggested by 'sally' above; cf. *Ham.*, I.
ii. 129, etc.

7. *unheedful*] not taking due heed or
care.

12.] see n. to S.D. above.

13. *Whither, my lord!*] 'Lucy impa-
siently echoes the question, which he
tcorns to answer. His concern is with
the person from whom, not the one to
whom, he is sent' (Brooke).

bought and sold] a common expression
= betrayed (cf. 39), with an allusion
to Judas, e.g. Luke, xxii. 44–8; cf. *R3*,
v. iii. 305; *John*, v. iv. 10; etc. The

imagery of the passage (cf. 15, 16, 18,
21, 25) is drawn from the betrayal, the
agony of Gethsemane, and the Crucifixion.

14. *ring'd about*] encircled; cf. sc. iii,
'wall'd', 'hemm'd about', 'bounded',
etc.

16. *legions*] The emendation is possibly corroborated from the imagery
of Gethsemane (Matt., xxvi. 53),
though it does not imply that Talbot
had large forces.

18. *bloody sweat*] from the Litany; cf.
Luke, xx. 44, 'His sweat was like
droppes of blood'; and notes at iii. 42
and 13 above.

19. *in advantage lingering*] 'Protract-
ing his resistance by the advantage of
a strong post' (Johnson); 'or perhaps,
endeavouring by every means that he
can, with advantage to himself, to
linger out the action' (Malone).

20. *trust*] trustee; cf. *Tit.*, I. i. 181.

Keep off aloof with worthless emulation.
Let not your private discord keep away
The levied succours that should lend him aid,
While he, renowned noble gentleman,
Yield up his life unto a world of odds.   25
Orleans the Bastard, Charles, Burgundy,
Alençon, Reignier, compass him about,
And Talbot perisheth by your default.

Som. York set him on; York should have sent him aid.

Lucy. And York as fast upon your Grace exclaims,   30
Swearing that you withhold his levied horse,
Collected for this expedition.

Som. York lies; he might have sent and had the horse:
I owe him little duty, and less love,
And take foul scorn to fawn on him by sending.   35

Lucy. The fraud of England, not the force of France,
Hath now entrapp'd the noble-minded Talbot:
Never to England shall he bear his life,
But dies betray'd to fortune by your strife.

Som. Come, go; I will dispatch the horsemen straight: 40
Within six hours they will be at his side.

Lucy. Too late comes rescue: he is ta'en or slain,
For fly he could not if he would have fled;
And fly would Talbot never though he might.

Som. If he be dead, brave Talbot, then, adieu!   45

Lucy. His fame lives in the world, his shame in you.   *Exeunt.*

---

27. Reignier] *F (Reignard).*   31. horse] *Hanmer, conj. Theobald;* hoast *F.*
41. side] *This edn;* ayde *F.*

21. *worthless emulation*] 'mean, un-worthy rivalry; merely rivalry, not a struggle for superior exellence'c (John-son). The phrase continues the refer-ence to the Last Supper, through the conduct of the Disciples.
22. *private*] personal.
discord] disagreement.
25. *Yield*] This is 'subjunctive after "While"' (Wilson).
a world of] immense; cf. II. ii. 48 —a common Shakespearean expres-sion.
28. *default*] shortcoming.
29. *set him on*] incited him.

30. *upon . . . exclaims*] accuses loudly.
31. *his levied horse*] for the 'horse', cf. IV. i. 165; IV. iii. 10–11; and 33 and 40 below.
35. *take foul scorn*] passive of the common expression 'to think scorn'.
36. *fraud . . . force*] cf. *3H6*, IV. iv. 33; a standard collocation.
41. *side*] F 'at his *ayde*' is unidiomatic and highly improbable, and 'ayde' derives partly from similarity with 'syde' and partly from association with 'ayde' in 11, 23, and 29. Cf. also I. i. 95, 'to his side'; and see Intro., p. xxi.
46. *fame*] L. *fama* = reputation.

[SCENE V.—*The English camp near Bordeaux.*]

Enter TALBOT *and his Son.*

Tal. O young John Talbot, I did send for thee
        To tutor thee in stratagems of war,
        That Talbot's name might be in thee reviv'd,
        When sapless age and weak unable limbs
        Should bring thy father to his drooping chair.   5
        But—O malignant and ill-boding stars!—
        Now thou art come unto a feast of death,
        A terrible and unavoided danger;
        Therefore, dear boy, mount on my swiftest horse,
        And I'll direct thee how thou shalt escape   10
        By sudden flight. Come, dally not, be gone.
John. Is my name Talbot? and am I your son?
        And shall I fly? O, if you love my mother,
        Dishonour not her honourable name,
        To make a bastard and a slave of me!   15
        The world will say, he is not Talbot's blood
        That basely fled when noble Talbot stood.
Tal. Fly, to revenge my death if I be slain.
John. He that flies so will ne'er return again.
Tal. If we both stay, we both are sure to die.   20
John. Then let me stay; and, father, do you fly.
        Your loss is great, so your regard should be;
        My worth unknown, no loss is known in me.
        Upon my death the French can little boast;

Scene v

SCENE V] *Capell; not in F.*   The English . . . Bordeaux.] *Malone; not in F.*

The age of Talbot's son is deliberately lowered (Hall, 229), and the
style deliberately made more formal
(cf. the rhymed couplets, stichomy-
thia, and word-patterns) as fitting the
more poetic emotion and treatment.

4–5. *sapless . . . drooping chair*] cf. II. v.
12, 'That droops his sapless branches
to the ground'; and *2H6*, v. ii. 48, 'in
thy reverence, and thy chairdays'.

6. *malignant*] of evil or baneful influence.

ill-boding] inauspicious.

7. *a feast of death*] 'a field where death
will be feasted with slaughter' (Johnson).

8. *unavoided*] unavoidable, inevitable; cf. *R2*, II. i. 268; *R3*, IV. iv. 217.

22, 23. *is* . . . / . . . *is*] would be . . .'
. . . would be.

22. *your regard*] 'your care of your
own safety' (Johnson).

23. *My worth unknown*] cf. *Sonn.*, cxvi.
7–8, 'the star. . . . Whose worth's unknown', glossed by Palgrave as 'Whose
stellar influence is uncalculated'.

In yours they will, in you all hopes are lost.   25
Flight cannot stain the honour you have won;
But mine it will, that no exploit have done.
You fled for vantage, every one will swear;
But if I bow, they'll say it was for fear.
There is no hope that ever I will stay   30
If the first hour I shrink and run away.
Here, on my knee, I beg mortality,
Rather than life preserv'd with infamy.

Tal. Shall all thy mother's hopes lie in one tomb?

John. Ay, rather than I'll shame my mother's womb.   35

Tal. Upon my blessing, I command thee go.

John. To fight I will, but not to fly the foe.

Tal. Part of thy father may be sav'd in thee.

John. No part of him but will be sham'd in me.

Tal. Thou never hadst renown, nor canst not lose it.   40

John. Yes, your renowned name: shall flight abuse it?

Tal. Thy father's charge shall clear thee from that stain.

John. You cannot witness for me, being slain.
If death be so apparent, then both fly.

Tal. And leave my followers here to fight and die?   45
My age was never tainted with such shame.

John. And shall my youth be guilty of such blame?
No more can I be sever'd from your side
Than can yourself yourself in twain divide.
Stay, go, do what you will, the like do I;   50
For live I will not, if my father die.

Tal. Then here I take my leave of thee, fair son,
Born to eclipse thy life this afternoon.
Come, side by side, together live and die,
And soul with soul from France to heaven fly.   *Exeunt.*

---

39. sham'd] *Hudson, conj. S. Walker;* shame *F.*   55. S.D.] *F (Exit).*

27. *mine . . . that*] = of me . . . who.
29. *bow*] yield.
31. *shrink*] yield, give away.
32. *mortality*] death.
39. *sham'd*] an *e/d* misreading in F.
41. *abuse*] disgrace, dishonour.
43. *being slain*] L. construction = if you are slain.

44. *apparent*] evident, certain.
46. *age*] lifetime.
tainted] cf. attainted.
52, 53. *son . . . eclipse*] the pun is frequent in Shakespeare, e.g. *R3*, I. i. 2; cf. also the references above, stars (6), and worth (23), and throughout the play.

[SCENE VI.—*A field of battle.*]

Alarum: excursions, wherein TALBOT'S *Son is hemmed about, and* TALBOT *rescues him.*

Tal. Saint George and victory! Fight, soldiers, fight:
  The Regent hath with Talbot broke his word,
  And left us to the rage of France his sword.
  Where is John Talbot? Pause and take thy breath;
  I gave thee life and rescu'd thee from death.   5
John. O, twice my father, twice am I thy son!
  The life thou gav'st me first was lost and done,
  Till with thy warlike sword, despite of fate,
  To my determin'd time thou gav'st new date.
Tal. When from the Dauphin's crest thy sword struck fire, 10
  It warm'd thy father's heart with proud desire
  Of bold-fac'd victory. Then leaden age,
  Quicken'd with youthful spleen and warlike rage,
  Beat down Alençon, Orleans, Burgundy,
  And from the pride of Gallia rescu'd thee.   15
  The ireful Bastard Orleans, that drew blood
  From thee, my boy, and had the maidenhood
  Of thy first fight, I soon encountered,
  And, interchanging blows, I quickly shed
  Some of his bastard blood, and in disgrace   20
  Bespoke him thus: 'Contaminated, base,
  And misbegotten blood I spill of thine,

Scene VI

SCENE VI] *Capell; not in* F.   *A field of battle.*] *Capell; not in* F.   21. him thus: 'Contaminated] F; him: 'This contaminated *conj. Vaughan.*

S.D. hemmed about] authorial; cf. IV. iii. 21.

2. *Regent*] York; see IV. i. 163, and cf. V. iii. 1.

3. *France his*] cf. II. i. 1 and n.

9. *determin'd*] legal = to which a terminus or end has been set.

date] limit or term; cf. *Sonn.*, xiv. 14, 'beauty's doom and date'.

13. *Quicken'd*] brought to life again; cf. quick = alive, in 'the quick and the dead'.

spleen] fiery impetuosity (Wilson); ardour.

15. *pride*] full power (Schmidt); cf. III. ii. 40.

17–18. *maidenhood . . . first fight*] blood drawn from a foe in his first fight (Wilson).

20. *in disgrace*] treating him with contempt; to insult him.

21, 22. *Contaminated . . . misbegotten*] continuing the slur implied in 'Bastard' above.

Mean and right poor, for that pure blood of mine
Which thou didst force from Talbot, my brave boy'.
Here, purposing the Bastard to destroy,   25
Came in strong rescue. Speak, thy father's care,
Art thou not weary, John? How dost thou fare?
Wilt thou yet leave the battle, boy, and fly,
Now thou art seal'd the son of chivalry?
Fly, to revenge my death when I am dead;   30
The help of one stands me in little stead.
O, too much folly is it, well I wot,
To hazard all our lives in one small boat!
If I to-day die not with Frenchmen's rage,
To-morrow I shall die with mickle age: 35
By me they nothing gain and if I stay:
'Tis but the shortening of my life one day;
In thee thy mother dies, our household's name,
My death's revenge, thy youth, and England's fame:
All these and more we hazard by thy stay;   40
All these are sav'd if thou wilt fly away.
John. The sword of Orleans hath not made me smart;
These words of yours draw life-blood from my heart.
On that advantage, bought with such a shame,
To save a paltry life and slay bright fame,   45
Before young Talbot from old Talbot fly,
The coward horse that bears me fall and die!
And like me to the peasant boys of France,
To be shame's scorn and subject of mischance!
Surely, by all the glory you have won,   50
And if I fly, I am not Talbot's son.
Then talk no more of flight, it is no boot;
If son to Talbot, die at Talbot's foot.

25. *purposing*] while I was purposing
—an absolute use.

29. *seal'd*] 'Compare the Biblical
use of sealed as consecrated' (Carter).

32–3.] cf. Tilley, 209, 'Venture not
all in one bottom'; and *Mer. V.*, I. i. 42.

35. *mickle*] great, as still used provincially; cf. *2H6*, v. i. 174.

42. *smart*] suffer.

44. *On that advantage*] referring to
39–41—to gain these benefits, i.e. revenge for Talbot, youth (and life), and
England's fame, as partly repeated in
45.

48. *like*] liken, i.e. reduce to a level
with (Johnson).

49. *subject of mischance*] subjected to
misfortune.

52. *boot*] advantage; use.

Tal. Then follow thou thy desperate sire of Crete,
         Thou Icarus; thy life to me is sweet: 55
         If thou wilt fight, fight by thy father's side,
         And, commendable prov'd, let's die in pride.   *Exeunt.*

[SCENE VII.—*Another part of the field.*]

Alarum: excursions. Enter old TALBOT *led [by a Servant].*

Tal. Where is my other life? Mine own is gone.
         O, where's young Talbot? Where is valiant John?
         Triumphant Death, smear'd with captivity,
         Young Talbot's valour makes me smile at thee.
         When he perceiv'd me shrink and on my knee,   5
         His bloody sword he brandish'd over me,
         And like a hungry lion did commence
         Rough deeds of rage and stern impatience;
         But when my angry guardant stood alone,
         Tendering my ruin and assail'd of none,   10
         Dizzy-ey'd fury and great rage of heart
         Suddenly made him from my side to start

---

55. Icarus;] *edd.; Icarus, | F.*   57. S.D.] *F (Exit.).*

Scene VII

SCENE VII] *Pope; not in F.*   *Another . . . field.] Malone; not in F.*   S.D. *by a Servant.] Cambridge; not in F.*

54–5. *sire of Crete, | Thou Icarus*] a favourite analogy of Shakespeare's, from Ovid, *Metam.*, viii; perhaps suggested by 'flight' (52). Icarus is associated, for Shakespeare, with 'pride', which comes before a fall; cf. IV. vii. 16; and see Armstrong, 36.

For the punctuation, see collation.

57. *commendable*] accented on the first syllable.

pride] honour, glory; and see n. to 54.

Scene VII

3. *Triumphant*] triumphing, holding a triumphal procession and leading captives after him; cf. I. i. 20–2.

smear'd with captivity] There is probably an allusion to Ephes.,

iv. 8, 'He led captivity captive'. Death triumphs over the captive Talbots, as over Henry V, and laughs them to scorn (18); but his victory is 'dishonourable', 'smear'd'; old Talbot smiles at him, and both old and young by their eternal fame ('coupled in bonds of perpetuity') evade his capture and 'scape mortality'.

5. *shrink*] yield, give way; cf. IV. v. 31.

8. *rage*] warlike ardour, fury.

impatience] anger, rage.

9. *guardant*] guard, protector.

10. *Tendering my ruin*] caring for me in my fall; 'Tend'ring' suggests both 'looking after' and 'affection'.

11. *Dizzy-ey'd*] dazzled with fury.

Into the clustering battle of the French;
And in that sea of blood my boy did drench
His over-mounting spirit; and there died   15
My Icarus, my blossom, in his pride.

Enter [Soldiers, bearing the body of] JOHN TALBOT.

Serv. O my dear lord, lo where your son is borne!
Tal. Thou antic Death, which laugh'st us here to scorn,
Anon, from thy insulting tyranny,
Coupled in bonds of perpetuity,   20
Two Talbots winged through the lither sky,
In thy despite shall scape mortality.
O thou whose wounds become hard-favour'd Death,
Speak to thy father ere thou yield thy breath!
Brave Death by speaking, whether he will or no;   25
Imagine him a Frenchman and thy foe.
Poor boy! he smiles, methinks, as who should say,
Had Death been French, then Death had died to-day.
Come, come, and lay him in his father's arms:
My spirit can no longer bear these harms.   30
Soldiers, adieu! I have what I would have,
Now my old arms are young John Talbot's grave.   *Dies.*

Enter CHARLES, ALENÇON, BURGUNDY, BASTARD, *and*
[LA] PUCELLE.

16. S.D.] *Alexander; Enter with Iohn Talbot, borne. | F.*

13. *clustering battle*] crowded ranks.
14. *drench*] drown.
15. *over-mounting*] excessively proud.
16. *pride*] cf. IV. vi. 16 and 57 n.; Icarus was naturally associated with the 'sea' (14); see Armstrong, *Sh.'s Imagination*, 38.
18. *antic*] grotesque figure, like, e.g., a gargoyle; cf. *R2*, III. ii. 162, 'keeps Death his court, and there the Antic sits, / Scoffing his state, and grinning at his pomp'.
19. *insulting*] L. *insultatio* = springing or leaping upon, hence, behaving violently and contemptuously; cf. I. ii. 138; and *R3*, II. iv. 51, 'Insulting tyranny begins to jet'.

21.] a continuation of the Daedalus–Icarus imagery.
lither] yielding; *OED.*, A 4.
23. *hard-favour'd*] hard-featured; ill-looking; ugly; cf. *Ven.*, 931.
24. *yield thy breath*] Carter compares the 'thanksgiving after the receiving of the Lorde's Supper' in the Genevan Bible, 'His soule he gaue to torments great / And yeelded vp his breath'.
27. *methinks*] it seems to me.
30. *harms*] injuries.
32. *arms . . . grave*] cf. *3H6*, II. v. 114, 'These arms of mine shall be thy winding-sheet'; and Marlowe, *Jew of Malta*, III. ii. 11 (1192), 'These arms of mine shall be thy sepulchre'.

Cha. Had York and Somerset brought rescue in,
         We should have found a bloody day of this.
Bast. How the young whelp of Talbot's, raging-wood,   35
         Did flesh his puny sword in Frenchmen's blood!
Puc. Once I encounter'd him, and thus I said:
         'Thou maiden youth, be vanquish'd by a maid;'
         But with a proud majestical high scorn
         He answer'd thus: 'Young Talbot was not born   40
         To be the pillage of a giglot wench.'
         So, rushing in the bowels of the French,
         He left me proudly, as unworthy fight.
Bur. Doubtless he would have made a noble knight;
         See where he lies inhearsed in the arms   45
         Of the most bloody nurser of his harms.
Bast. Hew them to pieces, hack their bones asunder,
         Whose life was England's glory, Gallia's wonder.
Cha. O no, forbear! For that which we have fled
         During the life, let us not wrong it dead.   50

            Enter [*Sir* WILLIAM] LUCY [, *attended*].

Lucy. Conduct me to the Dauphin's tent, to know
         Who hath obtain'd the glory of the day.
Cha. On what submissive message art thou sent?
Lucy. Submission, Dauphin! 'Tis a mere French word:
         We English warriors wot not what it means.   55
         I come to know what prisoners thou hast ta'en
         And to survey the bodies of the dead.

---

50. S.D.] *Capell* (. . . *attended; Herald of the French preceding.*; *Enter Lucie.* | *F.*
51. Conduct . . . to know] *Pope;* Herald, conduct . . . | To know *F*+*edd.*

35. *whelp*] a quibble on 'talbot = hound' (Scott-Giles).

wood] mad.

36. *puny*] that of a junior or novice; (cf. puisne).

41. *giglot*] wanton; strumpet.

45. *inhearsed*] laid as in a coffin; cf. 32 above.

46. *his harms*] the injuries he has done us (Wilson).

47–50.] Hall, 178, from which this rebuke is adapted.

51–2.] see Intro., p. xviii. The prompter or adapter, in order to eliminate Lucy from the cast (cf. IV. ii. 16), presumably jotted 'Herald' above the speech-prefix here as an indication to the scribe who made out the 'parts'; hence its erroneous incorporation in the F text. The line was then further adjusted for length by over-running, and this produced the unnatural 'sent/tent' rhyme; and spoiled the metre.

54. *mere*] L. *merus* = pure; 'a word exclusively French'.

Cha. For prisoners ask'st thou? Hell our prison is.
　　　But tell me whom thou seek'st.
Lucy. But where's the great Alcides of the field,　　　60
　　　Valiant Lord Talbot, Earl of Shrewsbury,
　　　Created for his rare success in arms
　　　Great Earl of Washford, Waterford, and Valence,
　　　Lord Talbot of Goodrig and Urchinfield,
　　　Lord Strange of Blackmere, Lord Verdun of Alton,　65
　　　Cromwell of Wingfield, Furnival of Sheffield,
　　　The thrice victorious Lord of Falconbridge,
　　　Knight of the noble Order of Saint George,
　　　Worthy Saint Michael, and the Golden Fleece,
　　　Great Marshal to Henry the Sixth　　　　　　　70
　　　Of all his wars within the realm of France?
Puc. Here is a silly-stately style indeed!
　　　The Turk, that two and fifty kingdoms hath,
　　　Writes not so tedious a style as this.
　　　Him that thou magnifiest with all these titles,　　75
　　　Stinking and fly-blown lies here at our feet.
Lucy. Is Talbot slain—the Frenchmen's only Scourge,

---

66. Cromwell] *This edn, conj. Capell;* Lord *Cromwell* | *F.*　　　Furnival] *This edn,*
conj. Capell; Lord *Furniuall* | *F.*　　70. Henry] *F;* our King Henry *F2.*　　72. Here
is] *Pope;* Heere's *F.*　　silly-stately] *Dyce, conj. S. Walker;* silly stately *F.*

60. *But where's*] The short line, 59, and the double 'But' may indicate that something has been cut or omitted.

Alcides] Hercules, as the descendant (grandson) of Alceus.

60 ff.] 'The passage reminds us of how Homer reduced the bright glory of his heroes to the shabby indignity of death. . . At the same time he [Shakespeare] uses this intolerable humiliation to dismiss Talbot from the play and from our minds' (Price, 34).

61 ff.] Cf. Dekker, *Satiromastix,* I. ii. 312–13, 'thy tytle's longer than the Stile a the big Turkes'.

No contemporary or earlier source is known for this epitaph. It appeared in a similar form in Richard Crompton's *Mansion of Magnanimitie* (1599), sig. E 4, from which it was copied into

Ralph Brooke's *Catalogue and Succession of the Kings* (ed. 1619, p. 196). This passage has been the basis of theories of revision or later adaptation.

It occurred earlier in Roger Cotton's *Armor of Proofe,* 1596 (Miss J. Pearce in *MLN.,* LIX. 327–9), and was probably known earlier (cf. *W.S.,* I. 293).

63. *Washford*] old name for Wexford, in Ireland.

66.] For the intrusive F titles, see Intro., p. xx.

72. *style*] titles added to a name.

73. *The Turk*] technical expression for the Turkish Sultan, the Grand Turk. Bajazeth in *2 Tamb.,* III. i. 1–7, has 130 kingdoms.

77–8. *Scourge . . . Terror*] cf. IV. ii. 16 and n.

Your kingdom's Terror and black Nemesis?
O, were mine eye-balls into bullets turn'd,
That I in rage might shoot them at your faces!   80
O that I could but call these dead to life!
It were enough to fright the realm of France.
Were but his picture left amongst you here,
It would amaze the proudest of you all.
Give me their bodies, that I bear them hence   85
And give them burial as beseems their worth.

Puc. I think this upstart is old Talbot's ghost,
He speaks with such a proud commanding spirit.
For God's sake, let him have them; to keep them here,
They would but stink and putrefy the air.   90

Cha. Go, take their bodies hence.

Lucy.   I'll bear them hence;
But from their ashes shall be rear'd
A phoenix that shall make all France afeard.

      [Exeunt Lucy and Attendants with the bodies.]

Cha. So we be rid, do with them what thou wilt.
And now to Paris in this conquering vein: 95
All will be ours now bloody Talbot's slain.   *Exeunt.*

---

85. bear] *This edn;* may beare *F.*   89. have them] *Theobald* (... 'em) *;* have him
F.   91–3.] *as Pope;* Go ... hence. / *Lucy.* Ile ... reard / A ... affear'd. *F.*
92. ashes] *F;* ashes, Dauphin, *Pope;* noble ashes *conj. this edn.*   93. S.D.] *Capell*
(*subst.*) *; not in F.*   94. rid] *Capell;* rid of them *F.*   them] *F2, Theobald* ('em) *;*
him *F.*   96. S.D.] *Rowe; Exit. | F.*

78. *Nemesis*] the goddess of justice,
who punished pride and arrogance;
retribution.

79–80.] cf. Jonson, *EMO.*, I. i. 26–7,
'cast / Mine eye-balls forth'; and *Volp.*,
v. viii. 2.

85–94.] an 'improving' hand, possibly tempted by the profusion of pro-
nouns and ellipses, has clearly been at
work.

87. *upstart*] overbearing fellow.

93. *phoenix*] cf. *3H6*, I. iv. 35.

[ACT V]

SCENE I. [—*London. The Palace.*]

Sennet. Enter KING, GLOUCESTER, *and* EXETER.

K. Hen. Have you perus'd the letters from the Pope,
    The Emperor, and the Earl of Armagnac?
Glou. I have, my lord; and their intent is this:
    They humbly sue unto your Excellence
    To have a godly peace concluded of   5
    Between the realms of England and of France.
K. Hen. How doth your Grace affect their motion?
Glou. Well, my good lord, and as the only means
    To stop effusion of our Christian blood
    And stablish quietness on every side.   10
K. Hen. Ay, marry, uncle, for I always thought

ACT V
Scene I

ACT V SCENE I] *Capell; Scena secunda.* | *F.*   *London. The Palace.*] *Cambridge,
after Capell; not in F.*   2, 17. Armagnac] *F* (Arminack(e)).

This Act seals England's disastrous loss of France, and future subservience to French influence. The keynote is sounded at once in (*a*) the peace proposals of the Emperor Sigismund and the Pope (Hall, 166, 174), and (*b*) the Armagnac proffer of marriage (1442) to Henry (Hall, 203), which has Gloucester's approval (cf. v. v. 25), but which is however ousted—a breach of faith—by Suffolk's still more disastrous scheme for Henry's marriage with Margaret of Anjou.

The Act, while completing the fall of Joan, (*a*) arranges for her immediate replacement as the English scourge by Margaret, (*b*) aggravates thereby the quarrel of Winchester and Gloucester, and (*c*) emphasizes the grief of York

and Warwick at the loss of Anjou and Maine—Margaret's dowry—foreshadowing the entire loss of France to the English throne, to which York aspires. Suffolk's triumph, and the prospective marriage of Henry and Margaret, lead straight into *2 Henry VI*, where the intestine divisions of the nobles under a weak king and a French queen will be continued *in England*, with further disastrous results for them, but even more for the country itself.

5. *godly peace*] Hol.; Hall has 'godly concorde' (175).

7. *affect*] stand affected to; like. *motion*] proposal, offer.

9. *effusion . . . blood*] Hall, 203; *Homily . . . Rebellion.*

108

It was both impious and unnatural
That such immanity and bloody strife
Should reign among professors of one faith.

Glou. Beside, my lord, the sooner to effect   15
And surer bind this knot of amity,
The Earl of Armagnac, near knit to Charles,
A man of great authority in France,
Proffers his only daughter to your Grace
In marriage, with a large and sumptuous dowry.   20

K. Hen. Marriage, uncle! Alas, my years are young!
And fitter is my study and my books
Than wanton dalliance with a paramour.
Yet call th' ambassadors, and, as you please,
So let them have their answers every one: 25
I shall be well content with any choice
Tends to God's glory and my country's weal.

Enter WINCHESTER [*in Cardinal's habit, a Legate*] *and two Ambassadors.*

Exe. What! is my Lord of Winchester install'd,
And call'd unto a cardinal's degree?
Then I perceive that will be verified   30
Henry the Fifth did sometime prophesy:
'If once he come to be a cardinal,
He'll make his cap co-equal with the crown.'

K. Hen. My Lords Ambassadors, your several suits
Have been consider'd and debated on.   35
Your purpose is both good and reasonable;

---

17. knit] *F;* kin *Pope.*   27. S.D.] *Cambridge, after Capell; Enter Winchester, and three Ambassadors. | F.*

13. *immanity*] barbarity; atrocious savagery.

20. *dowry*] Hall, 202–3.

21. *young*] Henry was actually twenty-one; but this vagueness helps to maintain the difficult feat of presenting him in a play at the beginning of which he was nine months old.

22. *study . . . books*] typical of Henry; cf. *2H6*, I. i. 259.

26–7. *choice | Tends*] on the omission of the relative, cf. Abbott, 244.

28 ff.] Exeter's surprise is, of course, inconsistent with I. iii. 19 ff. The inconsistency may be Shakespeare's, or due to other causes; it is not necessarily a sign of revision or multiple authorship; see Intro., p. xiv.

29. *degree*] rank.

30. *be verified*] come true.

31. *sometime*] formerly.

32–3.] Hall, 139.

34. *several*] separate, respective (legal sense).

And therefore are we certainly resolv'd
To draw conditions of a friendly peace,
Which by my Lord of Winchester we mean
Shall be transported presently to France.   40
Glou. And for the proffer of my lord your master,
I have inform'd his Highness so at large,
As, liking of the lady's virtuous gifts,
Her beauty, and the value of her dower,
He doth intend she shall be England's Queen.   45
K. Hen. In argument and proof of which contract,
Bear her this jewel, pledge of my affection,
And so, my Lord Protector, see them guarded
And safely brought to Dover; where, inshipp'd,
Commit them to the fortune of the sea.   50
                    Exeunt [all but Winchester and Legate].
Win. Stay, my Lord Legate; you shall first receive
The sum of money which I promised
Should be deliver'd to his Holiness
For clothing me in these grave ornaments.
Leg. I will attend upon your lordship's leisure.   *[Exit.]* 55
Win. Now Winchester will not submit, I trow,
Or be inferior to the proudest peer.
Humphrey of Gloucester, thou shalt well perceive
That neither in birth nor for authority
The Bishop will be overborne by thee;   60
I'll either make thee stoop and bend thy knee,
Or sack this country with a mutiny.   *Exit.*

---

49. where, inshipp'd] *F4+edd.; wherein ship'd F.*   50. S.D.] *edd.; Exeunt. | F.*
55. S.D.] *Dyce and Staunton; not in F.*   59. nor] *Hanmer; or F.*   for] *F; in
Marshall.*   62. sack] *F; rack conj. Vaughan.*   62. S.D. Exit.] *Dyce and Staunton;
Exeunt. | F.*

38. *draw*] draw up, draft.
40. *presently*] Elizabethan sense—immediately.
42. *at large*] fully, in detail.
42–3. *so . . . As*] Abbott, 275.
46. *argument*] evidence, proof; *OED.*, 1. i.
52 ff.] probably due to a misunderstanding of Hall, 139, which states that Winchester *purchased* (i.e. obtained)
at Rome a 'Bull legatyne' (Wilson).
54. *grave ornaments*] important robes of office.
55. *attend*] L. sense = wait.
59. *in birth . . .*] 'Thou shalt not rule me, though thy birth is legitimate, and thy authority supreme' (Johnson).
60. *overborne*] over-ruled; subdued; cf. III. i. 53.
62. *mutiny*] discord, dissension.

SCENE II. [—*France. Plains in Anjou.*]

Enter CHARLES, BURGUNDY, ALENÇON, BASTARD, REIGNIER,
and LA PUCELLE.

Cha.　These news, my lords, may cheer our drooping
　　　spirits:
　　'Tis said the stout Parisians do revolt
　　And turn again unto the warlike French.
Alen.　Then march to Paris, royal Charles of France,
　　And keep not back your powers in dalliance.　　　　5
Puc.　Peace be amongst them, if they turn to us;
　　Else ruin come within their palaces!

Enter Scout.

Scout.　Success unto our valiant general,
　　And happiness to his accomplices!
Cha.　What tidings send our scouts? I prithee speak.　　10
Scout.　The English army, that divided was
　　Into two parties, is now conjoin'd in one,
　　And means to give you battle presently.
Cha.　Somewhat too sudden, sirs, the warning is;
　　But we will presently provide for them.　　　　15
Bur.　I trust the ghost of Talbot is not there:
　　Now he is gone, my lord, you need not fear.

Scene II

SCENE II] *Capell; Scœna Tertia. | F.*　　*France.*] *Pope; not in F.*　　*Plains in Anjou.*]
Capell; not in F.　　S.D. *La Pucelle*] F (*Ione*).　7. come within] *This edn;* combat
with *F.*　　12. is now conioyn'd] *F;* now conjoins *conj. this edn.*

2. *Parisians . . . revolt*] Hall, 179.
　3. *turn again*] like Frenchmen; cf. III.
iii. 85.
　5. *powers*] forces.
　dalliance] trifling; idle waste of time.
　6. *Peace be . . .*] cf. Ps., cxxii. 6, 7,
'Peace be within thy walls, and prosperity within thy palaces' (Carter).
　7.] *ruin combat with* is, as Wilson remarks, 'a strange expression'. It may
well be a scribal misinterpretation influenced by I. i. 54, '*Combat with* adverse planets . . .' The source (n.

above) suggests 'come within', or 'be
within'. See Intro., p. xxii.
　Else,] if not; otherwise.
　9. *accomplices*] colleagues; assistants.
　12. *conjoin'd in one*] united into one
force. The line is probably corrupt,
and should read 'parties, now conjoins'. The corruption may have arisen
from a misreading of 'conjoine' as
'conjoin'd', with subsequent addition
of 'is' for the sense.
　13, 15. *presently*] immediately—
Elizabethan sense.

Puc. Of all base passions, fear is most accurs'd.
　　　Command the conquest, Charles, it shall be thine:
　　　Let Henry fret and all the world repine.　　　　　20
Cha. Then on, my lords; and France be fortunate.　　*Exeunt.*

[SCENE III.—*Before Angiers.*]

Alarum: excursions. Enter LA PUCELLE.

Puc. The Regent conquers and the Frenchmen fly.
　　　Now help, ye charming spells and periapts;
　　　And ye choice spirits that admonish me,
　　　And give me signs of future accidents:　　　*Thunder.*
　　　You speedy helpers that are substitutes　　　5
　　　Under the lordly monarch of the north,
　　　Appear and aid me in this enterprise!

Enter Fiends.

This speed and quick appearance argues proof
Of your accustom'd diligence to me.

Scene III

SCENE III] *Capell; not in F.*　　*Before Angiers.*] *Cambridge; not in F; Under Angiers. |
Capell.*　　S.D. *La Pucelle*] F (*Ione de Pucell*).　　8. speed and quick] *Dyce;* speedy
and quicke *F;* speedy quick *Pope.*

18. *passions*] any kind of emotion by
which the mind is powerfully moved,
or *suffers* (L. *patior, passus*).
　21. *fortunate*] have Fortune on their
side; be successful or victorious.

Scene III
Source: Hall, 156–7.
　1. *Regent*] York; see iv. i. 163 and
iv. vi. 2. Historically Bedford was still
alive and Regent at this time.
　2. *charming*] acting as charms; cf. 31.
　periapts] amulets; inscribed band-
ages or charms 'worn about the neck
as preservatives against disease or
danger. Of these, the first chapter of
St John's Gospel was deemed the
most efficacious' (Steevens); cf.
Scot, *Discoverie of Witchcraft,* xii. xi,

'periapts, amulets and charms'.
　3. *admonish*] notify, inform in any
way.
　4. *accidents*] chance happenings of
any kind; cf. Cooper, *Thesaurus,* 'Acci-
dens = that chanceth or happeneth'.
　5. *substitutes*] those placed under (L.
sub + stare), servants, agents.
　6. *the lordly monarch of the north*] the
ruler of all evil spirits, variously named
by Scot (Zimimar) and Greene, *Frier
Bacon* (Asmenoth). Milton assembles
his rebel angels in the north (Johnson);
cf. Lucifer, in Isa., xiv. 13.
　8. *speed*] F was probably affected by
'speedy' at 5 above.
　quick] live; in living form; cf. 'the
quick and the dead'.
　9. *diligence*] assiduity in service.

Now, ye familiar spirits that are cull'd   10
Out of the powerful regions under earth,
Help me this once, that France may get the field.
                              They walk, and speak not
O, hold me not with silence over-long!
Where I was wont to feed you with my blood,
I'll lop a member off and give it you   15
In earnest of a further benefit,
So you do condescend to help me now.
                              They hang their heads.
No hope to have redress? My body shall
Pay recompense if you will grant my suit.
                              They shake their heads.
Cannot my body nor blood-sacrifice   20
Entreat you to your wonted furtherance?
Then take my soul; my body, soul, and all,
Before that England give the French the foil. *They depart.*
See! they forsake me. Now the time is come
That France must vail her lofty-plumed crest   25
And let her head fall into England's lap.
My ancient incantations are too weak,
And hell too strong for me to buckle with:
Now, France, thy glory droopeth to the dust.   *Exit.*

Excursions. BURGUNDY *and* YORK *fight hand to hand.*
[*The*] *French fly* [, *leaving* LA PUCELLE *in* YORK'S *power*].

11. regions] *F;* legions *Singer, conj. Warburton.*   29. S.D. *The French . . . power.*]
Tucker Brooke; French flye. | F; La Pucelle is taken. The French fly. | Cambridge.

10 ff. *familiar spirits*] cf. 1 Sam.,
xxviii. 8; a familiar or attendant spirit
was a link with the powers of hell pos-
sessed by witches; cf. Saul's consulta-
tion of the Witch of Endor: 'I pray
thee coniecture vnto mee by thy familiar spirite, and bring mee him vp
whom I shal name vnto thee' (Noble);
cf. III. ii. 122.
    11. *regions under earth*] the homes of
the powerful fiends, i.e. Erebus; cf.
2 Tamb., 4011-12, 'O thou that swaiest
the region vnder earth . . . a king as
absolute as Ioue'.
    12. *get the field*] win the battle.

14. *Where*] whereas.
    17. *condescend*] cf. *Man. Voc.*, 'con-
descende = consentire'; agree.
    18. *redress*] relief from trouble; assist-
ance.
    23. *give . . . the foil*] defeat.
    25. *vail*] lower; cf. *Mer. V.*, I. i. 28.
    27. *ancient*] former (Fr. *ancien*).
    28. *buckle with*] grapple, close with.
    29. S.D.] There is obviously some
discrepancy between Joan's *Exit* and
the absence of a re-entry. 'Modern
editors make the fight take place between Joan and York, but without
justification. Joan's power has now

York. Damsel of France, I think I have you fast: 30
    Unchain your spirits now with spelling charms,
    And try if they can gain your liberty.
    A goodly prize, fit for the devil's grace!
    See how the ugly witch doth bend her brows,
    As if, with Circe, she would change my shape!   35
Puc. Chang'd to a worser shape thou canst not be.
York. O, Charles the Dauphin is a proper man:
    No shape but his can please your dainty eye.
Puc. A plaguing mischief light on Charles and thee!
    And may ye both be suddenly surpris'd   40
    By bloody hands, in sleeping on your beds!
York. Fell banning hag, enchantress, hold thy tongue!
Puc. I prithee, give me leave to curse awhile.
York. Curse, miscreant, when thou comest to the stake.

                                      Exeunt.

    Alarum. Enter SUFFOLK, *with* MARGARET *in his hand.*

Suf. Be what thou wilt, thou art my prisoner. *Gazes on her.* 45
    O fairest beauty, do not fear nor fly!
    For I will touch thee but with reverent hands,
    And lay them gently on thy tender side.

---

32. your] *F;* you *conj. anon. (in Cambridge).*   44. comest] *Rowe;* comst *F.*
47. reverent] *F* (reverend).

disappeared and her part is passive. Probably the *Exit.* after line 29 . . . should be omitted, leaving Joan a spectator of the fight which follows' (Brooke).

31. *spelling*] which work spells.

33. *the devil's grace*] ironical and paradoxical.

35. *with*] in the same way as; *OED.*, 15.

37. *proper*] handsome, good-looking.

40. *surpris'd*] captured.

42. *Fell*] fierce.

banning] cursing; cf. Joan's successor, Margaret, in *2H6*, III. ii. 299 ff.

44. *miscreant*] mis-created; cf. 'misconceived', v. iv. 49.

44. S.D.] Some editors have made a new scene here, probably on the strength of the S.D. '*Alarum.*' Scene iii

takes place at Compiègne, where Joan was captured; while Reignier's castle is in Anjou. But Reignier and Margaret are supposed to be with the French army, and Joan taken in the same battle. Exact localities are avoided.

It is no accident that, as one captured French 'enchantress' is led off prisoner, another, her direct successor, is led on, 'prisoner'.

The scene is a deliberate and immediate threat to Henry's contract with the Earl of Armagnac's daughter (v. i), and will both illustrate the weakness of Henry and create new intestine divisions among the nobles.

The incident is fictitious, being merely suggested by the language of Hall, 218–19.

48–9.] For the rearrangement of

I kiss these fingers for eternal peace.

Who art thou, say, that I may honour thee?　　　50

Mar. Margaret my name, and daughter to a king,

The King of Naples—whosoe'er thou art.

Suf. An earl I am, and Suffolk am I call'd.

Be not offended, nature's miracle,

Thou art allotted to be ta'en by me:　　　55

So doth the swan her downy cygnets save,

Keeping them prisoner underneath her wings.

Yet, if this servile usage once offend,

Go and be free again as Suffolk's friend.　　*She is going.*

O, stay!—I have no power to let her pass;　　　60

My hand would free her, but my heart says no.

As plays the sun upon the glassy streams,

Twinkling another counterfeited beam,

So seems this gorgeous beauty to mine eyes.

Fain would I woo her, yet I dare not speak:　　　65

I'll call for pen and ink, and write my mind.

Fie, de la Pole! disable not thyself;

Hast not a tongue? Is she not prisoner here?

48, 49.] *Capell;* 49, 48 *F.*　　57. her] *F3;* his *F.*　　68. prisoner here?] *This ed.;* heere? *F;* heere thy prisoner? *F2.*

lines, cf. I. iv. 86–8, and see Intro., p. xxiii. The scribe (or compositor) has omitted, and wrongly inserted, a line. Some scholars would defend the F arrangement thus: Suffolk begins with a general reassurance. 'For I will touch thee...' Then, suiting the action to the word, he proceeds to the details: 'I kiss these fingers', i.e. 'I am now kissing these fingers of mine in your honour'; 'And lay them...', i.e. 'I am now laying them...'

In the rearrangement, however, 'lay' can equally well be future: 'I will touch... and (I will) lay them...' More important, Suffolk will obviously lay *hands*, not fingers, on Margaret's side. Carter finds a reference to John, xx. 27 (cf. finger... hand... side).

49. *for*] in token of—kissing his fingers; cf. Malvolio in *Tw. N.*, III. iv. 36.

50.] The F line is in the interrogative form of 'Say who thou art, that I may honour thee'; i.e. it is one statement, which becomes one question. The interrogation mark therefore comes best at the end.

55. *allotted*] appointed (by fate).

58. *servile usage*] treatment as a slave (L. *servus*).

62. *glassy*] like a glass or mirror; reflecting; cf. *Ham.*, IV. vii. 168

63. *Twinkling... beam*] 'That is, each twinkling beam, reflected by the water seems doubled' (Brooke).

67. *de la Pole*] Suffolk's family name; cf. *2H6*, IV. i.

disable] disqualify; treat your abilities as unequal to the occasion; cf. *AYL.*, V. iv. 80, 'he disabled my judgment'.

68.] The F1 line is incomplete; F2's reading sounds like a conjecture; though the word 'prisoner' (cf. 45, 57,

Wilt thou be daunted at a woman's sight?
Ay, beauty's princely majesty is such   70
Confounds the tongue and makes the senses rough.
Mar. Say, Earl of Suffolk, if thy name be so,
What ransom must I pay before I pass?
For I perceive I am thy prisoner.
Suf. How canst thou tell she will deny thy suit,   75
Before thou make a trial of her love?
Mar. Why speak'st thou not? What ransom must I pay?
Suf. She's beautiful, and therefore to be woo'd;
She is a woman, therefore to be won.
Mar. Wilt thou accept of ransom, yea or no?   80
Suf. Fond man, remember that thou hast a wife;
Then how can Margaret be thy paramour?
Mar. 'Twere best to leave him, for he will not hear.
Suf. There all is marr'd; there lies a cooling card.
Mar. He talks at random; sure, the man is mad.   85
Suf. And yet a dispensation may be had.
Mar. And yet I would that you would answer me.
Suf. I'll win this Lady Margaret. For whom?
Why, for my king! Tush, that's a wooden thing!
Mar. He talks of wood: it is some carpenter.   90
Suf. Yet so my fancy may be satisfied,
And peace established between these realms.
But there remains a scruple in that too;

71. makes the senses rough.] *F; mocks the sense of touch. Collier;* Makes the senses nought. *conj. Vaughan.*   83. 'Twere] *Pope;* I were *F.*

74) seems required by the context.

69. *a woman's sight*] the sight of a woman.

71. *Confounds*] that it confounds or destroys the power of.

makes the senses rough] The phrase may mean 'disturbs the senses like troubled waters, ruffles them' (Schmidt), or dulls the senses, if indeed it means anything as it stands.

78-9.] a cliché; cf. *Tit.,* II. i. 82-3; *R3,* I. ii. 227-8; Greene, *Planetomachia* (Grosart, v. 110).

81. *Fond*] Elizabethan sense = foolish.

82. *paramour*] mistress.

83. *'Twere*] an easy mistake in F, the correction of which improves the metre.

84. *cooling card*] a card (played by one's adversary) which dashes one's hope (Brooke)—a common Elizabethan expression.

85. *at random*] recklessly; cf. *Gent.,* II. i. 100.

89. *wooden thing*] (*a*) expressionless, insensible thing—referring to the king (Hart); (*b*) an awkward business, an undertaking not likely to succeed (Steevens).

91. *fancy*] amorous inclination, love (the commonest Shakespearean sense).

For though her father be the King of Naples,
Duke of Anjou and Maine, yet is he poor,   95
And our nobility will scorn the match.
Mar. Hear ye, captain, are you not at leisure?
Suf. It shall be so, disdain they ne'er so much;
Henry is youthful, and will quickly yield.—
Madam, I have a secret to reveal.   100
Mar. What though I be enthrall'd? He seems a knight,
And will not any way dishonour me.
Suf. Lady, vouchsafe to listen what I say.
Mar. Perhaps I shall be rescu'd by the French;
And then I need not crave his courtesy.   105
Suf. Sweet madam, give me hearing in a cause—
Mar. Tush, women have been captivate ere now.
Suf. Lady, wherefore talk you so?
Mar. I cry you mercy, 'tis but *quid* for *quo*.
Suf. Say, gentle Princess, would you not suppose   110
Your bondage happy, to be made a queen?
Mar. To be a queen in bondage is more vile
Than is a slave in base servility;
For princes should be free.
Suf.   And so shall you,
If happy England's royal king be free.   115
Mar. Why, what concerns his freedom unto me?
Suf. I'll undertake to make thee Henry's queen,
To put a golden sceptre in thy hand
And set a precious crown upon thy head,
If thou wilt condescend to be my—
Mar.   What?   120
Suf. His love.

---

108. Lady,] *F;* Lady, sweet lady, *conj. Lettsom;* Nay, hear me, lady, *Capell.*
120. to be my] *F;* to *Dyce²*, *conj. Steevens.*

98. *disdain*] show contempt.
101. *enthrall'd*] in its original sense =
made thrall or captive.
106. *cause*] case (in law); possibly
also implying 'in Henry's cause or behalf'.
107. *captivate*] taken prisoner or captive, literally and metaphorically.
109. *cry you mercy*] ask your pardon—
a common Elizabethan expression.

quid *for* quo] L. *quid pro quo* = tit for
tat.
110. *gentle*] noble.
111. *to be*] if you were in consequence
(Brooke).
112. *vile*] L. *vilis* . cheap, worthless; with a play on *servile*.
113. *servility*] slavery (L. *servus*).
120. *condescend*] agree; cf. v. iii.
17.

Mar. I am unworthy to be Henry's wife.

Suf. No, gentle madam, I unworthy am
To woo so fair a dame to be his wife,
And have no portion in the choice myself.   125
How say you, madam, are ye so content?

Mar. And if my father please, I am content.

Suf. Then call our captains and our colours forth!
And, madam, at your father's castle walls
We'll crave a parley, to confer with him.   130

Sound [a parley]. Enter REIGNIER *on the walls.*

See, Reignier, see, thy daughter prisoner!

Reig. To whom?

Suf.   To me.

Reig.   Suffolk, what remedy?
I am a soldier, and unapt to weep
Or to exclaim on fortune's fickleness.

Suf. Yes, there is remedy enough, my lord: 135
Consent, and for thy honour give consent,
Thy daughter shall be wedded to my king,
Whom I with pain have woo'd and won thereto;
And this her easy-held imprisonment
Hath gain'd thy daughter princely liberty.   140

Reig. Speaks Suffolk as he thinks?

Suf.   Fair Margaret knows
That Suffolk doth not flatter, face, or feign.

Reig. Upon thy princely warrant I descend
To give thee answer of thy just demand.

                              [*Exit from the walls.*]

Suf. And here will I expect thy coming.   145

Trumpets sound. Enter REIGNIER [, *below*].

130. S.D. *Sound a parley.*] *after Capell; Sound. | F.*   144. S.D.] *Capell; not in F.*
145. coming.] *F; coming, Reignier. Capell.*   145. S.D. *below*] *Capell; not in F.*

125. *choice*] ambiguous—(*a*) an act of choice; (*b*) the object chosen.

132. *what remedy?*] there's no help for it.

134. *exclaim on*] accuse; cf. III. iii. 60.

136.] not clear, and probably corrupt.

142. *face*] put a false face on the matter, deceive; 'play the hypocrite' (Johnson).

145. *expect*] await.

S.D. *below*] Reignier descends from the upper stage (the walls) to the lower. 'The fanfare gives . . .

Reig. Welcome, brave Earl, into our territories;
　　　Command in Anjou what your Honour please.
Suf. Thanks, Reignier, happy for so sweet a child,
　　　Fit to be made companion with a king.
　　　What answer makes your Grace unto my suit?　　　150
Reig. Since thou dost deign to woo her little worth
　　　To be the princely bride of such a lord,
　　　Upon condition I may quietly
　　　Enjoy mine own, the country Maine, and Anjou,
　　　Free from oppression or the stroke of war,　　　155
　　　My daughter shall be Henry's, if he please.
Suf. That is her ransom; I deliver her;
　　　And those two counties I will undertake
　　　Your Grace shall well and quietly enjoy.
Reig. And I again, in Henry's royal name,　　　160
　　　As deputy unto that gracious king,
　　　Give thee her hand for sign of plighted faith.
Suf. Reignier of France, I give thee kingly thanks,
　　　Because this is in traffic of a king.
　　　[*Aside.*] And yet, methinks, I could be well content　165
　　　To be mine own attorney in this case.
　　　I'll over then to England with this news
　　　And make this marriage to be solemniz'd.
　　　So farewell, Reignier: set this diamond safe
　　　In golden palaces, as it becomes.　　　170
Reig. I do embrace thee, as I would embrace
　　　The Christian prince, King Henry, were he here.
Mar. Farewell, my lord. Good wishes, praise, and prayers
　　　Shall Suffolk ever have of Margaret.　　　*She is going.*
Suf. Farewell, sweet maid; but hark you, Margaret:　175

---

147. please] *This edn;* pleases *F.*　　154. country] *F;* countries *Capell;* county
Malone.　165. S.D. *Aside.*] *Rowe; not in F.*　175. maid] *This edn.;* Madam *F.*

---

time for Reignier's descent' (Wilson).
　147. *please*] cf. 156, 'if he please'.
　151. *worth*] worthiness, excellence.
　154. *country*] cf. 158; a possible F
mis-reading. But Hall, 119, has 'coun-
trys'.
　155. *the stroke of war*] a standard
term, like 'stroke of death' (Hart); cf.
1 Tamb., 717.
　160. *again*] in return.

161. *deputy*] referring to 'thee' (162)
=Suffolk.
　164. *traffic*] business.
　165. *methinks*] it seems to me.
　166. *mine own attorney*] my own agent,
i.e. acting on my own behalf; cf. *Err.,*
v. i. 100.
　170. *as it becomes*] as is fitting.
　175. *maid*] For the F scribal error,
see Intro., p. xxi.

No princely commendations to my king?

Mar. Such commendations as becomes a maid,
A virgin, and his servant, say to him.

Suf. Words sweetly plac'd and modestly directed;
But, madam, I must trouble you again: 180
No loving token to his Majesty?

Mar. Yes, my good lord; a pure unspotted heart,
Never yet taint with love, I send the King.

Suf. And this withal.   *Kiss her.*

Mar. That for thyself: I will not so presume   185
To send such peevish tokens to a king.

> [*Exeunt Reignier and Margaret.*]

Suf. O, wert thou for myself! But, Suffolk, stay;
Thou may'st not wander in that labyrinth:
There Minotaurs and ugly treasons lurk.
Solicit Henry with her wondrous praise.   190
Bethink thee on her virtues that surmount,
And natural graces that extinguish art;
Repeat their semblance often on the seas,
That, when thou com'st to kneel at Henry's feet,
Thou may'st bereave him of his wits with wonder.   *Exit.*

---

184. S.D.] F (*Kisse her.*).   186. S.D.] *Capell; not in F.*   188, 195. may'st] F
(mayest).   192. And] *Capell;* Mad F; 'Mid *Dover Wilson.*

179. *plac'd*] arranged, disposed; cf.
III. ii. 3.

182. *unspotted*] James, i. 27; and cf.
2H6, III. i. 100.

183. *taint*] pa. pple—tainted, tinged.

184. *withal*] in addition.

186. *peevish*] silly, foolish, trifling.

188–9. *labyrinth . . . Minotaurs*] referring of course to the maze of King
Minos in Crete, where lived the de-
vouring monster.

190. *Solicit*] move, excite.

her wondrous praise] the praise of her,
who is full of wonders.

191. *surmount*] excel, are pre-
eminent.

192. *extinguish art*] a contrast of
nature and art; extinguish = eclipse.

193. *Repeat . . . semblance*] revive the
idea or image of them, by description.

[SCENE IV.—*Camp of the Duke of York in Anjou.*]

Enter YORK, WARWICK[, *and Others*].

York. Bring forth that sorceress condemn'd to burn.

Enter [LA] PUCELLE [*guarded, and a*] *Shepherd.*

Shep. Ah, Joan, this kills thy father's heart outright!
    Have I sought every country far and near,
    And, now it is my chance to find thee out,
    Must I behold thy timeless cruel death?   5
    Ah, Joan, sweet daughter, Joan I'll die with thee!
Puc. Decrepit miser! base ignoble wretch!
    I am descended of a gentler blood:
    Thou art no father nor no friend of mine.
Shep. Out, out! My lords, and please you, 'tis not so;   10
    I did beget her, all the parish knows:
    Her mother liveth yet, can testify
    She was the first fruit of my bachelorship.

Scene IV

SCENE IV] *Capell; not in* F.   *Camp* . . . *Anjou.*] *Capell; not in* F.   S.D. *and*
Others.] *Capell; Shepheard, Pucell.* | F.   1. S.D.] *edd., after Capell;* F, *before l. 1.*

The first part of this scene (1–93) has particularly offended modern sentiment, and is partly responsible for the desire to exonerate Shakespeare from the authorship of much of the play. It is, however, derived straight from Hall and Holinshed, and is typical enough of anti-French sentiment in Elizabethan times.

The conclusion of peace apparently gives victory to the English; but (*a*) Suffolk has already arranged for cession of Maine and Anjou, and (*b*) York and Warwick find a new source of discontent in the terms of the treaty.

Dr Brooks compares Lodge and Greene, *A Looking Glasse for London and England*, III. ii, where Radagon repudiates Samia his mother (and his father, Alcon). Both episodes end in a curse and death by fire; the shepherd and Alcon appeal to the parish for proof of parentage; blessing is refused; and there are some slight resemblances of phrase.

2. *kills* . . . *heart*] a common Elizabethan expression = causes great distress or grief.

3. *sought*] searched; cf. *Err.*, I. i. 136.

4. *it* . . . *chance*] I have happened.

5. *timeless*] untimely, premature.

7. *Decrepit*] worn with age; cf. *LLL.*, I. i. 139.

miser] wretch (L. *miser* = wretch, wretched man); cf. *F.Q.*, II. i. 9; II. iii. 8.

ignoble] not of noble blood.

8. *gentler*] more noble.

9. *friend*] relative.

12. *yet, can*] On the omission of the relative, see Abbott, 244.

13. *first fruit*] first born, with a possible allusion to 'first fruits', dedicated to the church.

War. Graceless, wilt thou deny thy parentage?
York. This argues what her kind of life hath been,   15
          Wicked and vile; and so her death concludes.
Shep. Fie, Joan, that thou wilt be so obstacle!
          God knows thou art a collop of my flesh;
          And for thy sake have I shed many a tear.
          Deny me not, I prithee, gentle Joan.   20
Puc. Peasant, avaunt! You have suborn'd this man
          Of purpose to obscure my noble birth.
Shep. 'Tis true, I gave a noble to the priest
          The morn that I was wedded to her mother.
          Kneel down and take my blessing, good my girl.   25
          Wilt thou not stoop? Now cursed be the time
          Of thy nativity! I would the milk
          Thy mother gave thee when thou suck'dst her breast
          Had been a little ratsbane for thy sake;
          Or else, when thou didst keep my lambs a-field,   30
          I wish some ravenous wolf had eaten thee.
          Dost thou deny thy father, cursed drab?
          O, burn her, burn her: hanging is too good.   *Exit.*
York. Take her away, for she hath liv'd too long,
          To fill the world with vicious qualities.   35
Puc. First let me tell you whom you have condemn'd:
          Not one begotten of a shepherd swain,

28. suck'dst] *F* (suck'st).   37. one] *Marshall, conj. Malone;* me *F.*

14, 20, 32. *deny*] disown; cf. *Rom.,* II.
ii. 34.
15. *argues*] betokens, implies; cf.
2H6, III. iii. 30, 'So bad a death argues
a monstrous life'.
16. *concludes*] (*a*) proves the truth of
the argument; (*b*) ends the case (i.e.
her life).
17. *obstacle*] 'an old vulgar corruption of "obstinate", which, I think, has
oddly lasted . . . till now' (Johnson).
The intention was probably to charac-
terize the rusticity of the shepherd. Cf.
Man. Voc., 'Obstacle, *pertinax, obsti-
natus*'.
18. *collop*] slice, fragment; cf. Golding's *Ovid,* v. 650–1, 'my daughter . . . /
A collop of mine owne flesh cut as well
out of thine'.

22–3. *noble*] the pun, or misunderstanding, is intended further to charac-
terize the shepherd. The noble was a
coin worth 6s. 8d.
27. *nativity*] birth.
29. *ratsbane*] white arsenic, used as
rat poison.
30. *keep . . . lambs*] Hol., iii. 604 (cf.
I. ii. 76); not in Hall.
32. *drab*] strumpet; cf. 'a beggers
brat', Hall, 157.
37. *one*] for the F error in reverse
(one/me), cf. *Shr.,* I. ii. 169, and *Tw.
N.,* III. iii. 7.
37 ff.] 'Joan is here drawing on
Gospel narrative, first in the call to the
Virgin (Luke, i), and next in the reference to the way the corrupted Jewish
leaders attributed Christ's miracles to

But issued from the progeny of kings;
Virtuous and holy, chosen from above,
By inspiration of celestial grace,   40
To work exceeding miracles on earth.
I never had to do with wicked spirits;
But you, that are polluted with your lusts,
Stain'd with the guiltless blood of innocents,
Corrupt and tainted with a thousand vices,   45
Because you want the grace that others have,
You judge it straight a thing impossible
To compass wonders but by help of devils.
No, misconceived Joan of Aire hath been
A virgin from her tender infancy,   50
Chaste and immaculate in very thought;
Whose maiden blood, thus rigorously effus'd,
Will cry for vengeance at the gates of heaven.

York. Ay, ay; away with her to execution!
War. And hark ye, sirs; because she is a maid,   55
Spare for no faggots, let there be enow:
Place barrels of pitch upon the fatal stake,
That so her torture may be shortened.

Puc. Will nothing turn your unrelenting hearts?
Then, Joan, discover thine infirmity   60
That warranteth by law to be thy privilege:

---

49. No, misconceived] *F4, Marshall;* No misconceyued, *F;* No. misconceived! *Steevens;* No, misconceivers: *Capell.*   Aire] *F;* Arc *Rowe+edd.*   61. to be thy] *F;* thy *Hanmer.*

Beelzebub (Matt., xii. 24, 27). The last two lines (52–3) are reminiscent of Abel the first martyr, whose blood called to Heaven for vengeance' (Noble). See Gen., iv. 10; and cf. *R2,* i. i. 104–6.

38. *progeny*] ancestry, *OED.,* 5; cf. III. iii. 61.

40. *inspiration . . .*] Hall, 157.

41. *exceeding*] exceptional, outstanding.

44. *the blood of innocents*] cf. Deut., xxi. 9, 'the cry of innocent blood', and the mediaeval representations of the Massacre of the Innocents.

49. *misconceived*] The F1 (and editorial) reading gives an active where a passive is wanted; and the application is not to York, but to Joan herself. This is appropriate to the context—as the F1 reading is not—and adds a typical ironic turn to the speech; 'misconceived' means (a) misunderstood, (b) misbegotten (cf. 37). Though not in *OED.,* it seems inevitable as a parallel to 'misbegotten'; cf. *Sp. Tragedy,* III. i. 89.

Aire] see II. ii. 20 and n.

56. *enow*] enough.

60. *discover*] uncover, reveal.

61. *privilege*] The legal 'privilege' is presumably due to the Roman law

I am with child, ye bloody homicides;
Murder not then the fruit within my womb,
Although ye hale me to a violent death.

York. Now heaven forfend! The holy maid with child!   65
War. The greatest miracle that e'er ye wrought!
Is all your strict preciseness come to this?
York. She and the Dauphin have been juggling:
I did imagine what would be her refuge.
War. Well, go to; we will have no bastards live,   70
Especially since Charles must father it.
Puc. You are deceiv'd; my child is none of his:
It was Alençon that enjoy'd my love.
York. Alençon, that notorious Machiavel!
It dies and if it had a thousand lives.   75
Puc. O, give me leave, I have deluded you:
'Twas neither Charles, nor yet the Duke I nam'd,
But Reignier, King of Naples, that prevail'd.
War. A married man! that's most intolerable.
York. Why, here's a girl! I think she knows not well—   80
There were so many—whom she may accuse.
War. It's sign she hath been liberal and free.
York. And yet, forsooth, she is a virgin pure!
Strumpet, thy words condemn thy brat and thee:
Use no entreaty, for it is in vain.   85
Puc. Then lead me hence, with whom I leave my curse:
May never glorious sun reflex his beams

---

70. we will] *F2;* we'll *F.*   74. Machiavel] *F* (Macheuile?).

maxim 'nasciturus pro nato'; Joan's execution would thus involve the death of the innocent. Cf. Hol., III. 604.

63. *the fruit*] cf. Ps., cxxvii. 3; Gen., xxx. 2 (Noble).

67. *preciseness*] strict morality; Puritanism.

68. *juggling*] See *Sh. Bawdy,* and cf. *Troil.,* v. ii. 24.

69. *refuge*] final defence or excuse.

73, 74. *Alençon . . . Machiavel*] Gentillet's translation of Machiavelli's *Il Principe* was dedicated to a later Alençon, who was suitor to Queen Eliza-beth (c. 1580), and afterwards became Henri III. As Duc d'Anjou he had taken part in the Massacre of St Bartholomew, and was author of the 'French fury' in Antwerp in 1583. Both events, very unpopular in England, were carried out on what were supposed to be Machiavelli's principles, as interpreted by Gentillet.

84. *brat*] child (with no necessary pejorative sense but implying insignificance).

87. *reflex*] cast; cf. Marlowe, *1 Tamb.*, 970, 'Nor Sun reflexe his vertuous beames thereon'.

Upon the country where you make abode;
But darkness and the gloomy shade of death
Environ you, till mischief and despair   90
Drive you to break your necks or hang yourselves!

Exit [*guarded*].

York. Break thou in pieces and consume to ashes,
Thou foul accursed minister of hell!

Enter Cardinal [BEAUFORT, *Bishop of* WINCHESTER, *attended*].

Win. Lord Regent, I do greet your Excellence
With letters of commission from the King.   95
For know, my lords, the states of Christendom,
Mov'd with remorse of these outrageous broils,
Have earnestly implor'd a general peace
Betwixt our nation and the aspiring French;
And here at hand the Dauphin and his train   100
Approacheth to confer about the same.
York. Is all our travail turn'd to this effect?
After the slaughter of so many peers,
So many captains, gentlemen, and soldiers,
That in this quarrel have been overthrown   105
And sold their bodies for their country's benefit,
Shall we at last conclude effeminate peace?
Have we not lost most part of all the towns,
By treason, falsehood, and by treachery,
Our great progenitors had conquered?   110
O, Warwick, Warwick! I foresee with grief
The utter loss of all the realm of France.
War. Be patient, York: if we conclude a peace,

---

91. S.D.] *Theobald; Exit* | F.   93. S.D.] *Capell; Enter Cardinall.* | F (*after 91*).
101. the same] *This edn;* some matter F.

---

89. *darkness . . . death*] Malone
compares Matt., iv. 16, 'them that
sit in darkness and the shadow of
death'.
90. *mischief*] misfortune, calamity.
93. *minister*] servant.
97. *remorse*] pity, compassion.
99. *aspiring*] ambitious; cf. 'aspiring
. . . Lancaster', *3H6,* v. vi. 61.

101. *confer*] converse, discuss.
the same] The subject of discussion is
not vague, as implied by F 'some'; it is
the 'general peace'. An omission (of
'the') with subsequent rationalization,
taking 'same' for 'some', would account for F. 'The same' is Shakespearean, 'some matter' not.
102. *travail*] toil.

It shall be with such strict and several covenants
As little shall the Frenchmen gain thereby.   115

Enter CHARLES, ALENÇON, BASTARD, REIGNIER,
[*and Others*].

Cha. Since, lords of England, it is thus agreed
That peaceful truce shall be proclaim'd in France,
We come to be informed by yourselves
What the conditions of that league must be.
York. Speak, Winchester, for boiling choler chokes   120
The hollow passage of my poison'd voice
By sight of these our baleful enemies.
Win. Charles and the rest, it is enacted thus:
That, in regard King Henry gives consent,
Of mere compassion and of lenity,   125
To ease your country of distressful war,
And suffer you to breathe in fruitful peace,
You shall become true liegemen to his crown.
And, Charles, upon condition thou wilt swear
To pay him tribute and submit thyself,   130
Thou shalt be plac'd as viceroy under him,
And still enjoy thy regal dignity.
Alen. Must he be then as shadow of himself?
Adorn his temples with a coronet,
And yet, in substance and authority,   135
Retain but privilege of a private man?
This proffer is absurd and reasonless.
Cha. 'Tis known already that I am possess'd
With more than half the Gallian territories,
And therein reverenc'd for their lawful king: 140

114. several] *This edn, conj. Vaughan;* seuere *F.*   115. S.D. *and Others.*] *Capell;* not in F.

114. *several*] F 'seuere' is (*a*) superfluous, (*b*) always accented on the second syllable, and will not fit the metre (the example in *Meas.,* II. ii. 41, can be explained as the result of transposition in a memorially contaminated text). 'Several' gives metre and (legal) sense = enforceable against each of the parties.

115. *As*] that; see Abbott, 109.

121–2. *poison'd voice | By sight . . . baleful enemies.*] For the split adj. phrase, see Abbott, 419a. The allusion is to the fabulous basilisk, that killed by its breath and look; cf. *2H6,* III. ii. 52, 324.

124. *in regard*] inasmuch as, since.

125. *mere . . . lenity*] pure . . . mildness.

134. *coronet*] crown; cf. *Lr.,* I. i. 141.

Shall I, for lucre of the rest unvanquish'd,
Detract so much from that prerogative
As to be call'd but viceroy of the whole?
No, Lord Ambassador, I'll rather keep
That which I have than, coveting for more,   145
Be cast from possibility of all.

York. Insulting Charles! Hast thou by secret means
Us'd intercession to obtain a league,
And, now the matter grows to compromise,
Stand'st thou aloof upon comparison?   150
Either accept the title thou usurp'st,
Of benefit proceeding from our king
And not of any challenge of desert,
Or we will plague thee with incessant wars.

Reig. [*Aside to Charles.*] My lord, you do not well in
        obstinacy   155
To cavil in the course of this contract;
If once it be neglected, ten to one
We shall not find like opportunity.

Alen. [*Aside to Charles.*] To say the truth, it is your policy
To save your subjects from such massacre   160
And ruthless slaughters as are daily seen
By our proceeding in hostility;
And therefore take this compact of a truce,
Although you break it when your pleasure serves.

War. How say'st thou, Charles? shall our condition stand?
Cha. It shall; only reserv'd you claim no interest   166
In any of our towns of garrison.

York. Then swear allegiance to his Majesty:
As thou art knight, never to disobey
Nor be rebellious to the crown of England,   170

---

155. S.D.] *Hanmer* (*To the Dauphin aside.*).   159. S.D.] *Pope* (*Aside to the Dauphin.*).
165.] *as Pope;* ... *Charles?* / Shall ... *F.*

141. *lucre*] gain, acquisition.
142. *Detract*] take away, subtract.
146. *cast*] driven, excluded; cf. *Cym.*, v. iv. 60.
149. *grows to compromise*] is approaching an amicable settlement.
150. *Stand'st* . . . *upon comparison*] make a point of comparing your present state with the terms we offer.
152. *Of benefit*] by way of bounty (Brooke); as the (legal) beneficiary of (Johnson).
153. *challenge*] claim.
159. *policy*] politic course. Note Alençon's change of front, typically Machiavellian; cf. n. at 73.

Thou, nor thy nobles, to the crown of England.
         [*Charles and the rest give tokens of fealty.*]
So, now dismiss your army when ye please;
Hang up your ensigns, let your drums be still,
For here we entertain a solemn peace.   *Exeunt.*

[SCENE] V. [—*London. The royal palace.*]

Enter SUFFOLK *in conference with the* KING, GLOUCESTER,
and EXETER.

K. Hen. Your wondrous rare description, noble Earl,
    Of beauteous Margaret hath astonish'd me:
    Her virtues graced with external gifts
    Do breed love's settled passions in my heart:
    And like as rigour of tempestuous gusts   5
    Provokes the mightiest hulk against the tide,
    So am I driven by breath of her renown
    Either to suffer shipwreck, or arrive
    Where I may have fruition of her love.
Suf. Tush, my good lord, this superficial tale   10
    Is but a preface of her worthy praise;

171. S.D.] *Johnson; not in F.*

Scene v

SCENE V] *Capell; Actus Quintus. | F.*   *London. The royal palace.*] *Capell+edd.;*
not in F.

171. *to the crown . . .*] 'puerile repetition' (Wilson); possibly a typical error
of the scribe; for which see Intro.,
p. xxi.
  174. *entertain*] accept, bring in.

Scene v

Hall introduces Gloucester's opposition to the Anjou marriage for the
first time here; and does not show him
supporting the Armagnac contract.
Shakespeare, however, has extended
Gloucester's opposition to include this
positive support, and to aggravate his
opposition to Suffolk. The oath-
breach, as in the later historical plays
in the series, is vital.

1, 3. *wondrous . . . virtues*] cf. v. iii.
190, 'her wondrous praise . . . virtues',
Hall, 204.
  5 ff.] The imagery used here becomes dominant in *3H6.* It is symbolical, for Shakespeare, of the conflicting
currents of the civil wars, as it is here of
Henry's easy desertion of Armagnac
for Anjou.
  6. *Provokes*] impels.
  8. *arrive*] with the usual Elizabethan
implication of reaching shore (L. *ad +
ripa*).
  10. *superficial*] concerning her 'external gifts'.
  11. *her worthy praise*] L. construction
= the praise of her worth.

The chief perfections of that lovely dame,
Had I sufficient skill to utter them,
Would make a volume of enticing lines,
Able to ravish any dull conceit;   15
And, which is more, she is not so divine,
So full replete with choice of all delights,
But with as humble lowliness of mind
She is content to be at your command;
Command, I mean, of virtuous chaste intents,   20
To love and honour Henry as her lord.

K. Hen. And otherwise will Henry ne'er presume.
Therefore, my Lord Protector, give consent
That Margaret may be England's royal Queen.

Glou. So should I give consent to flatter sin.   25
You know, my lord, your Highness is betroth'd
Unto another lady of esteem;
How shall we then dispense with that contract,
And not deface your honour with reproach.

Suf. As doth a ruler with unlawful oaths;   30
Or one that, at a triumph, having vow'd
To try his strength, forsaketh yet the lists
By reason of his adversary's odds:
A poor earl's daughter is unequal odds,
And therefore may be broke without offence.   35

Glou. Why, what, I pray, is Margaret more than that?
Her father is no better than an earl,
Although in glorious titles he excel.

Suf. Yes, my lord, her father is a king,
The King of Naples and Jerusalem;   40
And of such great authority in France
As his alliance will confirm our peace,
And keep the Frenchmen in allegiance.

---

39. my] *F; my good F2.*

15. *conceit*] Elizabethan sense = imagination.

17. *full*] fully.

25. *flatter*] gloss over, palliate.

28. *dispense with*] set aside, neglect (Hart).

contract] normal Elizabethan ac-cent, on the second syllable.

29. *deface*] disfigure, soil.

30. *oaths*] The breaking of oaths is a recurrent theme in this series of plays.

31. *triumph*] tournament.

41–2. *such ... / As*] Abbott, 107.

42. *confirm*] strengthen.

Glou. And so the Earl of Armagnac may do,
    Because he is near kinsman unto Charles.   45
Exe. Beside, his wealth doth warrant a liberal dower,
    Where Reignier sooner will receive than give.
Suf. A dower, my lords! Disgrace not so your king,
    That he should be so abject, base, and poor,
    To choose for wealth and not for perfect love.   50
    Henry is able to enrich his queen,
    And not to seek a queen to make him rich:
    So worthless peasants bargain for their wives,
    As market-men for oxen, sheep, or horse.
    Marriage is a matter of more worth   55
    Than to be dealt in by attorneyship;
    Not whom we will, but whom his Grace affects,
    Must be companion of his nuptial bed;
    And therefore, lords, since he affects her most,
    [That] most of all these reasons bindeth us   60
    In our opinions she should be preferr'd.
    For what is wedlock forced but a hell,
    An age of discord and continual strife?
    Whereas the contrary bringeth bliss,
    And is a pattern of celestial peace.   65
    Whom should we match with Henry, being a king,
    But Margaret, that is daughter to a king?
    Her peerless feature, joined with her birth,
    Approves her fit for none but for a king;
    Her valiant courage and undaunted spirit,   70
    More than in women commonly is seen,
    Will answer our hope in issue of a king;
    For Henry, son unto a conqueror,
    Is likely to beget more conquerors,

---

44. Armagnac] *F* (Arminacke).   60. [That] most] *This edn;* Most *F;* Which
most *Dover Wilson;* It most *Rowe.*   72. answer our] *F;* answer *Hudson, conj.*
Steevens.

46. *warrant*] guarantee.   60. *That*]] see Intro., p. xxvii.
47. *Where*] whereas.   62-3.] cf. Prov., xvii. 1.
54. *market-men*] cf. III. ii. 4; peasants   65. *pattern*] example, instance.
who haggle over their transactions in   68. *feature*] form of body (Brooke).
open market.   69. *Approves*] proves.
56. *attorneyship*] proxy.   70. *courage*] spirit, disposition; cf.
57. *affects*] loves.   App. I (2) (Hall, 205).

If with a lady of so high resolve   75
As is fair Margaret he be link'd in love.
Then yield, my lords; and here conclude with me
That Margaret shall be Queen, and none but she.
K. Hen. Whether it be through force of your report,
My noble Lord of Suffolk, or for that   80
My tender youth was never yet attaint
With any passion of inflaming love,
I cannot tell; but this I am assur'd,
I feel such sharp dissension in my breast,
Such fierce alarums both of hope and fear,   85
As I am sick with working of my thoughts.
Take therefore shipping; post, my lord, to France;
Agree to any covenants, and procure
That Lady Margaret do vouchsafe to come
To cross the seas to England and be crown'd   90
King Henry's faithful and anointed queen.
For your expenses and sufficient charge,
Among the people gather up a tenth.
Be gone, I say; for till you do return
I rest perplexed with a thousand cares.   95
And you, good uncle, banish all offence;
If you do censure me by what you were,
Not what you are, I know it will excuse
This sudden execution of my will.
And so conduct me where from company   100
I may revolve and ruminate my grief.   *Exit.*
Glou. Ay, grief, I fear me, both at first and last.
                        Exeunt Gloucester [and Exeter].

---

82. love] *F2+edd.;* Ioue *F.*   90. To cross] *F;* Across *Hudson, conj. S. Walker.*
102. S.D.] *Capell; Exit Glocester. | F.*

80. *for that*] because.
81. *attaint*] pa. pple.
86. *working*] applied to the motion or labours of the mind (Schmidt).
88. *procure*] contrive.
92. *charge*] money to spend (Brooke).
93. *a tenth*] Hall says 'a fifteenth' as in *2H6*, I. i. 131; a tax on incomes.
97. *censure*] judge (no blame is implied).

what you were] an allusion to Gloucester's affair with Lady Jaquet, the wife of John, Duke of Brabant (Hall, 116, 128–9). For its bearing on the priority of *1H6*, see Intro., p. li.
100. *from company*] in solitude.
101. *revolve and ruminate*] occurs in *Troil.*, II. iii. 182–3.
101, 102. *grief*] (*a*) pain, uneasiness; (*b*) sorrow (Johnson).

Suf. Thus Suffolk hath prevail'd; and thus he goes,
    As did the youthful Paris once to Greece;
    With hope to find the like event in love,   105
    But prosper better than the Trojan did.
    Margaret shall now be Queen, and rule the King;
    But I will rule both her, the King, and realm.   *Exit.*

---

105. *event*] L. *eventus* = outcome, result—the Elizabethan sense.

108.] cf. Hall, 207; Suffolk 'by the meanes of the Quene, was shortely erected to the estate and degree of a Duke, and ruled the Kyng at his pleasure'. This leads on to *2H6*. Political order is to be completely reversed, and the anarchy of the Roses follows automatically.

Appendix I

(a) From Edward Hall's *The Union of the Two Noble and Illustre Famelies of Lancastre and Yorke*, 1548

References are to (i) the 1548 edition, (ii) the reprint of 1809

lxxviii 108 Durying this siege [of Meaux] was borne at Wynsore on the daie of S. Nicholas the kynges sonne Henry. . . [Henry V] gave thankes to his Creator. . . But when he heard reported the place of his nativitie, whether he fantasied some old blind prophesy, or had some foreknowledge, or els judged of his sonnes fortune, he sayd . . . these wordes. 'My lorde, I Henry borne at Monmoth shall small tyme reigne & much get, & Henry borne at Wyndsore shall long reigne and al lese, but as God will so be it.'   III. i. 195–9

lxxx^v 112 [1422] And as touchyng the estate of my realmes, Fyrst I commaund you to loue and ioyne together in one leage or concord and in one vnfained amitie, kepyng continual peace and amitie with Philip duke of Burgoyn. And neuer make treatie with Charles that calleth him selfe dolphyn of Vyen, by the whiche any part either of the croune of Fraunce or of the duchies of Normandy or Guyan may be appaired or diminished. Let the duke of Orleance and the other princes styl remayne prisoners til my sonne come to his lawful age, lest his returnyng home againe may kyndle more fier in one day then may be well quenched in thre. If / you thinke it necessary I would my brother Vmfrey should be Protector of England duryng the minoritie of my child, prohibityng him once to passe out of the realme. And my brother of Bedford with the helpe of the duke of Burgoyne I wyll shall rule and be regent of the realme of Fraunce, com-   I. i. 162–4

lxxxi

133

maundyng him with fyre and sworde to perse-
cute Charles callyng him selfe dolphyn, to thentent either to bryng him to reason & obeysaunce,
or to dryue and expel him out of the realme of
Fraunce admonishyng you to lese no tyme, nor
to spare no cost in recoueryng that whiche to
you is now offered. And what thynges either I
haue gotten or you shal obtaine, I charge you
kepe it, I commaund you to defend it, and I desire you to norishe it: for experience teacheth
that there is no lesse praise to be geuen to the
keper then to the getter, for verely gettyng is a
chaunce and kepyng a wit. . . .

The noble men present promised to obserue
his preceptes and performe his desires. . . .

This Henry was a kyng whose life was im-   1. i. 6 ff.
maculate & his liuyng without spot. This kyng
was a prince whom all men loued & of none disdained, This prince was a capitaine against
whom fortune neuer frowned nor mischance
once spurned. . . His vertues were nomore notable then his qualities were worthy of praise . . . /
xxxi ᵛ 113   He had suche knowledge in orderyng and guyd-
yng an armye and suche a grace in encouragyng
his people, that the Frenchmen sayd he could
not be vanquished in battel. . . . What should I
say, he was the blasyng comete and apparant
lanterne in his daies, he was the myrror of Christ-
endome & the glory of his countrey, he was the
floure of kynges passed, and a glasse to them that
should succede. . . . No prince had lesse of his
subiectes and neuer kyng conquered more:
whose fame by his death as liuely florisheth as
his actes in his life wer sene and remembred . . . /
lxxxii   . . . His body was enbaumed & closed in lede &
layde in a charet royal richely apparaled with
114   cloth of gold, . . . On this Charet / gaue attend-
ance Iames kyng of Scottes the principal mor-
ner, the duke of Exceter Thomas his uncle,
therle of Warwike Richard, therle of Marche
Edmond, therle of Stafford Humfrey, the erle
of Mortaine Edmond Beaufford. . . . The Hache-
mentes wer borne onely by capitaines to the

nombre of xii. and round about the charet rode
CCCCC. men of armes al in blacke harnes &
their horses barded blacke. . . . With this funeral
pompe he was conveighed . . . thorough London
to Westminster, where he was buried with suche
solempne ceremonies, / . . . as neuer was before
that day sene in the realme of Englande.

lxxxii^v

lxxxiii
115

[The i. yere (1422)] . . . And the custody of   L. i. 171
this young prince [Henry VI] was apoyncted to
Thomas duke of Excester, and to Henry Beaufford bishopp of Wynchester: the duke of Bedford was deputed to be Regent of Fraunce, and   84
the duke of Gloucester was assigned Protector   37
of Englande.

lxxxiv^v
116

Humfrey duke of Gloucester either blynded   v. v. 97
with ambicion or dotyng for love, married the
lady Jaquet . . . whiche was lawfull wife to Jhon
duke of Brabant then livyng, whiche mariage
was not onely woundered at of the comon
people, but also detested of the nobilite, & abhorred of the Clergie. But suerly the swete tast,
of this pleasant mariage, brought after a sower
sauce, bothe to the amorous housbande, and to
the wanton wife. For Jhon duke of Brabant,
what with force, and what with spirituall com-
pulsaries, never left of, till he had recovered his
Lady out of the Duke of Gloucesters possession.

xcii^v 128

[The iii. yere (1424–5)] Edmonde Mortimer,   II. v
the last Erle of Marche of that name (whiche   III. i. 61–3,
long tyme had been restrained from his liberty,   149 ff.
and finally waxed lame) disceased without issue,
whose inheritaunce discended to lorde Richarde
Plantagenet, sonne and heire to Richard erle of
Cambridge, beheded, as you haue heard before,
at the toune of Southhampton. Whiche Richard
within lesse then xxx. yeres, as heire to this
erle Edmond, in open parliament claimed the
croune and scepter of this realme . . .

xciii 129

The duke of Gloucester . . . by wanton affec-   I. i. 39
cion blinded, toke to his wife Elianor Cobham

doughter to the lord Cobham, of Sterberow, whiche before (as the fame went) was his soueraigne lady and paramour, to his great slaunder and reproche. And if he wer vnquieted with his other pretensed wife, truly he / was tenne tymes more vexed, by occasion of this woman, as you shall herafter plainly perceiue: so that he began his mariage with euill, and ended it with worse.

xciii^v

xciiii 130   [iiii. yere. (1426–7)] In this season fell a greate   i. i. 32–56
diuision in the realme of England, whiche, of a sparcle was like to growe to a greate flame: For whether the bishop of Winchester called Henry Beaufort, sonne to Ihon Duke of Lancastre . . . enuied the authoritee of Humfrey duke of Gloucester Protector of the realme, or whether the duke had taken disdain at the riches and pompous estate of the bishop, sure it is that the whole realme was troubled with them and their partakers: so that the citezens of London fearyng   iii. i
that that should insue vpon the matter, wer faine to kepe daily and nightly, watches, as though their enemies were at hande, to besiege and destroye them: In so muche that all the shoppes within the cite of London wer shut in for feare of the fauorers of those two greate personages, for eche parte had assembled no small nombre of people. . . .

The duke of Bedford beyng sore greued and   i. i. 44 ff.,
vnquieted with these newes, . . . returned again   69 ff.
ciiii^v   ouer the seas into England. . . . / The xxv. daie of Marche after his commyng to London, a parliament began at the toune of Leicester, where the Duke of Bedford openly rebuked the Lordes in generall, because that thei in the tyme of warre, through their priuie malice and inwarde grudge, had almoste moued the people to warre and commocion. . . . In this parliament the Duke of Gloucester, laied certain articles to the bishoppe   iii. i. 1–13
of Wynchesters charge . . .

First, where as he beyng protector and defendor of this lande, desired the toure to be opened   i. iii. 1–56
to hym, and to lodge hym therein, Richard

Woodeuile esquire, hauyng at that tyme the
charge of the kepyng of the toure, refused his
desire, and kepte thesame toure against hym,
vnduly and against reason, by the commaunde-
ment of my saied Lorde of Winchester; and
afterward in approuyng of thesaid refuse, he receiued thesaid Wodeuile, and cherished hym
against the state and worship of the kyng, and
of my saied lorde of Gloucester.

131   ITEM my said lorde of Winchester, without   I. i. 175-7
the aduise and assente of my said lorde of Glou-
cester, or the kynges counsail, purposed and disposed hym to set hande on the kynges persone,
and to haue remoued hym from Eltham, the
place that he was in to Windsore, to the entent to put hym in suche gouernaunce as hym
list.

ITEM, that where my said lorde of Glouces-   III. i. 22-3
ter, . . . determinyng to haue gone to Eltham
vnto the kyng, to haue prouided as the cause required. My saied lorde of Winchester, vntruly
and against the kynges peace, to the entent to
trouble my said lord of Gloucester goyng to the
kyng purposyng his death in case that he had
gone that waie, set men of armes and archers,
at thende of London bridge next Southwerke:
xcv   . . . and set men in chambers, sellers and win-
dowes, with bowes / and arrowes and other
weapons, to thentent to bryng to final destruccion my saied lorde of Gloucesters persone, aswell as of those that then should come with
hym. . . .

ITEM . . . Gloucester saith . . . there was on a   I. iii. 33-4
night a man espied and taken behynd a tapet of
the . . . chambre, the whiche . . . confessed that
he was there by the steryng up and procuryng
of my saied Lorde of Winchester, ordained to
have slain thesaied prince in his bedde.

xcix^v 137   . . . it was decreed . . . that every ech of my   III. i. 126 ff.
lordes of Gloucester and Winchester should take
either other by the hande, in the presence of the
kyng and all the parliament, in signe and token
of good love and accord, the whiche was doen

and the Parliament was adjourned till after
Easter.

138   . . . the greate fire of this discencion . . . was thus   III. i. 149 ff.
. . . vtterly quenched out . . . For ioy whereof, the
kyng caused a solempne feast, to be kept on
Whitson sondaie, on the whiche daie, he created
Richard Plantagenet, sonne and heire to the
erle of Cambridge (whom his father at Hamp-
ton, had put to execucion, as you before haue
hearde) Duke of Yorke, not forseyng before, that
this preferment should be his destruccion, nor
that his sede should, of his generacion, bee the
extreme ende and finall confusion.

Cᵛ 139   [v. yere (1427–8)] . . . The Duke of Bedforde   v. i. 28 ff.
. . . landed at Calice, with whom also passed the
seas, Henry bishop of Winchester, whiche in thesaied toune was inuested with the Habite, Hatte
and dignitie of a Cardinall, with all Ceremonies
to it appertainyng. Whiche degree, kyng Henry
the fifth knowyng the haute corage, and the am-
bicious mynde of the man, prohibited hym on
his allegeaunce once, either to sue for or to take,
meanyng that Cardinalles Hattes should not
presume to bee egall with Princes. But now the
kyng beyng young and the Regent his frende,
he obteined that dignitie, to his greate profite,
and to the empouerishyng of the spiritualtie.
For by a Bull legatyue, whiche he purchased at
Rome, he gathered so much treasure, that no
man in maner had money but he, and so was he
surnamed the riche Cardinall of Winchester,
and nether called learned bishop, nor verteous   I. i. 33–44
priest.

Cii 141   . . . the lord Talbot, was made gouernor, of   I. v. ff.
Aniow and Mayne, and sir Ihon Fastolffe was
assigned to another place: whiche lorde Talbot,
beyng bothe of noble birthe, and haute corage,
after his comming into Fraunce, obteined so
many glorious victories of his enemies, that his
only name was, and yet is dredful to the French
nacion, and muche renoumed emongest al other
people. This ioly capitan, and sonne of the vali-

ant Mars, entered into Mayn and slewe men,
destroyed castles, and brent tounes, . . .

Ciii 142 The duke of Alaunson, whiche . . . was late   I. vi–II
deliuered out of Englande, reuiued again the
dull spirites of the Dolphyn, and . . . determined
to do some notable feate against thenglishe men.
Then happened a chaunce vnloked for, or vn-
thought of, euen as thei would haue . . . desired,
for not onely the Magistrates, but chiefly the
spiritual persons of the citee of Mauns, knowyng
that the duke of Britayne and his brother, were
reuerted and turned to the French partie, . . .
determined and fully concluded, to aduertise of
their myndes and determinacions, the capitaines of Charles the dolphyn, . . .

When the daie assigned . . . was come, the
Frenche capitaines priuely approched the toune,
makyng a litle fire on an hill in the sight of the
toune, to signifie their commyng and approch-
yng. The citezens, whiche by the great church
wer loking for their approch, shewed a burnyng
Cresset out of the steple, whiche sodainly was   III. ii. 20
put out & quenched. What should I saie, the
capitaines on horssebacke came to the gate, and
the traytors within slewe the porters and watche
men, and let in their frendes, the footemen entered firste, and the men of armes waited at the
143 barriers, to the intent that if muche nede / required or necessitie compelled, thei might fight
in the open feld. And in the meane season many
Englishmen wer slain, and a greate claymor and
a houge noyse was hard through the toune. . . . /
Ciiiᵛ The erle of Suffolke, whiche was gouernour of
the toune, . . . entered into the Castle which
standeth at the gate of Sainct Vincent, . . . whether also fled so many Englishemen, that the
place was pestured, and there if thei wer not
rescued, likely to be famished . . . But all their
hardines had not serued, . . . if thei had not
priuely sent a messenger to the lorde Talbot,
whiche then laie at Alanson, certefiyng hym in
what case thei stoode. . . The lorde Talbot her-
yng these newes, neither slept nor banquetted,

but with all hast assembled together his valiaunt
capitaines, . . . and in the mornyng came to a
castle . . . twoo myles from Mauns, and from
thence sent as an espial Matthew Gough. . .
Matthew Gough so well sped, that priuely in the
night he came into the castle, where he knew
how that the French men beyng lordes of the
citee, and now castyng no perels nor fearyng any
creature, began to waxe wanton and felle to
riote, as though their enemies could do to them
no damage: thynkyng that the Englishemen
whiche wer shutte vp in the Castle, studied nothyng but how to escape . . . Matthew Gough
. . . priuely returned again, and within a mile of
the citee met with the lorde Talbot and the
Lorde Scales, . . . whiche to spede the matter,
because the daie approched, with al hast possible came to the posterne gate, and alighted
from their horses, and about sixe of the clocke in
the mornyng thei issued out of the castle criyng   II. i. 38 S.D
sainct George, Talbot. The French men which
wer scarce vp, and thought of nothyng lesse
then of this sodain approchement, some rose out
of their beddes in their shertes, and lepte ouer   II. ii. 22 -5
the walles, other ranne naked out of the gates
for sauyng of their liues, leuyng behynde theim   II. i.
all their apparell, horsses, armure / and riches.   77 S.D.–81

Ciiii

143   [The vi. yere. (1428–9)] The citee of Mauns
thus beyng reduced into the Englishe mennes
handes, the Lorde Talbot departed to the toune
of Alanson. After whiche marciall feat manly
acheued, the erle of Warwicke departed into
Englande, to bee gouernor of the young kyng,
in steade of Thomas duke of Excester, late departed to God. In whose stede was sent into
144   Fraunce, / the lorde Thomas Mountacute erle
of Salisbury with fiue thousande men, whiche
landed at Calice and so came to the Duke of
Bedford in Paris. Where he consultyng with the   I. ii; I. iv
duke of Bedforde, concernyng the affaires of the
realme of Fraunce: seyng all thynges prosper-
ously succede on the Englishe part, began mer-

uailously to phantesie the citee and countrey of
Orliance, standyng on the riuer of Loyre. But
because the cite was well fortified bothe by the
nature of the situacion of the place, and by the
pollicie of man, he imagined it not the woorke of
one daie, nor the study of one houre. Wherfore
he remitted it to a farther deliberacion, yet he
was the man at that tyme, by whose wit, strength
and pollicie, the Englishe name was muche fearfull and terrible to the French nacion, whiche
of hymself might bothe appoynt, commaunde
and do all thynges, in maner at his pleasure, in
whose power, (as it appeared after his deathe) a
greate part of the conquest consisted and was
estemed, because he was a man both painful and
diligent, redy to withstand thynges perilous and
imminent, and prompt in counsail, and with no
labor be weried, nor yet his corage at any tyme
abated or appalled, so that all men put no more
trust in any one man, nor no synguler person gat
more the hartes of all men. After this greate
enterprise, had long been debated and argued,
in the priuie counsaill, the erle of Salisburies
deuise, (although it semed harde and straunge
to all other, and to hym as it wer a thyng pre-
destinate very easie) was graunted and allowed,
which enterprise was the finall conclusion of his
naturall destiny . . . Thus he replenished with
good hope of victory, & furnished with artilery,
and municions apperteinyng to so greate a siege,
accompanied with the erle of Suffolke and the
lorde Talbot, and with a valiaunt company, to
the nombre of tenne thousande men, departed
from Paris . . .

II. ii. 4 ff.

Ciiii^v

After this in the moneth of Septembre, he
laied his siege on the one side of the water of
Loyre, before whose commyng, the Bastarde of
Orleaunce, and the bishop of the citee and a
great nombre of Scottes, hearyng of therles intent, made diuerse fortificacions about the toune
and destroyed the suburbes . . . Thei cut also
doune al the vines, trees and bushes within
fiue leages of the toune, so that the English-

men should haue neither comfort, refuge nor succor.

This coragious Bastard [of Orleans], after the
siege had continued thre wekes ful, issued out of
the gate of the bridge, and fought with the Englishemen, but thei receiued hym with so fierce
and terrible strokes, that he was with all his
company compelled to retire and flie back into
the citee: but the Englishemen folowed theim
so faste, in killyng and takyng of their enemies,
that thei entred with them the Bulwarke of the
bridge, whiche with a greate toure, standing at
thende of thesame, was taken incontinent by
thenglishemen. In whiche conflict many Frenche
men were taken, but mo were slain, and the
kepyng of the toure and Bulwerke was committed to William Glasdale esquier. When he had
gotten this Bulwarke, he was sure that, by that
waie neither man nor vitaill could passe or
come. After that, he made certayne Bulwarkes
rounde about the citee, castyng trenches betwene the one and the other, laiyng ordinaunce
in euery part, where he saw that any battery
might be deuised. When thei within perceiued
that thei were enuironed with fortresses and
ordinance, thei laied gonne against gonne, and
fortefied toures against bulwarkes, and within
made new rampires, and buylded new mud-
walles to auoyde crackes and breches, whiche
might by violent shot sodainly insue. Thei appoynted the Bastard of Orleance, and Stephen
Veignold called the Heire, to se the walles and
watches kept, & the bishop sawe y^t thinhabi-
tantes within the cite: wer put in good ordre,
and that vitaill wer not wantonly consumed,
nor vainly spent.

In the toure that was taken at the bridge ende,
. . . there was a high chamber hauyng a grate
full of barres of yron by the whiche a man might
loke al the length of the bridge into the cite at
which, grate many of the chief capitaines stode
diuerse times, vieuyng the cite & deuisyng in
what place it was best assautable. Thei within

the citee perceiued well this totyng hole, and
laied a pece of ordynaunce directly against the
wyndowe. It so chaunced that the lix. daie after
the siege laied before the citee, therle of Salisbury, sir Thomas Gargraue and William Glasdale and diuerse other, went into thesaid toure
and so into the high chambre, and loked out at
the grate, and within a short space, the sonne of
the Master gonner, perceiued men lokyng out
at the wyndowe, tooke his matche, as his father

Cv^v   had taught hym, / whiche was gone doune to
dinner, and fired the gonne, whiche brake &
sheuered ye yron barres of the grate, whereof,
one strake therle so strongly on the hed, that it
stroke away one of his iyes and the side of his
cheke. Sir Thomas Gargraue was likewise strik-
en, so that he died within two daies. Therle was
conueyed to Meum vpon Loyre, where he laie
beyng wounded viii. daies . . . whose body was
conueyed into England, with al funerall and
pompe, and buried . . . What detriment, what

146   damage, / what losse succeded to the Englishe   cf. 1. i. 57 ff.
publique wealthe, by the sodain death of this
valiaunt capitain, not long after his departure,
manifestly apered. For high prosperitie, and
great glory of the Englishe nacion in the parties
beyond the sea, began shortely to fall, and litle
and litle to vanishe awaie: whiche thyng, although the Englishe people like a valient &
strong body, at the firste tyme did not perceiue,
yet after y^t thei felt it grow like a pestilent
humor, which successiuely a litle and litle corrupteth all the membres, and destroyeth the
body. For after the death of this noble man,
fortune of warre began to change, and triumphant victory began to be darckened. . . .

Cvi 147   The Erle of Suffolke . . . continued his siege,   III. iii. 17 ff.
and euery daie almoste, skirmished with his
enemies, whiche, being in dispaire of all succors,
began to commen emongest theimself, how thei
might rendre the toune, to their moste honoure

Cvi^v   and profite. . . . / they thought to find a meane
waye to saue themselfes, and their cite from the

captiuitie of their enemies, and deuised to submit their citee, themselfes, & al theirs vnder the
obeysance of Phillip duke of Burgoyn because
he was brought out of the stocke and bloud
royall of the auncient hous of Fraunce: thinkyng
by this meanes (as thei did in deede) to breke or
minishe the great amitie betwene the Englishemen & hym.

After this poynt concluded, thei made open &
sent to the duke al their deuises and intentes
whiche certified them that he would gladly receiue their offre, so that the Regent of Fraunce
would therto agre & consent. And therupon dis-
patched certain ambassadors to the duke of Bedford, to whom these newes wer straunge and not
very pleasaunt, vpon whiche poynt, he assembled a great counsaill. Some thought that
maner of yeldyng to be bothe honorable and
profitable to the king of Englande, by reason
wherof, so greate a citee, & so riche a countrey,
should be brought out of the possession of their
enemies, into the handes of their trusty frendes,
without farther cost or bloudshed. The Duke of
Bedford & other, wer of a contrary opinion,
thinkyng it bothe dishonorable and vnprofit-
able to the realme of England, to se a cite so long
besieged at the costes & expenses of the kyng of
England, & almoste brought to the poynt of
yeldyng, to be yelded to any other foren prince
or potestate, and not to hym or his Regent, the
example wherof might prouoke other tounes
herafter to do thesame. This reason toke place,
and the Regent answered the dukes ambassadors, that it was not honorable nor yet con-
sonaunte to reason, that the kyng of England
should beate the bushe and the duke of Burgoyne should haue the birdes: Wherfore sithe
the right was his, the war was his, and the
charge was his, he saied that ye citie ought not to
be yelded to no other person, but to hym or to his
vse and profite. By this litle chance, succeded a
great change in thenglishe affaires, for a double
mischief of this answere rose and sprang out.

For first the duke of Burgoyne, began to con-
ceiue a certain priuye grudge against thenglishmen for this cause: thynkyng them to enuy &
beare malice against his glory and profite, for
the whiche in continuance of time he became
their enemy, and cleued to the French Kyng.
Secondly, the Englishemen lefte the siege of
Orleaunce, whiche by this treaty thei might
haue had to frend, or to haue continued neutre,
till their Lord the duke of Orleaunce, or the erle
of Angulosie his brother wer deliuered out of the
captiuitie of the English people . . .

I. ii. 46 ff.

While this treaty of the Orleaunces was in
hand, Charles the / dolphin, daily studied . . .
to plucke the fauor and hartes of the nobilitie of
Fraunce, from the Englishe nacion . . . While he
was studiyng . . . this matter, there happened to
hym, a straunge chaunce . . .

I. iv. 100–II. i

For . . . there came to hym beyng at Chynon,
a mayd of the age of xx. yeres, and in mans apparell, named Ione, borne in Burgoyne in a
toune called Droymy beside Vancolour, which
was a greate space a chamberleyn in a commen
hostrey, and was a rampe of suche boldnesse,
that she would course horses and ride theim to
water, and do thynges, that other yong maidens,
bothe abhorred & wer ashamed to do: yet as
some say, whether it wer because of her foule
face, that no man would desire it, either she had
made a vowe to liue chaste, she kept her may-
denhed, and preserued her virginitie. She (as a
monster) was sent to the Dolphin, by sir Robert
Bandrencort capitain of Vancolour, to whom
she declared, that she was sent from God, bothe
to aide the miserable citee of Orleaunce, and
also to remit hym, to the possession of his realme,
out of the whiche, he was expulsed . . . : rehersyng
to hym, visions, traunses, and fables, full of blas-
phemy, supersticion and hypocrisy, that I mar-
uell much that wise men did beleue her, and
lerned clarkes would write suche phantasies.
What should I reherse, how thei saie, she knewe
and called hym her kyng, whom she neuer saw

before. What should I speake how she had by
reuelacion a swerde, to her appoynted in the
churche of saincte Katheryn, of Fierboys in To-
rayne where she neuer had been. What should I
write, how she declared suche priuy messages
from God, our lady, and other sainctes, to the
dolphyn, that she made the teres ronne doune
from his iyes. So was he deluded, so was he
blynded, & so was he deceiued by the deuils
meanes which suffred her to begynne her race,
and inconclusion rewarded her with a shameful
fal. But in the meane season suche credite was
geuen to her, that she was honoured as a sainct,
of the religious, and beleued as one sent from
God of the temporaltie, in so muche that she
(armed at all poyntes) rode from Poytiers to
Bloys, and ther found men of war vitail, and
municions, redy to be conueyed to Orleaunce.
The Englishmen perceiuyng that thei within
could not long continue, for faute of vitaile &
pouder, kepte not their watche so diligently as
thei wer accustomed, nor scoured not the countrey enuirond, as thei before had ordained:
which negligence, the citezens shut in perceiuing, sent worde therof to the Frenche capitaines,
whiche with *Pucelle* in the dedde tyme of the
night, and in a greate rayne and thundre, with
all their vitaile and artilery entered into the   I. iv. 97
citee. . . . And the next daie the Englishemen
boldely assauted the toune, promisyng to theim
Cvii^v   that / best scaled the walles great rewardes.
Then men mounted on ladders coragiously, and
with gonnes, arrowes and pikes, bette their enemies from the walles.

The Frenchemen, although thei marueiled at
the fierce fightyng of the English people, yet thei
wer not amased, but thei defended theim selfes
to the darke night. . . The Bastard of Orleaunce
(seying the puyssaunce of thenglishe nacion)
began to feare the sequele of the matter: wherfore he sent worde to the duke of Alaunson, ad-
uertisyng him in what case the toune then
stoode, and that it could not long continue

without his hasty spede, and quicke diligence.
Whiche delaiyng no tyme . . . came with al his
army within two leagues of the citee, and sent
woorde to the capitaines, that on the next
morowe thei should be redy to receiue theim.
Whiche thyng, the next daie thei accomplished,
for the Englishemen thought it to be muche to
their auaile, if so greate a multitude entered into
the citee, vexed with famyne & replenished with
scarsenes. On the next daie in the mornyng, the
Frenchemen altogether issued out of the toune,
and assauted the fortresse or Bastile, . . . the
whiche with great force and no litle losse thei
toke and set it on fire, and after assauted the
toure at the bridge foote, whiche was manfully
defended. But the Frenchemen beyng more in
nombre, so fiersely assauted it, that thei toke it
or the Lorde Talbot could come to succors: in
the whiche Willyam Gladdisdale the capitain
was slain . . .

The Frenchemen puffed vp with this good
lucke, seyng the strong fortres . . . vngotten,
whiche was vnder the defence of the lorde Talbot, fetched a compasse aboute, and in good
ordre of battaile marched thether ward. The
lord Talbot like a capitain, without feare or /
dred of so great a multitude, issued out of his
Bastile, and so fiersly fought with the Frenchemen, that thei not able to withstande his puyssaunce, fled (like shepe before the Wolffe) again
into the citee, with greate losse of men and small
artilerie: and of the Englishemen wer lost in the
two Bastyles sixe hundred persones. Then the
erle of Suffolke, the Lorde Talbot, the Lorde
Scales, and other capitaines, assembled together, where causes wer shewed, that it was
bothe necessary and conueniente either to leue
the siege for euer, or to deferre it till another
tyme, more luckey & conuenient. . . .

After this siege thus broken vp, to tel you,
what triumphes wer made in the citee of Orleaunce, what wood was spente in fiers, what
wyne was dronke in houses, what songes wer

49

Cviii

I. vi;
II. i. 11 ff.

song in the stretes, what melody was made in
Tauernes, what roundes were daunced, in large
and brode places, what lightes were set vp in the
churches, what anthemes, wer song in Cha-
pelles, and what ioye was shewed in euery place,
it were a long woorke . . . After the Englishmen,
wer thus retired from the siege of Orleaunce, . . .
the duke of Alaunson, the Bastard of Orleaunce,
Ione the puzell, the lorde of Gancort, & diuerse
other Frenche men came before the toune of
Iargeaux . . .

[The vii. yere. (1429–30)] After the gaynyng of
the toune . . . the same army cam to Meum. . . /
. . . met with the duke of Alaunson, Arthur of
Britayne . . . newly made Constable of Fraunce
. . . with whom was the lord Delabret with xii. C.
men: to whom daily repaired freshe aide out of
euery parte, as the Erle of Vandosme, and other,
to the nombre of xx. or xxiii. M. men. All these
men of warre, determined to go to Meum, and
to take the toune, but / . . . as thei marched forwarde, . . . thei had perfite knowledge, that the
lorde Talbot with v. thousand men, / was commyng to Meum. Wherfore, thei intendyng to
stop hym a tyde, conueyed their company to a
small village called Patay, whiche way, thei
knewe that the Englishmen must nedes passe by.
And first thei appoynted their horsemen, whiche
were well and richely furnished, to go before,
and sodainly to set on the Englishmen, or thei
wer, either ware or set in ordre. The Englishmen
commyng forwarde, perceiued the horsemen,
and, imaginyng to deceiue their enemies, commaunded the fotemen, to enuirone & enclose
themselfes about, with their stakes, but the
French horsmen came on so fiersly, that the
archers had no leyser, to set themselfes in a raie.
There was no remedy, but to fight at aduenture.
This battaill, continued by the space of thre long
houres. And, although thenglishmen wer ouer-
pressed, with the nombre of their aduersaries,
yet thei neuer fledde backe one foote, til their

1. i. 113

1. i. 103 ff.

Cviii^v

150

capitain the lorde Talbot, was sore wounded at
the backe, and so taken. Then their hartes began to faint, & thei fled, in whiche flight, there
wer slain aboue xii. C. and taken xl. wherof the
lorde Talbot, the lord Scales, the lord Hungerford, & sir Thomas Rampston, were the chief:
howbeit diuerse archers whiche had shot all
their arrowes, hauyng only their swerdes, defended themself, and with the help of some of
the horsmen, cam safe to Meum.

. . . From this battaill, departed without any
stroke striken, sir Ihon Fastolffe, thesame yere
for his valiauntnes elected into the ordre of the
Garter. For whiche cause the Duke of Bedford,
in a great anger, toke from hym the Image of
sainct George, and his Garter: but afterward,
by meane of frendes, and apparant causes of
good excuse by hym alledged, he was restored
to the order again, against the mynd of the lorde
Talbot.

I. iv. 34
IV. i. 93 ff

Cix 150 Charles . . . when he had thus conquered
Reyns, he in the presence of all the noblemen
of his faccion, and the dukes of Lorayne and
Barre, was sacred kyng of Fraunce, by the name
of Charles the vi. with all rites and ceremonies
therto apperteinyng . . .

151 The Duke of Bedford, hearyng that these
tounes and soyssons also, had returned to the
part of his aduersaries, and that Charles late
Dolphyn had taken vpon hym the name and
estate of the kyng of Fraunce, . . . he hauyng together x. M. good Englishemen, (beside Nor-
mans) departed out of Paris, in warlike fashion
. . . and sente by . . . his herault letters to the
Cix^v Frenche kyng, alledgyng to hym that he contrary to the lawes of God and man . . . / onely
allured and intised by a deuilishe wytche, and
a sathanicall enchaunterese, had . . . craftely,
taken vpon hym, the name, title and dignitie of
the kyng of Fraunce . . .

Cxi 153 [The viii. yere. (1430–1)] On the vi. day of
Nouembre . . . kyng Henry, . . . was, at West-

minster with all pompe and honor, crouned
kyng of this realme of England . . .

154   . . . kyng Charles / . . . although he muche re-
ioysed, at the good successe, that Fortune had to
hym sente, yet he was somwhat desperate, how
to recouer his countrey from the possession of
the Englishemen, except he vnknitted the knotte
and league, betwene the duke of Burgoyn and
them. Wherfore, he sent his Chauncellor, &
diuerse Ambassadors to the duke of Burgoyn,
first, excusyng himself of the death & murder,
of duke Ihon his father, & after, declaryng to
him, that there could be nothing more foule,
Cxi^v   more dis/honest, nor more detestable, then, for
his awne peculiar cause, & priuate displeasure,
to ioyne with his auncient enemies, and per-
petual aduersaries, against his natiue countrey
and naturall nacion: not onely requiryng hym,
of concord, peace, and amitie, but also promisyng golden mountaines, and many more bene-
fites, then at that tyme, he was either able or
could performe. This message was not so secrete
. . . but the Duke of Bedford, therof was plainly
informed. Whiche, beyng sore troubled, and vnquieted in his mind, because he sawe the power
of thenglishe nacion, daily waxe lesse . . .

Cxiii 156   [The ix. yere. (1431–2)] In this very season, the
Englishemen in the colde moneth of Decembre,
besieged the toune of Laigny, in the whiche was
the Puzel and diuerse other good capitaines. But
the weither was so cold, & the raine so greate
and so continuall, that thei, of force compelled,
not by their enemies, but by intemperate season,
reised their siege: and in their returne, the
Puzell and all the garrison within the toune,
issued out and fought with thenglishmen, where,
(after long fightyng) bothe parties departed
without either greate gain or losse. After this
enterprise doen, the duke of Burgoyne, accompanied with the erles of Arundell and Suffolke,
. . . and with a great puissance, besieged the
toune of Champeigne: whiche toune was well

walled, manned, and vitailed, so that the be-
siegers, must either by assaut or long tariyng,
wery or famishe theim within the toune. So thei
caste trenches, and made moynes, and studied
al the waies that thei could deuise, how to compasse their conquest and enterprise. And it happened in the night of the Assencion of our lorde,
that Pothon of Xentraxles, Ione the Puzell, and
fiue or sixe hundred men of armes, issued out of
Champeigne, by the gate of the bridge towarde

Mowntdedier, intendyng to set fire in / the
tentes and lodgynges of the lord of Baudo, which
was then gone to Marigny, for the Duke of Bur-
goyns affaires. At whiche tyme, sir Ihon of Lux-
enborough, with eight other gentlemen (whiche
had riden aboute the toune to serche and vieue,
in what place the toune might be moste aptly
and conueniently assauted or scaled) were come
nere to the lodges of the lorde of Baudo, where
thei espied the Frenchmen, whiche began to cut
doune tentes, ouerthrowe pauilions, and kil men
in their beddes. Wherefore, shortely thei assembled a greate nombre of men, as well Englishe
as Burgonions, and coragiously set on the
Frenchmen. Sore was the fight and greate was

the slaughter, in so / muche that the Frenchemen, not able lenger to indure, fled into the
toune so faste, that one letted the other to entre.
In which chace was taken, Ione the Puzell, and
diuerse other: whiche Ione was sent to the duke

of Bedford to Roan, wher, (after long examina-
cion) she was brent to ashes. This wytch or manly woman, (called the maide of GOD) the
Frenchemen greatly glorified and highly ex-
tolled, alledgyng that by her Orleaunce was
vitailed: by her, kyng Charles was sacred at
Reynes, and that by her, the Englishmen wer
often tymes put backe and ouerthrowen. O
Lorde, what dispraise is this to the nobilitie of
Fraunce? What blotte is this to the Frenche
nacion? What more rebuke can be imputed to
a renoumed region, then to affirme, write &
confesse, that all notable victories, and honor-

able conquestes, which neither the kyng with
his power, nor the nobilitie with their valiaunt-
nesse, nor the counsaill with their wit, nor the
commonaltie with their strenght, could compasse or obtain, were gotten and achiued by a
shepherdes daughter, a chamberlein in an hos- v. iv
trie, and a beggers brat: whiche blindyng the
wittes of the French nacion, by reuelacions,
dreames & phantasticall visions, made them
beleue thynges not to be supposed, and to geue
faithe to thynges impossible. For surely, if credite maie be geuen to the actes of the Clergie,
openly doen, and commonly shewed, this wo-
man was not inspired with the holy ghost, nor I. ii. 140 ff.
sent from God, (as the Frenchmen beleue) but
an enchanteresse, an orgayne of the deuill, sent
from Sathan, to blind the people and bryng
them in vnbelife: . . .

Cxv 159   And when she saw that the fatall daie of her v. iii, iv
obstinacie was come, she openly confessed, that
the spirites, whiche to her often did appere, were
euill and false, . . . and that their promes, which
thei had made, to deliuer her out of captiuitie,
was false and vntrue: affirmyng her self, by those
spirites to bee often beguiled, blynded, and
mocked. And so beyng in good mynde, she was
by the Iustices, caried to the olde market, within
the citee of Roan, and there by the fire, consumed to asshes, in the sight of all the people. . . .

Cxvᵛ   . . . where was her shamefastnes, when she
daily and nightly, was conuersant with comen
souldiors, and men of warre, emongest whom,
is small honestie, lesse vertue, and shamefast-
nesse, least of all exercised or vsed? Where was
her womanly pitie, when she takyng to her, the
harte of a cruell beaste, slewe, man, woman, and
childe, where she might haue the vpper hand?
Where was her womanly behauor, when she
cladde her self in a mannes clothyng, and was
conuersaunt with euery losell, geuyng occasion
to all men to iudge, and speake euill of her, and
her doynges. Then these thynges, beyng thus
plainly true, all men must nedes confesse, . . .

she was no good woman, . . . she was no sainct.[1]

Cxvi 160	[The x. yere. (1432–3)] In the moneth of No-uembre, he [Henry] remoued from Roan . . . to the intent to make his entrie, into the citee of Paris, and there to be sacred kyng of Fraunce, and to receiue, the sceptre and Croune of the realme and countrey.	IV. i. 1 ff.
Cxvi[v]	There wer in his company . . . his vncle the Car/dinall of Winchester, the Cardinall and Archebishoppe of Yorke, the Dukes of Bedforde,	
161	Yorke, and Norffolke, the / Erles of Warwicke, Salisbury, Oxford, Huntyngdon, Ormond, Mortayn, Suffolke. . . . And . . . he was met at the Chapell, in the meane waie, by Sir Simon Moruer prouost of Paris, with a greate com-	
Cxvii	pany . . . / And on the xvii. of thesaied moneth . . . he was anoynted and crouned kyng of Fraunce, by the Cardinal of Winchester . . .	
Cxviii[v] 164	. . . Emongest the capitaines was found pri-soner, the valiaunt capitain, called Poynton of	I. iv. 22 ff.
Cxix	Sanc/trailes, (whiche without delay,) was ex-chaunged for the lorde Talbot, before taken prisoner, at the battaill of Patay. . . .	
Cxx 165	While the Englishe and Frenche nacions, thus stroue, . . . by the vnreasonable rage of warre in Fraunce, the rich men were spoyled of their goodes, . . . the common people wer slain, mur-dred, and trode vnder the foote, . . . tounes wer destroied and wasted, toune dwellers and cite-zens, wer robbed and exiled, beautiful buyld-ynges wer cruelly brent, nothyng was spared, by the crueltie of Mars: whiche by fire, bloud,	III. iii. 44 ff.
	or famyne, might be catched or destroied, be-side a hundred more calamities, that daily vexed and troubled the miserable French nacion . . .	IV. ii. 10–11
Cxxi[v] 168	The Duke of Burgoyne, (whose mynde began to incline, a litle and litle, toward kyng Charles) was sore greued and angry, that the duke of Bedforde, was ioyned in affinitie, with the noble and famous hous of Luxemborough: by the whiche he sawe, that the power of the English-	III. iii. 41 ff.

1. Cf. the account of Joan in Holinshed, below.

men, should be greatly aduaunced. But the
mariage was fully ended, and he could finde no
remedy.

Cxxvii[v] 176 [The xiii. yere (1435–6)] . . . the Frenchemen   III. iii. 41 ff.
and the Burgonyons began familiarly to com-
mon of a peace, and talke of an amitie, to the
whiche mocion, Phillip duke of Burgoyne, was
neither deiffe nor straunge: for he in the begin-
nyng of his rule, beyng muche desirous to reuenge and punishe the shamefull murder doen
to his father, and to kepe hymself in his high
estate . . . began to be associate, and to reigne
with thenglishe power, and to serue the kyng of
England thinking, that by his amity and ioyn-
yng, that he should neither harme nor hurte,
the common wealth of the countrey, whereof at
that tyme he bare the whole rule . . . But when
it happened, contrary to his expectacion, that
the kyng of Englande, by the right course of inheritaunce, tooke vpon hym the whole rule and
gouernaunce, within the realme of Fraunce, . . .
& that the duke iudged, that he was not had in
great confidence, nor in perfite truste, as he
thought, because the Duke of Bedforde, would
not suffre the toune of Orleaunce, to be render-
ed to hym, (as you before haue heard): He ther-
fore imagined, & determined with hymself, to
returne into the pathe again, from the whiche
he had straied and erred, and to take part, and
ioyne with his awne bloud and nacion: so that
some honest meane, might be sought by other,
and not by hymself, least paraduenture by his
awne sekyng, he might bind himself in condicions hurtfull, & sore inconueniences, to the
Frenche kyng, and also be noted of vntruth, and
traiterous behauor, toward the king of Englande
and his nacion: . . . And so, shadowed with this
counsaill, without long argument or prolongyng
Cxxviii   of tyme, he tooke a determinate peace . . . / This
concorde, was so pleasaunt to the Frenche kyng,
that he, not only sent for hym: but . . . met hym
in proper persone . . .

177   When this league was sworne, and this knot
          was knit, the duke of Burgoyne, to sette a vayle,
          before the kyng of Englandes iyes, sent Thoison
          Dor, his kyng at Armes, to kyng Henry with
Cxxviii^v   letters: that he . . . / was in maner compelled . . .   IV. i. 9–12
          to take a peace . . . with kyng Charles . . . with
          many flatteryng wordes . . .
             Here is to be noted, that the Duke of Bur-
          goyne, whiche thought hymself by this concord
          in maner dishonored, . . . sente his letters to the
          Kyng of Englande, rather to purge . . . hymselfe,
          of his vntruth. . . . not for any malice or displea-
          sure, whiche he bare to kyng Henry, or to the
          Englishe nacion. This letter was not alitle loked
          on, . . . of the kyng of England, and his sage
          counsaill: not onely for the waightines of the
          matter, but also for the sodain chaunge of the
          man, & for the straunge superscripcion of the
          letter, which was: *To the high and mightie Prince,*   IV. i. 51
          Henry, by the grace of GOD Kyng of Englande, his
          Welbeloued cosyn: Neither namyng hym kyng of
          Fraunce, nor his souereigne lorde, accordyng as,
          (euer before that tyme) he was accustomed to
          do.
Cxxix 178   This yere the xiiii. daie of September, died   III. ii. 41 ff.
          Ihon duke of Bedford, Regent of Fraunce, a
          man, as pollitique in peace, as hardy in war and
          yet no more hardy in warre, then mercifull,
          when he had victory, whose bodye was, with
          greate funerall solempnitie, buried in the Cathe-
          drall churche of our Lady, in Roan, on the
          Northside of the high aulter, vnder a sumptuous
          and costly monument: whiche . . . sepulture,
          when kyng Lewes the xi. sonne to this kyng
          Charles, which recouered again Normandy, did
          well aduise and behoulde, certayne noblemen
          in his company . . . counsailed hym to . . . plucke   IV. vii. 47 ff.
          doune the tombe, and to cast the deede carcasse
          into the feldes: . . . Kyng Lewes aunswered again
          saiyng: . . . . hym, whom in his life, neither my
          father, nor your progenitors, with all their
          power . . . wer once able, to make flie one foote
          backeward, but by his strength, witte, and pol-

licie, kepte theim all out of the principall domi-
nions, of the realme of Fraunce . . . : wherfore I
saie, first, God haue his soule, & let his body now
lye in reste, whiche, when he was a liue, would
haue disquieted the proudest of vs all: and as
for the tombe, I assure you, is not so decent, nor
conuenient for hym, as his honor and Actes de-
serued, although it wer muche richer, and more
beautifull.

Cxxix^v 179 [The xiiii yere. (1436–7)] . . . the Englishe
people . . . began the warre new again, and
appoynted for regent in Fraunce, Richard duke
of Yorke, sonne to Richard erle of Cambridge.
Although the duke of Yorke, bothe for birthe
and corage, was worthy of this honor and preferment, yet he was so disdained of Edmond
duke of Somerset, beyng cosin to the kyng, that
he was promoted to so high an office, (whiche
he in verie deede, gaped and loked for) that by
al waies and meanes possible, he bothe hindered
and detracted hym, glad of his losse, and sory
of his well-dooyng, causyng hym to linger in
Englande, without dispatche, till Paris and the
floure of Fraunce, were gotten by the Frenche
kyng. The duke of Yorke, perceiuyng his euill
will, openly dissimuled that, which he inwardly
thought priuely, eche workyng thynges, to the
others displesure. This cancard malice, and
pestiferous diuision, so long continued, in the
hartes of these twoo princes, till mortall warre
consumed theim bothe, and almoste all their
lynes and ofsprynges, . . .

Cxxx   . . . the losse of . . . the noble citee of Paris. For
where before tymes there were sent ouer, for the
aide and tuicion of the tounes, and citees, . . .
thousandes of men, apte and mete for the warre
. . . : now were sent into Fraunce, hundredes,
yea scores, some rascall, and some not able to
drawe a bowe, or cary a bill. . . . Whiche weake-
180   nes kyng Charles well perceiued. . . / The Parisians. . . . (whiche, euer with an Englishe countenaunce, couered a Frenche harte) perceiuyng

III. iv. 28 ff.
IV. i. 78 ff.
IV. iii–vii

v. ii
I. i. 61

the weaknes of the Englishemen, . . . signifiyng
to the Frenche capitaines, their mindes and intentes, willed them to come with all diligence. . . /

Cxxx^v   The Englishemen . . . with their small company,
defended their fortresse, tenne daies, lokyng for
aide, but when thei sawe that no comforte ap-
pered, thei yeilded their fortresse . . .

Cxl 193   [The xviii. yere. (1440)] . . . . the vnhappie de-   III. iii. 68 ff.
uision, betwene the two noble families, of Or-
leaunce and Burgoyne . . . this Duke of Orleaunce, was deteined thus long in captiuitie, . . .

Cxl^v 194   in the realme of England. . . . / . . . But the very
cause of his long deteinyng wer two: . . . you
haue heard before, how that Ihon Duke of Burgoyne father to Phillippe, shamefully and cruel-
ly, caused Lewes Duke of Orleaunce, father to
this Duke Charles, . . . to be murthered in the
citee of Paris: for the whiche murder, al the
alies and frendes to the Duke of Orleaunce, had
enuie against the hous and familie of Burgoyne,
. . . for the surety . . . of the duke of Burgoyne . . .
[the English] kepte still the duke of Orleaunce
in Englande, . . . But after that the duke of Burgoyn . . . had broken his promes, . . . and was
turned to the Frenche part, the counsaill of the
kyng of Englande, studied . . . how to deliuer the
duke of Orleaunce, to do displeasure to the duke
of Burgoyn.

Cxlii^v 197   [The xix. yere (1441–2)] . . . the Frenchemen   III. ii. 1–74
had taken the toune of Eureux, by treason of a
fisher. Sir Fraunces Arragonoys hearyng of that
chaunce, apparreled sixe strong men, like rus-
tical people with sackes and baskettes, as car-
riers of corne and vitaile, and sent them to the
Castle of Cornyll, in the whiche diuerse Englishemen were kept as prisoners: and he with
an imbusshement of Englishemen, laye in a
valey nye to the fortresse. These sixe compan-
ions entered into the Castle, vnsuspected and not
mistrusted, and straight came to the chambre of
the capitain, & laied handes vpon hym, geuyng

THE FIRST PART OF

knowledge therof to their imbushement, whiche
sodainly entered the Castle, and slew and toke
all the Frenchemen prisoners, and set at libertie
all the Englishemen, whiche thing doen, thei
set all the castle on fire, and departed with great
spoyle to the citee of Roan.

Cxliii   [The xx. yere (1442–3)] These bee in parte, the   III. i. 10–13
poyntes and Articles, whiche I Humfrey Duke
of Gloucester, . . . saied late, I would geue in
writyng . . .

Cxlvi^v 202   [The xxi. yere (1443–4)] About this season, the   III. iv. 20–6
kyng remembryng the valeaunt seruice, and
noble actes of Ihon Lorde Talbot, created hym
Erle of Shrewesburie . . . / . . . the Erle of Armin-   v. i. 15 ff.
acke . . . sent solempne Ambassadors to the kyng
of Englande, offeryng hym his doughter in mariage, not onely promisyng hym siluer hilles, and
golden mountaines with her, but also would be
bound, to deliuer into the kyng of Englandes
handes, all suche Castles and tounes, as he or
his auncestors deteined from hym, within the
203   whole duchie of Acquitayn or Guyen, . . . / . . .
offryng farther, to aide thesame kyng with
money, for the recouery of other citees, within
thesaied duchy . . . iniustely kept. . . This offre
semed bothe profitable, and honorable to kyng
Henry and his realme, and so the Ambassadors,
wer . . . louyngly enterteined . . . after whom
wer sent . . . an honorable company, whiche . . .
bothe concluded the mariage, and by proxie
affied the young Lady.

Cxlvii 203   [The xxii. yere. (1444–5)] . . . to appeace the   v. iii. 45 ff.
mortall warre . . . there was a greate diete ap-   v. v
poynted, to be kepte at the citee of Tours. . .
Many metynges wer had . . . but . . . a finall
concord could not be agreed, but in hope to
come to a peace, a certain truce . . . was concluded . . . for xviii. monethes . . .
   In the treatyng of this truce, the Erle of Suffolke, extendyng his commission to the vtter-

moste, without assent of his associates, imagen-
ed in his phantasie, that the nexte waie to come
to a perfite peace, was to moue some mariage,
betwene the Frenche kynges kynsewoman, and
kyng Henry his souereigne: & because the
Frenche kyng had no dough/ter of ripe age, to
be coupled in matrimony with the kyng his
Master, he desired to haue the Lady Margaret, /
cosyn to the Frenche kyng, and doughter to
Reyner duke of Aniow, callyng hymself kyng of
Scicile, Naples, and Hierusalem, hauyng onely
the name and stile of the same, without any
peny profite, or fote of possession. This mariage
was made straunge to therle a good space, in
somuche that he repented hym of the first mocion, but yet like a bold man, entendyng not to
take a foile in so greate a matter, desisted not
still, daily to sollicite and aduaunce forward his
cause. . . .

The erle of Suffolke . . . either corrupted with
bribes, or to muche affeccionate to this vnprofit-
able mariage, condiscended and agreed to their
mocion, that the Duchie of Aniow, and the
countie of Mayne, should be released and deliuered, to the kyng her father, demaundyng for
her mariage, neither peny nor farthyng: . . . the
Erle of Suffolke . . . came to the kyng to Westminster, and there openly before the kyng and
his counsail, declared how he had taken an
honorable truce . . . omitting nothyng, whiche
might extoll & setfurth, the personage of the
Ladie, nor forgetting any thyng, of the nobilitie
of her kinne, nor of her fathers high stile: as who
would saie, that she was of suche an excellent
beautie, and of so high a parentage, that almoste
no king or Emperor, was worthy to be her make.
Although this mariage, pleased well the kyng,
and diuerse of his counsaill, and especially suche
as wer adherentes, and fautors to the erle of
Suffolke, yet Humfrey duke of Gloucester, Protector of the realme, repugned and resisted as
muche as in him laie, this new alliaunce and
contriued matrimonie: alledgyng that it was

neither consonaunt to the lawe of GOD nor
man, nor honorable to a prince, to infrynge and
breake a promise or contracte, by hym made
and concluded, for the vtilitie and profite of his
realme and people, declaryng, that the kyng,
Cxlviii   by / his Ambassadors, sufficiently instructed and
authorised, had concluded and contracted, a
mariage betwene his highnes, & the doughter
of therle of Arminacke, vpon condicions, bothe
to hym and his realme, asmuche profitable as
honorable. Whiche offers and condicions, thesaid erle . . . is redy to yelde and performe, sai-
yng: that it was more conueniente for a Prince,
to marie a wife with riches and frendes, then to
take a make with nothyng, and disherite hymself and his realme of olde rightes and auncient
seigniories. The duke was not heard, but the
Erles doynges, were condiscended vnto, and allowed. Whiche facte engendered suche a flame,
that it neuer wente oute, till bothe the parties
with many other wer consumed and slain . . .

Cxlviii^v 205   [xxiii. yere (1445–6)] This woman excelled all   v. v. 68 ff.
other, aswell in beautie and fauor, as in wit and
pollicie, and was of stomack and corage, more
like to a man, then a woman. . . .
. . . for the fetchyng of her, the Marques of
Suffolke, demaunded a whole fiftene, in open
parliament: also for her mariage, the Duchie of
Aniow, the citee of Mauns, and the whole
countie of Mayne, were deliuered and released
to Kyng Reyner, her father, whiche countreis
wer the very stayes . . . of Normandy.

Clii 210   [The xxvi. yere. (1448–9)] . . . Henry Beaufford, bishop of Winchester, and called the
ryche Cardinall, . . . was sonne to Ihon of
Gaunte duke of Lancaster, discended of an
honorable lignage, but borne in Baste, more   III. i. 42
noble of blodd, then notable in learning, haut
in stomacke, and hygh in countenaunce, ryche
aboue measure of all men, & to fewe liberal, /
Clii^v   disdaynfull to his kynne and dreadfull to his

louers, preferrynge money before friendshippe.
... Hys couetous[1] insaciable, and hope of long
lyfe, made hym bothe to forget God, hys Prynce
and hym selfe, in hys latter daies ...

Clxiiii 227   [The xxxi. yere. (1453–4)] The counsaill of
Englande, not forgettinge the offer of the Gas-   IV. vi–vii
cons, and that thei might now haue the citie of
Burdeaux, with the countrey round about, by
offer and request, ... appointed the veterane
souldiour, and valiaunt Capitayn, Ihon lord
Clxiiii[v]   Talbot, and erle of Shrews/burye, to be chefe-
tayn of the armye, which should in all haste be
transported and conueyed into Acquitayn. The
lordes of Gascoyn, both well pleased and glad
of their aunswere, returned into their countrey.
... When the valiant Talbot, the hardy erle of
Shrewsbury was appointed to assemble an army
of men, and them to conuey into the duchie of
Acquitayn, Lord, how busy he was in muster-
ing, howe diligent in setting forward, and how
ientelly he entertayned his men of warre, as
though he went first to warre, and neuer had
taken payne, either to serue his prince or to gayn
honor. What should I speake, how that he
thought euery houre, as thre, till his armie were
ready, or write, what payne he toke to se them
shipped and vitayled. But verely men iudge,
that as this labor was the ende and extreme
point of all his worldly busynes so he should
shew him self: fearce, coragious, & fearEful to
his enemies in the extreme point of his death and
naturall departing. Thys English Hector &
marcial flower, elected to him, the most hardy
& coragious persons, which he could espye, preparing also, horses, municions, vitayles, and all
thinges necessarie to such an army, and to so
great an enterprise. When all thinges were shipped, and wynd and wether serued he toke his
chaunce, and sayled into Gascoyn, ... where he
reposed his army, beyng scant iii. M. men, and
destroyed all the countrey, betwene Burdeaux

1. Covetousness *or* covetise?

228 and Blay, . . . / This auncient Fox, and pollitique
Capitayne lost not one houre . . . till he came
before the citie of Burdeaux. The citezens . . .
opened one gate, and let in a great parte of the
Englishmen army. The French Capitaynes en-
tending to escape secretely, by a posterne, were
slayne and taken. . . After the regaynyng of Bur-
Clxv deaux, arriued / at Blay, the bastard of Somerset, syr Ihon Talbot, lord Lisle, by his wyfe
sonne to the sayd erle of Shrewesbury, . . . syr
Ihon Vernon with xxii. C. men with vitailes
and municions. . . . the erle of Shrewesbury . . .
firste . . . fortified Burdeaux with Englishmen &
victayle: after that, he rode into the countrey
abrode, where he obteined cities, and gat
townes without stroke or dent of swourde: . . .
The French kynge . . . assembled a great army to
the number of xxii. M. men . . . diuided his army
into two parties, wherof the one was gouerned
by the erle of Cleremont, . . . in the whiche were
xv. M. men, in whome consisted the wayght
and peyse of the whole enterprise. This army
he appointed to take the next way toward Burdeaux: the other army wherof he was Capitayn
and leadar him self, . . . he kept . . . The erle of
Shrewesbury . . . perceiuing that he must of
necessitie . . . fight with two armies, determined
w^t him selfe, first to assay the least power and
weeker puyssaunce: wherfore without longer
procrastinacion, he assembled togither viii. C.
horsemen, wherof the lord Lisle his sonne . . .
and syr Ihon Vernon were chefe, and so marched forward . . . , appoyntyng v. M. fote men . . .
Clxv^v 229 to folowe / hym with all spede. . . . / . . . The
Frenchmen . . . retired . . . into the place which
they had trenched, dytched, and fortefied with
ordenaunce. . . . The coragious erle . . . feryng,
leste through long taryeng the byrdes might be
flowen awaye, not tarieng till his fotemen were
come, set forward, toward his enemies, . . .
When the Englishmen were come to the place
where the Frenchmen were encamped, in the
which . . . were iii. C. peces of brasse, beside

diuers other small peces, and subtill Engynes
to the Englishmen vnknowen, and nothing sus-
pected, they lyghted al on fote, the erle of
Shrewesbury only except, which because of his
age, rode on a litle hakeney, and fought fiercely
with the Frenchmen, & gat thentre of their
campe, and by fyne force entered into thesame.
This conflicte continued in doutfull iudgement
of victory ii. longe houres: durynge which fight,
the lordes of Montamban and Humadayre, with
a great companye of Frenchmen entered the
battayle, and began a new felde, & sodaynly the
Gonners perceiuynge the Englishmen to ap-
proche nere, discharged their ordinaunce, and
slew iii. C. persons, nere to the erle, who perceiuynge the imminent ieopardy, and subtile
labirynth, in the which he and hys people were
enclosed and illaqueate, despicynge his awne
sauegarde, and desirynge the life of his entierly
and welbeloued sonne the lord Lisle, willed,
aduertised, and counsailled hym to departe out
of the felde, and to saue hym selfe. But when the
sonne had aunswered that it was neither honest
nor natural for him, to leue his father in the extreme ieopardye of his life, and that he woulde
taste of that draught, which his father and
Parent should assay and begyn: The noble erle
& comfortable capitayn sayd to him: Oh sonne
sonne, I thy father, which onely hath bene the
terror and scourge of the French people so many
yeres, which hath subuerted so many townes,
. . . neither can here dye, for the honor of my
countrey, without great laude and perpetuall
fame, nor flye or departe without perpetuall
shame and continualle infamy. But because this
is thy first iourney and enterprise, neither thy
flyeng shall redounde to thy shame, nor thy
death to thy glory: for as hardy a man wisely
flieth, as a temerarious person folishely abid-
ethe, / therefore ye fleyng of me shalbe ye dis-
honor, not only of me & my progenie, but also
a discomfiture of all my company: thy departure shall saue thy lyfe, and make the able an-

Clxvi

other tyme, if I be slayn to reuenge my death
and to do honor to thy Prince, and profyt to his
Realme. But nature so wrought in the sonne,
that neither desire of lyfe, nor thought of secu-
ritie, could withdraw or pluck him from his
natural father: Who consideryng the constancy
of his chyld, and the great daunger that they
stode in, comforted his souldiours, cheared his
Capitayns, and valeauntly set on his enemies,
and slew of them more in number than he had in
his company. But his enemies hauyng a greater
company of men, & more abundaunce of ordinaunce then before had bene sene in a battayle,
fyrst shot him through the thyghe with a hand-
gonne, and slew his horse, & cowardly killed
him, lyenge on the grounde, whome thei neuer
durste loke in the face, whyle he stode on his
fete, and with him, there dyed manfully hys
sonne the lord Lisle. . . . At this battayl . . . ended
his lyfe Ihon lord Talbot, and of his progenie yᵉ
fyrst erle of Shrewesbury, after that he with
muche fame, more glory, and moste victorie had
for his prince and countrey, by the space of
xxiiii. yeres and more, valeauntly made warre,
and serued the kyng in the partes beyond the
sea, whose corps was / left on the ground, &
after was found by hys frendes, & conueyed to
Whitchurch in Shropshyre, where it is intumu-
late. This man was to the French people, a very
scorge and a daily terror, in so much that as his
person was fearfull, and terrible to his aduersaries present: so his name and fame was spite-
full and dreadfull to the common people absent,
in so muche that women in Fraunce to feare
their yong children, would crye, the Talbot
commeth, the Talbot commeth.

230

(b) Holinshed, *Chronicles* (from the second edition, 1587)

600/2/2   In time of this siege at Orleance (French stories   I. ii
saie) the first weeke of March 1428 [i.e. 1429],
unto Charles the Dolphin, at Chinon . . . was
caried a yoong wench of an eighteene yeeres old,
called Jone Are, by name of hir father (a sorie
sheepheard) James of Are, and Isabell hir
mother, brought up poorelie in their trade of
keeping cattell . . . Of favour was she counted
likesome, of person stronglie made and manlie,
of courage great, hardie, and stout withall, an
understander of counsels though she were not
at them, great semblance of chastitie both of
bodie and behaviour, the name of Jesus in hir
mouth about all hir businesses, humble, obedient, and fasting diverse daies in the weeke. A
person (as their bookes make hir) raised up by
power divine, onelie for succour to the French
estate then deeplie in distresse; in whome, for
planting a credit the rather, first the companie
that toward the Dolphin did conduct hir,
through places all dangerous, as holden by the
English, (where she never was afore) all the
waie and by nightertale safelie did she lead:
then at the Dolphins sending by hir assigne-
ment, from saint Katharins church of Fierbois
in Touraine (where she never had beene and
knew not,) in a secret place there among old
iron, appointed she hir sword to be sought out
and brought hir, that with five floure delices
was graven on both sides, wherewith she fought
and did manie slaughters by hir owne hands.
On warfar rode she in armour cap a pie &
mustered as a man, before hir an ensigne all
white, wherin was Jesus Christ painted with a
floure delice in his hand.

Unto the Dolphin into his gallerie when first
she was brought, and he, shadowing himselfe
behind, setting other gaie lords before him to
trie hir cunning, from all the companie, with a
salutation, (that indeed marz all the matter),
she pickt him out alone; who thereupon had hir

to the end of the gallerie, where she held him
an houre in secret and private talke, that of his
privie chamber was thought verie long, and
therefore would have broken it off; but he made
them a signe to let hir saie on. In which (among
other), as likelie it was, she set out unto him the
singular feats (forsooth) given hir to understand by revelation divine, that in vertue of that
sword shee should atchive; which were, how
with honor and victorie shee would raise the
siege at Orleance, set him in state of the crowne
of France, and drive the English out of the coun-
trie, thereby he to injoie the kingdome alone.
Heereupon he hartened at full, appointed hir a
sufficient armie with absolute power to lead
them, and they obedientlie to doo as she bad
them. Then fell she to worke, and first defeated,
indeed, the siege at Orleance; by and by incouraged him to crowne himselfe king of France
at Reims, that a little before from the English
she had woone. Thus after pursued she manie
bold enterprises to our great displeasure a two
yeare togither, for the time she kept in state untill she were taken and for heresie and witcherie
burned.

604/1/55   Of hir lovers (the Frenchmen) reporteth one,   v. iii–iv
how in Compeigne thus besieged, Guillaume de
Flavie the capteine having sold hir aforehand
to the lord of Lutzenburgh, under colour of
hasting hir with a band out of the towne towards their king, for him with speed to come
and leavie the siege there, so gotten hir foorth
he shut the gates after hir, when anon by the
Burgognians set upon and overmatcht in the
conflict she was taken: marie yet (all things
accounted) to no small marvell how it could
come to passe, had she beene of any devotion or
of true beleefe, and no false miscreant, but all
holie as she made it . . . Tillet telleth it thus, that
she was caught at Compeigne by one of the earle
of Ligneis soldiers, from him had to Beaurevoir
castell, where kept a three months, she was after
for ten thousand pounds in monie and three

hundred pounds rent (all Turnois) sold into
the English hands.

In which for her pranks so uncouth and suspicious, the lord regent . . . caused hir life and
beleefe, after order of law, to be inquired upon
and examined. Wherein found though a virgin,
yet first, shamefullie rejecting hir sex abomin- cf. ii. i. 20–4
ablie in acts and apparell, to have counterfeit
mankind, and then, all damnablie faithlesse, to
be a pernicious instrument to hostilitie and
bloudshed in divelish witchcraft and sorcerie,
sentence accordinglie was pronounced against
hir. Howbeit, upon humble confession of hir
iniquities with a counterfeit contrition, pretend-
ing a carefull sorow for the same, execution
spared and all mollified into this, that from
thencefoorth she should cast off hir unnaturall
wearing of mans abilliments, and keepe hir to
garments of hir owne kind, abjure hir pernicious practises of sorcerie and witcherie, and
have life and leasure in perpetuall prison to be-
waile hir misdeeds. Which to performe (according to the maner of abjuration) a solemne oth
verie gladlie she tooke.

But herein (God helpe us) she fullie afore
possest of the feend, not able to hold her in anie
towardnesse of grace, falling streight waie into
hir former abominations, (and yet seeking to
eetch out life as long as she might,) stake not
(though the shift were shamefull) to confesse
hir selfe a strumpet, and (unmaried as she was)
to be with child. For triall, the lord regents
lenitie gave hir nine moneths staie, at the end
wherof she (found herein as false as wicked in
the rest) an eight daies after, upon a further de-
finitive sentence declared against hir to be relapse and a renouncer of hir oth and repentance,
was she thereupon delivered over to secular
power, and so executed by consumption of fire
in the old market place at Rone, in the selfe
same steed where now saint Michaels church
stands: hir ashes afterward without the towne
wals shaken into the wind. Now recounting

altogither, hir pastorall bringing up, rude,
without any vertuous instruction, hir campes-
trall conversation with wicked spirits, whome,
in hir first salutation to Charles the Dolphin,
she uttered to be our Ladie, saint Katherine,
and saint Annes, that in this behalfe came and   I. ii. 76 ff.
gave hir commandements from God hir maker,
as she kept hir fathers lambs in the fields.

(c) Robert Fabyan, *The New Chronicles of England and France*, 1516,
repr. 1811

clxxxv 595   [1425] . . . the xxix daye of October . . . the   III. i. 74–85
maire . . . was by the lorde protectour sente for
in spedy maner. . . . he gave to him streyght
commaundemente, that he shuld se that the
city wer surely watched in that night folowyng,
and so it was. Then upon the morowe folowinge
about ix of the clocke, certaine servauntes of the
forenamed bishop [Winchester] would have
entred by the bridge gate. But the rulers therof
would not suffer them in so greate number, but
kept them out by force, lyke as before they were
commaunded. Wherewith they beyng grevous-
ly discontented, gathered to them a more number of archers and men of armes, and assauted
the gate with shotte and other meanes of warre.
596   In so muche / that the Commons of the citee
hearyng thereof, shutte in their Shoppes and
sped them thither in greate nomber. And likely
it was to have ensued greate effusion of bloude
shortly thereupon, ne had been the discrecion of
the Maire and his brethren, that exhorted the
people by al politike meane to kepe the kinges
peace. . . . This was cleped of the common people
the parliament of battes. The cause was, for pro-
clamations were made, that men should leve
their sweardes and other weapons in their Innes,
the people toke great battes and staves in their
neckes, and so folowed their lordes and maisters,
unto the parliament. And when that weapon
was inhibited them, then they toke stones and

plumets of lede, and trussed them secretly in
their sleves and bosomes. Duryng the parla-
mente, among other notable thinges for the
weale of the realme, the variaunce that was betwene the forsayd lordes was herein debated
and argued. In so muche that the duke of Gloucester put in a bill of complaynt againste the
bishop conteyninge vi. articles.

THE HOUSES OF YORK AND LANCASTER

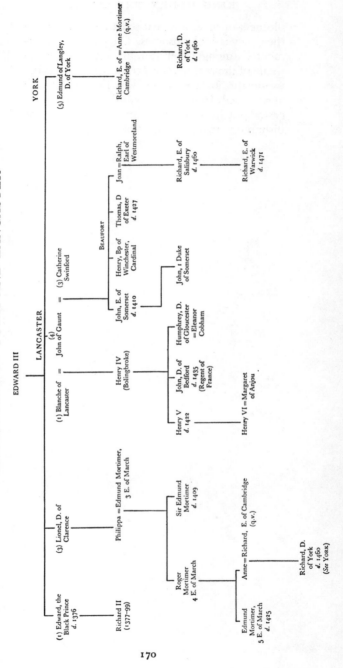

EDWARD III

LANCASTER

YORK

(1) Edward, the Black Prince *d.* 1376

(3) Lionel, D. of Clarence

(4) John of Gaunt

(3) Catherine Swinford

(5) Edmund of Langley, D. of York

Richard II (1377–99)

Philippa = Edmund Mortimer, 3 E. of March

(1) Blanche of Lancaster =

= (3) Catherine Swinford

Henry IV (Bolingbroke)

Richard, E. of = Anne Mortimer Cambridge (q.v.)

Richard, D. of York *d.* 1460

BEAUFORT

Sir Edmund Mortimer *d.* 1409

Roger Mortimer 4 E. of March

Henry V *d.* 1422

John, D. of Bedford *d.* 1435 (Regent of France)

Humphrey, D. of Gloucester = Eleanor Cobham

John, E. of Somerset *d.* 1410

Henry, Bp of Winchester, Cardinal

Thomas, D of Exeter *d.* 1427

Joan = Ralph, Earl of Westmoreland

Edmund Mortimer, 5 E. of March *d.* 1425

Anne = Richard, E. of Cambridge (q.v.)

Henry VI = Margaret of Anjou

John, 1 Duke of Somerset

Richard, E. of Salisbury *d.* 1460

Richard, D. of York *d.* 1460 (*See* YORK)

Richard, E. of Warwick *d.* 1471

APPENDIX III

SOME 'RECOLLECTIONS' FROM *1 HENRY VI* IN SHAKESPEAREAN QUARTOS

In each instance the quotations appear in the following order:
(*a*) the passage 'recollected' from *1 Henry VI*;
(*b*) the passage affected in F1;
(*c*) the form in which (*b*), as memorially influenced by (*a*), appears in the quarto (with page reference from vol. ix of the Cambridge Shakespeare, 1893).

1. Coniurers and Sorcerers   *1H6*, I. i. 26
   with Witches and with Coniurers,   *2H6*, II. i. 167
   wichcrafts, sorceries, and coniurings,   *Cont.*, 527

2. the dreadfull Iudgement-Day   *1H6*, I. i. 29 (*R3*, I. iv. 106)
   at my Tryall day.   *2H6*, III. i. 114
   at the iudgement day.   *Cont.*, 536

3. France is reuolted from the English quite,   *1H6*, I. i. 90
   What Newes from France?
   Som. That all your Interest in those Territories,
   Is vtterly bereft you: all is lost.   *2H6*, III. i. 84–5
   That France should haue reuolted from Englands rule.
                                                            Cont., 539

4. His Ransome there is none but I shall pay . . .
   His Crowne shall be the Ransome of my friend:
                                          1H6, I. i. 148, 150
      . . .   *omits*   . . .   *2H6*, IV. i
   thy life shall be the ransome I will haue   *Cont.*, 548

5. the troupes of armed men,   *1H6*, II. ii. 24 [only instance in Sh.]
      . . .   *omits*   . . .   *2H6*, III. i
   With troupes of Armed men   *Cont.*, 539

6. lauish tongue   *1H6*, II. v. 47
   . . . *omits* . . .   *2H6*
   lauish tongue   *Cont.*, 549 (cf. 510)

7. the lawfull Heire / Of *Edward* King,   *1H6*, II. v. 65–6
[only instance in Sh.]

I am King.   *2H6*, II. ii. 52

then am I lawfull heire vnto the kingdome   *Cont.*, 529

[lawful] heir   *True Tr.*, 612

8. . . . I deriued am
From *Lionel* Duke of Clarence, third Sonne
To King *Edward* the Third;   *1H6*, II. v. 74–6

. . . and the third,
Lionel, Duke of Clarence; . . .   *2H6*, II. ii. 12–13

The third Sonne, Duke of Clarence,
From whose Line I clayme the Crowne,   *2H6*, II. ii. 34–5

by her I claime the Crowne, as the true heire to
Lyonell Duke of Clarence, the third sonne
to Edward the third.   *Cont.*, 529

9. . . . that doth belong vnto the House of *Yorke*,
From whence you spring, by Lineall Descent. *1H6*, III. i. 165–6

. . . your opinion of my Title,
Which is infallible, to Englands Crowne.   *2H6*, II. ii. 4–5

The right and title of the house of Yorke,
To Englands Crowne by liniall desent.   *Cont.*, 528

10. What ransome must I pay before I passe?   *1H6*, v. iii. 73

Heere shall they make their ransome on the sand, *2H6*, IV. i. 10

And let them paie their ransomes ere they passe   *Cont.*, 548

11. Take her away, for she hath liu'd too long,   *1H6*, v. iv. 34

You Madame . . . Shall . . . Liue in your Countrey here, in
    Banishment . . .   *2H6*, II. iii. 9–11

King. . . . Away with her,
Elnor. Euen to my death, for I haue liued too long.
                Cont., 530 (Cf. *Ed. 2.* 2331, 2651)

12. a Lady of so high resolue   *1H6*, v. v. 75 [only instance in Sh.]

Women and Children of so high a courage,   *3H6*, v. iv. 50

Women and children of so high resolue   *True Tr.*, 629